Social Science Approaches to Health Services Research

Editorial Board

John R. Griffith
Chairman
The University of Michigan

Gary L. Filerman
*Association of University
Programs in Health
Administration*

Ronald Andersen
University of Chicago

R. Hopkins Holmberg
Boston University

Arnold D. Kaluzny
University of North Carolina

Donald C. Riedel
University of Washington

Lee F. Seidel
University of New Hampshire

David G. Warren
Duke University

health administration press

*The Press was established in 1972 with
the support of the W. K. Kellogg
Foundation as a joint endeavor of the
Association of University Programs in
Health Administration (Washington,
D.C.) and The University of Michigan
Program and Bureau of Hospital
Administration.*

Social Science Approaches to Health Services Research

Edited by

Thomas Choi
Jay N. Greenberg

Health Administration Press
Ann Arbor, Michigan 1982

WILLIAM MADISON RANDALL LIBRARY UNC AT WILMINGTON

Copyright © 1983 by the Regents of The University of Michigan. All rights reserved. Printed in the United States of America. This book or parts thereof may not be reproduced in any form without written permission of the publisher.

Library of Congress Cataloging in Publication Data

Main entry under title:

Social science approaches to health services research.

  Bibliography: p.
  Includes index.
  1. Medical care—Research. 2. Social sciences—
Methodology. I. Choi, Thomas. II. Greenberg, Jay N.
RA440.85.S63 1982   362.1'072   82-23225
ISBN 0-914904-83-3

Health Administration Press
The University of Michigan
School of Public Health
Ann Arbor, Michigan 48109
(313) 764-1380

RA440
.85
.S63
1982

Contents

233805

CHAPTER EIGHT
Health Services Research: A Cross-Disciplinary Retrospective

Foreword

This long-awaited book which, I am sure will be useful for years to come, provides a broad social science perspective to the common issues in health services research. My hope is that this volume can serve as the beginning of a common understanding of language, assumptions, theory, methods, and applications in health services research. Each chapter has a freshness to it as each is specifically written for this volume with the enthusiasm of a leading scholar. The authors show a true desire to inform and to span disciplinary boundaries in a way which will surely be clear and helpful to students of health services research.

The volume starts with an overview of the role of the social sciences in health services research and closes with a cross-disciplinary retrospective on each of the chapters represented by sociology, political science, jurisprudence, epidemiology, demography, and economics. I consider this book particularly useful for a large cross-section of the health-related community of practitioners and scholars who are interested in learning the basic orientation and approaches of each of the six perspectives: how the perspectives are alike, how they differ, and where they may potentially cooperate. I hope the reader will emerge from reading the chapters with a sense of expectation of how and why things are done from each perspective. The content should entice us to feel that we can all communicate with individuals outside of our particular disciplines on issues related to health services research whether we are graduate students, health care administrators, grant funders, practitioners, policy makers, or simply persons of intellectual curiosity. The point is that this book aims and I think succeeds in informing and bridging the communication gap.

The introductory and concluding chapters raise several provocative questions and issues regarding the nature of the work and work environment of health services researchers. Such information should help clients and sponsors understand the world of health services research and of course help those who aspire to enter the world of research. It also helps us understand the influences of various reference groups to which health services researchers seek a sense of identification.

At a time when federal funding is dwindling, this book gives us perspective on the history and future of health services research. It is an important perspective to have. Of equal value is the way all the contributors convey a theoretical and methodological frame of reference about their perspectives. While each chapter uses empirical examples, the contributions of the chapters are not limited by time-bound findings.

STUART H. ALTMAN
Dean, Florence Heller School,
Brandeis University, and
President-Elect, Association
for Health Services Research

Contributors

RALPH E. BERRY, JR. is an Adjunct Professor of Economics at the Heller Graduate School of Brandeis University and the President of Policy Analysis, Inc. He was formerly Professor of Economics at the Harvard School of Public Health and a faculty member of the John F. Kennedy School of Government, Harvard University. Dr. Berry received a Ph.D. in Economics from Harvard University and has taught health economics for more than 15 years. Dr. Berry has been a consultant to many government agencies, The Netherlands' National Hospital Institute, Argentina's National Development Council, and Kuwait's Ministry of Health. He is the author of *The Economic Cost of Alcohol Abuse, Evaluating Health Program Impact*, and numerous articles concerning hospital services, costs, and regulation.

ANDREW B. DUNHAM is an Assistant Professor of Political Science at Colorado College. He has written numerous articles on regulation and health care. His dissertation from the University of Chicago, an analysis of the impact of state certificate of need regulation on hospital growth, won the William Anderson Award from the American Political Science Association. He is currently studying the politics of developing alternatives to per diem hospital reimbursement.

ROGER D. FELDMAN is Associate Professor in the Center for Health Services Research and the Economics department at the University of Minnesota. He previously taught economics at the University of North Carolina and received a Ph.D. in Economics from the University of Rochester. Dr. Feldman's research applies the economic model of rational individual behavior to problems in health services. He serves as a research reviewer for the National Center for Health Services Research, the National Science Foundation, and several professional journals.

MICHEL A. IBRAHIM is Dean of the School of Public Health at the University of North Carolina at Chapel Hill. He previously held positions as Chairman of the University of North Carolina Department of Epidemiology; Deputy Health Commissioner of Erie County, New York; and Associate Professor at the University of New York School of Medicine at Buffalo. Dr. Ibrahim earned an M.D. degree from the University of Cairo and an MPH in Biostatistics and a Ph.D. in Epidemiology from the University of North Carolina at Chapel Hill. Chairman of the Editorial Board of the *American Journal of Public Health* and consultant to the National Institutes of Health, he has published on cardiovascular disease, cancer, and health care.

THEODORE R. MARMOR is Professor of Public Health and Political Science and Chairman, Center for Health Studies, at Yale University. He previously taught at the Universities of Minnesota, Wisconsin, Essex (England), and Chicago. Dr. Marmor received a Ph.D. in Political Science from Harvard University. He has written *The Politics of Medicine* and numerous articles on the politics and policies of the welfare state, emphasizing social security, national health insurance, and health planning. He is the editor of *Journal of Health Politics, Policy and Law* and editor of and contributor to *National Health Insurance: Conflicting Goals and Policy Choices.*

CARL J. SCHRAMM is Director of the Center for Hospital Finance and Management, School of Hygiene and Public Health, the Johns Hopkins University. He also serves as vice-chairman of the Maryland Health Services Cost Review Commission. He received a Ph.D. in Economics from the University of Wisconsin and a law degree from Georgetown University. Since 1979 he has been the Director of the Municipal Health Services Program, a project of the Robert Wood Johnson Foundation, the American Medical Association and the U.S. Conference of Mayors. In the 1976-1977 academic year he was a Robert Wood Johnson Health Policy Fellow at the Institute of Medicine, National Academy of Sciences.

STEPHEN M. SHORTELL is the A.C. Buehler Distinguished Professor of Hospital and Health Services Management and Professor of Organization Behavior in the J. L. Kellogg Graduate School of Management, Northwestern University. Dr. Shortell also serves as Professor of Sociology in the Department of Sociology at Northwestern. He is the author of numerous articles and author or co-author of several books and monographs including *Organizational Research in Hospitals* and *Health Program Evaluation.* He is currently conducting research on hospital-sponsored group practices and on hospital organizational responses to regulation. Dr. Shortell received his Ph.D. in the Behavioral Sciences, Graduate School of Business, University of Chicago.

LOIS M. VERBRUGGE is an Associate Research Scientist at the Center for Population Planning, School of Public Health, and a Faculty Associate in the Survey Research Center, Institute for Social Research, The University of Michigan. Her research concerns sex differences in health status, health behavior, and mortality. She has been Associate Editor of the *Journal of Health and Social Behavior*, and she publishes actively in social science and health journals. Dr. Verbrugge has a five-year career development award from the National Institute of Child Health and Human Development to pursue her work on health and mortality. Dr. Verbrugge received her Ph.D. degree in Sociology from The University of Michigan and was an Assistant Professor at Johns Hopkins University before joining The University of Michigan faculty.

Acknowledgments

A book such as this cannot be done without the help of many who spent time commenting on and extending upon the early drafts. Their time and conscientiousness are very much appreciated, and it is only appropriate that their contributions be publicly acknowledged. We are grateful to Leonard M. Schuman, M.D., MPH; Jeffrey C. Salloway, Ph.D.; John E. Brandl, Ph.D.; and a special thanks to Daniel J. McInerney, J.D., MPH, whose well-written comments should have been assigned a chapter of their own if only space had permitted. We are further grateful to two anonymous reviewers provided by our publisher whose comments helped to shape the final content and format of this volume. We also wish to thank Cynthia M. Stange for work she did on the indices of this book and to R. Jacquline Peterson, Theresa L. Duty, Ann Marie Mulally, and Peggy J. Lainen for typing and proofing the manuscript. Finally, we want to thank John E. Kralewski, Ph.D., Director of the Center for Health Services Research, University of Minnesota, for the support he gave us in producing this work.

THOMAS CHOI
JAY N. GREENBERG
Minneapolis, Minnesota
October 19, 1982

One

The Role of the Social Sciences in Health Services Research: An Overview

JAY N. GREENBERG and THOMAS CHOI

Introduction and Overview

Much has been written in recent years about the field of health services research (HSR). Yet, very few of these discussions analyze in any depth the contributions and role that the various social sciences have played in the development of the field. The central focus of this book is an examination of the methods, models and substance of various social science perspectives as they relate to HSR. The perspectives represented in the book are sociology, political science, epidemiology, jurisprudence, demography and economics. The chapters to follow will examine each perspective with regard to its conceptual framework, assumptions, methods and contributions to the field of health services research. The final chapter is devoted to an analysis of the similarities and differences across these perspectives. However, because of the confusion and controversy that often surround health services research, it is necessary to put the field into perspective first.

This chapter consists of three sections. The first briefly examines the history of health services research. The second deals with several problems, issues and dilemmas that face the field. In that section the various ways that HSR has been defined are explored, together with the implications of those definitions and some suggested relationships between HSR, discipline-based research and health policy analysis. We also raise the question of whether HSR can or should be something greater than the summation of its contributory parts. The third section provides a roadmap or overview of the book.

Historical Development

The history and development of health services research as a field of inquiry has been admirably detailed by Anderson (1966), as well as Flook and Sanazaro (1973). Our purpose here is not to present a detailed chronicle of events, but rather to put the relationship between the social sciences and HSR into an historical perspective so that the roots of current problems, dilemmas and issues can be better understood. This, in turn, will provide the context for examining the contributions that the various social sciences have made.

Our basic premise is that the changing role of the federal government as a major financier, provider, regulator and planner of health services has substantially impacted the nature of health services research and, to a large extent, is responsible for current disillusionment with the field. Indeed, it has been the federal government's rapidly increasing need for information about the quality, availability and cost of health services that has spawned the field.

Anderson suggests that the development of public policy consensus about the nature of a particular issue or set of issues establishes the basic framework within which research priorities are set.

> My thesis is that *systematic* data gathering and research do not appear until a public policy consensus emerges providing the framework for social and economic research bearing on policy. Such a framework quite unconsciously establishes the guidelines for the selection of data and research problems within the feasibilities of time, resources and research methods. Social research relating to public policy is then largely *instrumental*, serving to analyze the context in which public policy decisions are made to implement such decisions and to evaluate alternatives and their consequences in terms of the objectives sought. (Anderson 1966, p. 11, emphasis added)

Two key words emerge from Anderson's thesis: systematic and instrumental. He is not arguing that no research or data collection occurs prior to policy consensus, but rather large-scale, systematic data collection and analysis efforts only emerge (are funded) after the establishment of consensus on issues to be addressed by particular policies. Furthermore, the resulting research efforts become primarily instrumental in nature. The term "instrumental" refers to work that is oriented to the solution of specific management, program, or policy problems and tends to be constrained by very short time frames. We will argue below that much of the current criticism of HSR is directed at the field's apparent failure to meet its charge as developer of instrumental findings. We will also raise the following question: "Since social scientists obtain their primary rewards from theory building, does it follow that they would be most unlikely to systematically contribute information of an instrumental nature?" (Mechanic 1978, p. 131).

Prior to the 1960s, the primary focus of health policy was on the development of a delivery system that would provide equitable access to care. Furthermore, the role of the federal government was seen as a channel of resources to states, local governments, and nonprofit organizations. Indeed, relative to the current situation, much of the early research on the system was sponsored by philanthropic organizations (Flook and Sanazaro 1973, pp. 82-108). Major ongoing research programs did not really exist. Rather, research on the nature of the delivery system followed the decentralized patterns established by the policy process itself (Bice 1980, pp. 183-84). The

Chicago Medical Society's 1909 (Holmes 1908) study of the use of midwives, the first survey of hospitals conducted by the American Medical Association in 1909 the famed Flexner Report (1910), and the reports of the Committee on the Costs of Medical Care (1932) are prime examples of the decentralized nature of early research efforts.

The passage of the Hill-Burton Act in 1946 not only significantly altered the role that the federal government would play in the financing of health facilities construction, but it also marked the beginning of the focusing and centralizing of the sponsorship of health services research. In addition to soliciting grant applications from states for the purpose of the construction of health care facilities, the Hill-Burton Act also called for grants that would aid states in conducting inventories of existing facilities and in evaluating unmet needs for additional facilities (Wilson and Neuhauser 1974, pp. 152-54).

The centralization of the federal government as financier of the health delivery system accelerated in the 1960s as a result of dozens of pieces of social legislation. The federal government not only became a major financier of health services through the passages of Medicare and Medicaid, but it also began to take on responsibility for the development of new delivery systems. Direct federal funding of neighborhood health centers and mental health centers are examples of this expanded federal role. Research during this period began to focus more and more on the operation and performance of these various federal programs. Furthermore, the conditions of participation associated with Medicare and Medicaid would ultimately result in the federal government playing an important role in regulation of the health delivery system.

Many historians of health policy and health services research argue that HSR, as a distinguishable field of inquiry, really began in the 60s (Bice 1980, p. 173, 185; Mechanic 1978, p. 128). During this same period the National Center for Health Services Research and Development was established by the federal government. It is important to remember that HSR was developing as part of a much larger trend of using applied social science research to improve public decision making. Not only did the Johnson administration produce much social legislation, but both the Kennedy and Johnson administrations sincerely believed that many of our social ills could be cured by the application of social research to these problems. In large part, the activities and beliefs of the 1960s cemented the relationship between HSR and applied social science research. A question that we address below is whether HSR is or can be something more than social science inquiry applied to the health services arena.

The 1970s witnessed a shift in the policy consensus away from access and expansion and toward cost containment and "shrinking the system" (Bice 1980, p. 184). The policy instrument chosen to implement cost containment was control by regulation. Utilization review programs, certificate of need and 1122 review, restrictive Medicare and Medicaid reimbursement policies, rate review and rate regulation programs, and the introduction of professional standards review programs (PSROs) are examples of this regulatory thrust that have led to further centralization of control over the system by state and federal governments. With this came a great need for new knowledge about how to control the system effectively. To help ensure that research would be problem-oriented and would focus on desired policy issues, the federal government began to rely more heavily on the RFP (request for proposal) approach to grant letting (Kralewski and Greene 1980, p. 299). This is in contrast to investigator-oriented approaches of the past. The RFP approach resembles a contracting process more than it does a granting process. Thus, as the policy context became more centralized, HSR also became more centralized in sponsorship and focus. Furthermore, government officials began to judge the usefulness of research in terms of its ability to solve the problems at hand.

What impact has this changing orientation had upon the field? As Mechanic points out:

> Given the enormous growth of the health services field and the difficult problems associated with cost containment, regulation, quality assurance and improvement of health behavior of the population, it might be anticipated that HSR would be a growing and vigorous activity. Instead, the HSR field faces considerable skepticism among public officials and significant erosion of its research and training support. (Mechanic 1978, p. 127)

Indeed, according to Myers (1973), Lewis (1977) and others, HSR has made very little direct impact on the formulation of national health care policies. As a result, many people are now questioning the worth of the entire enterprise.

PROBLEMS, ISSUES, DILEMMAS

DEFINITIONS OF HSR

Much of the criticism of HSR results from a lack of general agreement as to the nature and role of the field. Associated with this lack of domain consensus is disagreement regarding where, in the knowledge-building process, HSR fits. In particular, there is little agreement as to the distinction among applied social science research related to the health delivery systems, health services research, and health policy analysis. Furthermore, the degree to which people are critical of the performance of HSR also seems to be tied to their perception of the policy formation process itself.

In a 1978 working paper, the Institute of Medicine's Committee on Health Services Research defined HSR as:

> . . . an interdisciplinary activity, directly relevant to health and intended to further the understanding of the many factors influencing the delivery of health care with the ultimate objective of improving the provision of health services and making more efficient use of resources. It encompasses a wide spectrum of activities ranging from fundamental research, the collection of statistical information, applied research development, testing and evaluation to policy analysis and long-range planning. Its substantive concerns are equally broad and include the planning, organization, financing, management, use and effectiveness of the health services delivery system. (Institute of Medicine 1978, pp. 1–2)

This rather global conception of HSR captures the essence of much of the confusion surrounding it. For example, the definition states that HSR is an interdisciplinary activity. What is meant by interdisciplinary? Do they simply mean that due to the multivariate nature of the issues, health services research is (should be) conducted by persons from various disciplines working together? If this is the case, then there is a built-in dilemma posed by the goals of the field. The Institute claims that the goal of HSR is to improve the health care system. Thus it is a problem-oriented field and, to use the terminology presented above, it is instrumental. Yet the persons doing the research are social scientists. The goal of these disciplines is theory development and not problem solving. We argue that this difference in emphasis toward theory development or problem solving is by no means trivial and may account for much of the dissatisfaction among producers, users and sponsors of the research. In particular it can account for many of the claims that HSR is irrelevant and insensitive to the needs of policy makers and managers.

The definition indicates that the activities encompassing the field range from fundamental research to policy analysis. We argue, as have Myers (1973) and others, that research and policy analysis are very different activities. The degree of objectivity/advocacy associated with each, the methods used, and the time frame needed are so different that it makes little sense to lump them into one category. Furthermore, this "lumping" has often led to mistaken expectations with regard to the nature of the end products.

In contrast, Shortell and LoGerfo (1978) simply state that "health services research is concerned with studying the relationships between consumers and providers as they affect and are affected by health care organizations, technology, financing and payment systems" (Shortell and LoGerfo 1978, p. 1). This definition is much closer to describing an applied area of research of the various social science disciplines. However, as is suggested by both definitions, there does seem to be almost unanimous agreement that HSR is primarily concerned with social processes as opposed to biological processes (Kralewski and Greene 1980, p. 295). But again one must ask if it necessarily follows that HSR should be performed by social science disciplinarians or that health services researchers should use the results of social science inquiry as inputs into their research. We will return to this question later in this section.

As Bice points out, much of the answer to the question of whether HSR has significantly contributed to public policy depends on one's definitions of public policy and the policy development process itself. He argues that one view of the policy formation process sees it as a set of explicit and authoritative decisions made by a set of identifiable public officials. This group of individuals would tend to evaluate the performance of HSR in terms of its direct impact on these decisions. Thus, information or knowledge is valued as input into the problem-solving process or for its instrumental usefulness (Bice 1980, p. 175). Using this criterion for evaluating the performance of HSR, there would seem to be a great deal of evidence to suggest that HSR has not been very successful (Myers 1973; Lewis 1977; Last 1977; Eichhorn and Bice 1973).

The other view of the policy formation process that Bice presents is one of decentralized, pluralistic activities, actions and decisions. Rather than being identified by the decisions of a select few, it is a more nebulous, generalized political process (Bice 1980, p. 175). The essence of this view of policy formation is captured by Anderson's definition of the process: "Public policy may be defined as any set of values, opinions and actions which moves decision in the political, social and economic systems in certain directions, regardless of source in a pluralistic society" (Anderson 1966, p. 42).

Under this definition of the policy formation process, the quality of HSR would be evaluated in terms of its general ability to shape debate and action. Thus, one would not expect to find that the results of a particular piece of research played a direct and central role in a particular decision. Rather, one would look toward the nature of issues being raised and the nature of the debate surrounding these issues. If HSR is having an impact, then we should be able to at least associate past and ongoing research with current policy issues and debates. From this perspective, many would argue that given its rather short history and limited research, HSR has been reasonably successful (Anderson 1966; Klarman 1980; Kralewski and Greene 1980; Mechanic 1978). They would argue that a body of knowledge is developing and that it has influenced the debate surrounding the health care system. Klarman (1980) suggests that past research on the inflationary impact of certain types of reimbursement mechanisms has led to policy discussions about altering reimbursement systems (Klarman 1980, p. 207). It is no accident that the term "prospective rate setting" is now part of the common language of those involved in the formation of health policy. It is also no accident that findings of low hospital utilization under prepaid group practice has given added life to the HMO movement under a policy consensus of cost containment. The work of Pollak (1973), Joe (1976) and others on the potential costs and benefits of community-based long-term care has certainly helped shape the debate in this increasingly important area. In trying to answer the question of whether HSR has an impact, we would do well to remember the words of John Maynard Keynes:

> Practical men, who believe themselves to be quite exempt from any intellectual influences, are usually the slaves of some defunct economist. . . . I am sure that the power of vested interests is vastly exaggerated compared with the gradual encroachment of ideas. . . . Not, indeed, immediately, but after a certain interval, for in the field of economic and political philosophy there are not many who are influenced by new theories after they are 25 or 30 years of age, so that the ideas which civil servants and politicians and even agitators apply to current events are not likely to be the newest. But soon or late, it is ideas, not vested interests, which are dangerous for good or evil. (Keynes 1964, pp. 383-84)

In conjunction with and in addition to the issues that surround the definitions of HSR, there are several related issues or problems that others have identified as important.

EXPECTATIONS AND THE SIZE OF INVESTMENT

One of the most serious problems the field of HSR faces is the implicit belief that a modest investment in HSR can produce solutions to complex issues which surround the health care system (Mechanic 1978, p. 129). By almost any criterion, past and present public investment in HSR has been very small. In fiscal 1976, the federal government spent approximately $43.6 billion on health care. Of this, only approximately $741 million (or 1.7 percent) was spent on health services research (Kralewski and Greene 1980, p. 297). In contrast, private sector corporations often spent over five percent of revenues on research and development. This figure ($741 million) also represents somewhere between five percent and ten percent of federal dollars spent on biomedical research (Williams 1978, p. 223). Williams argues that the "correct" amount to be spent on HSR has little to do with comparative expenditures and should be based upon the budgetary implications of federal decisions on health policy (Williams 1978, p. 225). Fein (1977, p. 375) suggests that for this very reason the proportion of resources going to HSR should be increased. He suggests that in the long run an investment in HSR may actually reduce health care costs.

Not only is the size of the investment a problem, but the nature of the investment can also be questioned. As was discussed above, federal agencies have been rapidly moving away from investigator-initiated inquiries toward an RFP approach. Furthermore, the nature of RFPs is moving away from general areas of inquiry to specific "researchable questions." In essence, most of our investment is going to answer a select group of "issues of the day." Fewer resources are being devoted to longer-range problem identification and issue development. Part of the reason for this shift can be attributed to the view of HSR as the producer of instrumental findings. This view would suggest a problem-oriented, management-contracting approach to the use of funds. Nevertheless, even if one subscribes to this view of the role of HSR, it would seem that a more balanced investment portfolio would be prudent— where the balancing has to do with short-term versus long-term investments and gains.

THE ENVIRONMENT

There are a number of environmental factors that do not bode well for the HSR enterprise. With regard to the external environment, HSR has rather reluctant receptors in the field of practice and tends to attract critics (Mechanic 1978; Kralewski and Greene 1980). As Mechanic so aptly put it,

> Surgeons hardly like the suggestion that they perform unnecessary surgery; hospitals dislike the implication that they are inefficient and wasteful, physicians recoil at suggestions that they create their own demand, offer ineffective care and maintain political control over the medical marketplace. One hardly expects these groups to serve as a constituency in support of health services research. (Mechanic 1978, p. 131)

Even the practitioners of HSR do not make a strong lobbying group. HSR is conducted by individuals from different disciplines who vary greatly with regard to perspective, methods, assumptions and language. Furthermore, they most often associate themselves with their disciplines and not with HSR, resulting in the absence of an organized constituency to promote the research.

Within the academic community, HSR has few strong advocates. Traditionally, applied research is given low status in universities. Theory development and not theory application is thought by many to be the principal role of university-based researchers—particularly in the social sciences. Thus, an area as applied as HSR is viewed with disfavor by academic departments.

The external and internal academic environments intersect to place HSR in a double bind. HSR must achieve a degree of scientific rigor that is satisfactory to the members of the academic community and, at the same time, it must present work to the field of practice so that it is easily understood. Researchers must often choose between being responsive to their clients/ sponsors and being "rigorous" as defined by their disciplines. Additional analyses on the setting of HSR and the relationship between health services research, clients/sponsors, and individual disciplines will be taken up in the last chapter.

SOCIAL SCIENTISTS AS HEALTH SERVICES RESEARCHERS

Very often, the dissatisfaction with HSR is blamed directly on the style of work of its practitioners. In particular, health services researchers are often accused of not communicating with each other, being insensitive to the constraints and political realities of the field of practice, disinterested in the relevance of their findings to policy, cavalier about deadlines, too compulsive about the need for the purity of their experimental designs, and reluctant to properly communicate their findings to the field of practice (Myers 1973; Eichhorn and Bice 1973; Bice 1980).

Two remedies for these ills are typically recommended. The first suggests closer communication among the various disciplines involved in HSR and better communication between the disciplines and the field of practice and policy makers. The second calls for disciplinarians to make concessions with regard to the elegance of their methodologies and the nature of acceptable evidence, in addition to more truly multidisciplinary approaches to health services research.

As a means of furthering the debate, we suggest that neither of the above recommendations will substantially change the nature of the research produced, nor will they improve the relevance of the research to the field of practice. Currently, most HSR is performed by persons who consider themselves social scientists. We think that an argument can be made that the goals and methods of the social sciences (vis-à-vis HSR) are antithetical to the needs of both the field of practice and the policy maker for rapidly developed instrumental knowledge.

Consider the nature of social science inquiry. The goal of social science disciplines is the development of parsimonious, generalizable theories about the behavior of individuals and collectivities of individuals. It has been pointed out by Ben-David (1973, p. 39) and others that the social sciences have modeled themselves after the field of physics. This approach to knowledge building assumes that the universe is orderly and capable of being completely comprehended. Thus, the disciplinarian views "events" as indicators of abstract concepts. These concepts, in turn, are related to each other via theoretical statements (in the form of propositions, hypotheses, findings). Finally, these various theoretical statements comprise theories—the end product or goal of the inquiry (Eichhorn and Bice 1973, p. 138). Furthermore, because of its complexities, the world is partitioned into different areas of inquiry. This partitioning process defines the domains of the various social sciences.

It is important to realize that the partitioning of domains is done with regard to independent or explanatory variables (which explain from a certain perspective why things are the way they are) and not dependent variables. Indeed, it has often been said that the disciplines are oriented toward independent variables. For example, in trying to explain the utilization of emergency room services, economists tend to focus on the price that the consumer faces, insurance coverage and income. Sociologists concentrate on independent variables related to culture and class. In contrast, the instrumental version of HSR is oriented toward dependent variables such as utilization rate, quality of care, and health outcome. We think that this difference in independent/dependent variable orientation is a consequence of a difference in mission and purpose—namely, the building of theories versus the solving of immediate problems. This partitioning of inquiry based upon independent variables has led to many divergent strains of thought and work in HSR with little indication of true convergence. Furthermore, as Bice (1980) points out, this partitioning may lead not only to partial answers but also to invalid conclusions (biased estimators of parameters), because independent variables are often not independent of each other. Also, the disciplinarian will trade additional explanatory power for conceptual purity and parsimony (Bice 1980, p. 193). That is, they are more concerned with limiting the explanatory power to variables derived strictly from their theories than they are with maximum explanation (from eclectic sources) of the independent variable.

If we accept as a premise that the mission or purpose of social science inquiry is theory development and that the social sciences have modeled their methods of inquiry after physics, then the desirability of leaving to social scientists the task of producing instrumental HSR is called into question. Consider the difference between the goals and methods of a physicist and an engineer. The engineer is problem-oriented—he/she seeks a solution to a particular problem. For example, there is a river that prevents goods from flowing between two cities. The goal of the engineer is to construct a mechanism to facilitate the exchange—e.g., a bridge, tunnel or two airports. The point is that the engineer is primarily interested in solving the flow of goods problem between these two cities. He/she is not interested, at that point, in whether or not the solution will generalize to other locations. The main goal is not to develop a theory of bridges or tunnels, but simply to get the goods moving. That is not to say that he/she would not rely on the work of physicists; indeed, physicists might be called upon to work on certain unsolved problems. The important point is that the engineer is not a physicist and the immediate goals of the project are not the same as those of a physicist, except by coincidence.

Using the physicist/engineer analogy, social scientists are the physicists. But who are the engineers? Currently, the engineers are nothing more than "applied physicists." They are, in fact, not engineers at all. What may well be needed is an area of study or group of professionals whose methods and objectives are related to problem solving and not theory building. This is not to suggest that the social sciences cannot contribute greatly to this new field (call it health services research). We think that the social sciences would have a great deal of knowledge to offer the health services researcher. However, from the perspective of this new field, social science knowledge is viewed as input into the health services research production process. It may not be the process itself.

What then is this new and different production process? Needless to say, we do not know exactly. We do think, however, that the issue of conceptualizing, developing and refining a new process of HSR production is essential to the field if it is to meet its charge as producer of instrumental knowledge. Some have suggested that the use of general systems theory (GST) may provide a unifying methodology for HSR. According to Kralewski and Greene (1979, p. 303):

> Several authors have noted the potential of general systems theory (GST) as a method of bridging the applied/theoretical research gap and bringing disciplines together to focus on a health services research program (Hearn 1976; Meyer and Kolins 1976; Rizzo 1976; and Sills 1976). Others note that GST permits investigators to focus on specific areas of inquiry without losing sight of the integrative relationships of the system; that it provides a framework to reorient disciplinary researchers from the independent variables focus common to their scientific approach to the dependent variable approach necessary in health services research; and that it will act to liberate the disciplines from their artificially created boundaries to view the world from a much broader perspective (Berg 1976; King 1976; and Sills 1976).

Does this imply that the conventional view of the relationship between HSR and applied social science research is incorrect or inappropriate? Again, it depends upon the goals of the inquiry. If the goal of the inquiry is a long-term investment with the future payoff being issues raised, hypotheses developed and agendas and policies questioned, then the notion of HSR as simply another area of applied social science (interdisciplinary or otherwise) seems appropriate. However, if the goal is short-term problem solving dealing with issues, programs or policies, then we may well want to consider a new approach such as GST. Having raised the issue here, we will return to it in the final chapter and explore some difficulties that are associated with this view of HSR.

Regardless of which view of HSR is taken, it is clear that the social sciences have and will continue to play an important role in its development. Therefore, it is essential that producers, users and funders of HSR have a better understanding of the methods, concepts and approaches that these various disciplines bring to bear on the problems of the health services sector. This type of examination will allow us to evaluate more intelligently the proper roles of the social sciences in HSR.

A ROADMAP TO THE BOOK

The remainder of the book consists of seven chapters. In each of the first six chapters a distinguished social scientist(s) was asked to present an overview of the concepts, methods and contributions that his/her respective field of inquiry has contributed to health services research. To make comparisons as easy as possible, each author or set of authors was asked to respond to the following common set of questions:

1. What theoretical framework or model of behavior underpins the empirical work of your discipline? Is there more than one dominant framework or model?

2. What are the critical shared assumptions that underpin the theoretical and empirical work of your discipline? What are the consequences of these assumptions?

3. What methods of data gathering are most often used by your discipline? Which methods are most often advocated?

4. What types of research design and empirical analysis are typically used? What are some of the limits that result from such methods?

5. What impact have the findings from your discipline had on policy or on the policy debate?

Thus, in each chapter the author(s) attempts to highlight four important dimensions: methods, discovery, explanation and evaluation.

SOCIOLOGY

Shortell suggests that in sociology there is not one, but a host of competing theories and paradigms which govern research. He delineates these competing theories and paradigms into three major perspectives: structural-functional, conflict, and symbolic interaction. Each of these approaches spawns the following paradigms: the social facts paradigm (emphasis on how social structure and institutions shape human behavior), the social definition paradigm (emphasis on human meaning), and the social behavior paradigm (emphasis on interaction between individual and environment).

Shortell sees the impact made by sociologists primarily through the social behaviorist paradigm which encompasses work related to the incentives and disincentives that shape human behavior. He sees sociology as having relevance and policy impact in implementation of policies to competing and conflicting interest groups. The values and expectations of these different interest groups and their social structure are obstacles which need to be reckoned with. He also sees the emphasis on open systems in sociology as an important contribution to understanding the interdependence of health care organizations. The nature of these interdependencies should lend itself to more enlightened health policy. Methodologically, Shortell sees sociology as contributing to the development of important independent variables such as culture, social norm, social sanction and organizational structure.

POLITICAL SCIENCE

Political science is similar to sociology in that there is no one overall theory or paradigm, though there are some principles and assumptions which underlie the large domain of political science. Marmor maintains that political science is the study of how men are governed. The focus is on social choices concerning the distribution of benefits and burdens within society. The benefits and burdens of interest are not just material but symbolic and psychological as well, involving power and status.

Marmor and Dunham shy away from identifying a distinct area called the politics of health in large measure because the health industry faces the same governmental arrangements as do most other industries. From a political science perspective, the health industry faces the same mixing and balancing between public and private responsibility, the same "marbled cake" of local, state and federal authorities, the same voting alignments and party systems, the same federal legislature representing local interests and divided into contained committees, the same political culture, social structure and so on.

While Marmor and Dunham acknowledge that there is no single politics of health (but politics throughout the health industry instead), they are quick to point out that the nature of these politics differ markedly depending on the political system: redistributive, regulatory or distributive. It is clear from their chapter that there is no shared theory in political science. Political scientists are joined rather by a common object of inquiry: the differences among us and how we resolve them.

Marmor and Dunham's basic view of political science contributions concerns how diverse elements combine to produce public policy, a sort of multipolitics perspective that runs counter to some current fashions in the discipline which place more stress on the social structure and less on the individual public actor. Yet their perspective is an important one. They see multiple forces contributing to health policy, and by so doing they refuse to mechanize their discipline. Marmor and Dunham show how to use political science to illuminate and change health policy. Nothing they say allows one to think that there is a separate political science of health.

JURISPRUDENCE

From the perspective of jurisprudence, Schramm sees health services delivery intertwined with legislative initiatives. He sees health services research as being concerned with developing change in the way the health care system operates, and health policy impacting health services, especially in the area of organizational change. Schramm argues that unless the process of legal decision making is understood, research on organizational change is incomplete. His analysis of the legal perspective uncovers no clear theoretical approaches. However, the law operates by way of precedents and as such, norms guide legal behavior. The understanding of these norms and their contrast to prevailing models in other perspectives provide insights into the underpinnings of legal action and its impact on health services.

Schramm sees two current models prevalent in health services research. The first he labels the rational-patient model, which describes the patient as the one making medical choices in a way which optimizes his/her enjoyment of life within the context of limited resources (e.g., consumer choice plans). The second model is the scientific-provider model which views health providers doing the utmost to intervene in patient problems, regardless of efficiency and efficacy (e.g., kidney dialysis, CT scanners). The two models are antithetical: patient choice vs. provider choice. Both models are goal-oriented. The incompatibility of the two models results in looking to the legislature for resolution.

In contrast, the legal perspective is process-oriented and perceives all medical transactions like all other contractual transactions. The lawyer (or at least the more recent breed of lawyers) is seen as the policy maker who knows precisely how to deal within the boundaries of the law.

EPIDEMIOLOGY

In contrast to the legal perspective, epidemiology deals directly with the outcome of health services—namely, the health status of the population. Ibrahim defines epidemiology as the study of the distribution and determination of disease, disability, death or health in population groups. Traditionally, epidemiology has been concerned with the understanding and ultimate control of communicable diseases. Thus, the emphasis was on the germ theory of disease. As such, epidemiology would not directly relate to the topic at hand. However, Ibrahim argues that many of man's modern plagues such as heart disease, hypertension, cancer, obesity and mental illness are such that the germ theory is insufficient to explain the occurrence of these conditions. Thus, modern epidemiology looks to the social and behavioral sciences as well as to the biological sciences for its explanation.

He sees epidemiology as having an impact on health services research in several ways: methodologically, epidemiology contributes to a way of thinking by the use of a set of techniques and methods established to answer certain questions. Techniques used include cohort study, historical cohort, cross-sectional analysis, case-control study, before–after design, experimental designs, and multivariate analysis. Substantively, epidemiology is seen as a perspective which contributes to clarifying the causes of the population's health status.

The several uses of epidemiology in health services research are discussed throughout the chapter. Many of these are illustrated by examples of health manpower.

DEMOGRAPHY

Verbrugge defines demography as the study of the structure and dynamics of human populations. It is composed of three major approaches: social demography deals with the way demographic variables such as fertility and mortality affect health services utilization; population dynamics or mathematical demography deals with the impact of population changes on health planning; and technical demography, which she sees as a set of useful tools for health services researchers and planners. She also discusses a new branch called health demography which investigates the relationship between demographic variables and health status.

Demography is a particular way of asking scientific questions and of analyzing data. It takes characteristics such as age, sex and marital status and provides a framework of reference as a set of independent variables to predict health services utilization. Verbrugge points out that unlike the other social sciences, demography treats these variables as central, not merely "control variables." Thus, its major theoretical contribution is in seeking explanations to population differentials rather than just acknowledging them.

Verbrugge sees demography's major methodological contribution as the development and refinement of survey research techniques. She presents several examples of their use throughout the chapter.

ECONOMICS

Berry and Feldman view economics as primarily a science of scarcity. As such, three predominant themes emerge in health care economics: (1) What goods and services will be produced? (2) How will they be produced? (3) How will they be distributed? The theoretical framework of economics, as the authors see it, deals with the choice and economic activities of health care providers and consumers in the health market. The underlying assumption is that each actor in the market, whether provider or consumer, wants to maximize gains subject to certain constraints. The basic model of the economist is the intersection of supply and demand in the health services marketplace. Demand comes from individual consumers or household units that are assumed to be maximizing their utility or satisfaction subject to an income constraint, and the prices given in the several markets for the various goods and services among which they may choose. On the supply side, producers are assumed to be maximizing their profit subject to the constraints imposed by the technology available, market demand and prices they face in hiring or purchasing inputs or resources. The market is the basic mechanism for allocating scarce resources. The authors go on to discuss the nature of the market for health services, the problems associated with that market, and the economic and policy implications of market imperfections and "nonstandard" provider behavior.

They present several examples of the types of empirical studies that health economists have conducted. These range from estimation of production processes to estimation of the impact that a price change would have on the quantity of a service demanded. The authors also suggest that economics has contributed rather significantly to the methodological sophistication of the field.

Berry and Feldman conclude the chapter with an interesting discussion of several areas of inquiry that lend themselves well to collaborative research among disciplines. These areas include the role of physicians as consumers' agents, theories of hospital behavior, and the effect of group practice on physicians' incentives.

The eighth and final chapter summarizes and compares the preceding chapters, taking into account the various theoretical frames of references, the approaches taken toward data analysis, the contributions made through research findings, and the work setting of health services research.

REFERENCES

Anderson, O. W. 1966. Influences of social and economic research on public policy in the health field: A review. *Milbank Memorial Fund Quarterly* 44(July): 1, 11.

Ben-David, J. 1973. How to organize research in the social sciences. *Daedalus* 102:39-51.

Berg, L. E. 1976. Applied systems analysis in the delivery of comprehensive health services. In *Health research: The systems approach*, eds. H. H. Werley, A. Zuzich, and A. D. Zagornik. New York: Springer.

Bice, T. 1980. Social science and health services research: Contributions to public policy. *Health and Society: Milbank Memorial Fund Quarterly* 58(Spring):173-200.

Committee on the Costs of Medical Care. 1932. *The Five-Year Program of the Committee on the Cost of Medical Care.* Washington, D.C.

Eichhorn, R., and Bice, T. W. 1973. Academic disciplines and health services research. In *Health services research and R&D in perspective*, eds. E. E. Flook and P. J. Sanazaro. Ann Arbor, MI: Health Administration Press.

Fein, R. 1977. The economics of health research. In *The Horizons of health*, eds. H. Wechsler, J. Gurin, and G. F. Cahill. Cambridge: Harvard University Press.

Flexner, A. 1910. *Medical education in the United States and Canada: A report to the Carnegie Foundation for the advancement of teaching.* New York: Carnegie Foundation.

Flook, E. E., and Sanazaro, P. J. 1973. Health services research: Origins and milestones. In *Health services research and R&D in perspective*, eds. E. E. Flook and P. J. Sanazaro. Ann Arbor, MI: Health Administration Press.

Hearn, G. 1976. The client as the focal subsystem. In *Health research: The systems approach*, eds. H. H. Werley et al. New York: Springer.

Holmes, R. W., et al. 1908. Midwives of Chicago. *Journal of the American Medical Association* 50(April 25):1346-50.

Institute of Medicine. 1978. Working Paper of the Committee on Health Services Research, January, pp. 1-2. Washington, D.C.: The Institute.

Joe, T. Policies and strategies for long-term care. 1976. San Francisco: University of California, Health Policy Program.

Keynes, J. M. 1964. *The general theory of employment, interest, and money.* New York: Harcourt Brace.

King, I. M. The health care system: Nursing intervention subsystem. In *Health research: The systems approach*, eds. H. H. Werley et al. New York: Springer.

Klarman, H. E. 1980. Observations on health services research and health policy analysis. *Health and Society: Milbank Memorial Fund Quarterly* 58(Spring):201-16.

Kralewski, J. E., and Greene, B. R. 1980. Health services research and the evolving health systems. In *Health management for tomorrow*, eds. S. Levey and T. McCarthy, pp. 293-307. Philadelphia: J. B. Lippincott Company.

Last, J. M. 1977. Health services research: Does it make a difference? *New England Journal of Medicine* 297(November 10):1073.

Lewis, C. D. 1977. Health-services research and innovations in health-care delivery. *Science* 297:423-27.

Mechanic, D. 1974. *Politics, medicine and social science.* New York: Wiley.

————. 1978. Prospects and problems in health services research. *Health and Society: Milbank Memorial Fund Quarterly* 56(Spring)127-39.

Meyer, R., and Kolins, M. 1976. Systems approach to studying community health. In *Health research: The systems approach*, eds. H. H. Werley et al. New York: Springer.

Myers, B. A. 1973. Health services research and health policy: Interactions. *Medical Care* 11(July-August):352-58.

Pollack, W. Utilization of alternative care settings by the elderly. Working Paper 963-12. Washington, D.C.: The Urban Institute.

Rizzo, N. D. 1976. General systems theory: Its impact in the health fields. In *Health research: The systems approach*, eds. H. H. Werley et al. New York: Springer.

Shortell, S. M. and LoGerfo, J. P. 1978. Health services research and public policy: Definitions, accomplishments, and potential. Paper prepared for the Institute of Medicine Steering Committee on Health Services Research.

Sills, G. M. 1976. Bridging the gap between systems theory and research. In *Health research: The systems approach*, eds. H. H. Werley et al. New York: Springer.

Wilson, F. A., and Neuhauser, D. 1974. *Health services in the United States.* Cambridge: Ballinger Publishing Company.

Williams, A. P. 1978. Improving health services research. *Health Services Research* 13(Fall):223-26.

Two

The Contribution and Relevance of Sociology to Health Services Research

STEPHEN M. SHORTELL

INTRODUCTION

> Whatever hope there may be of using intelligence effectively must be in the application of adequate research methods to the creation of some organized and validated understanding of the principles of human behavior, social interaction, and the nature of organizations. (Farris 1964, p. 3)

The above quotation expresses not only the common desire of the social sciences, but also the concerns of many Americans about the delivery of health services in the United States—concerns that are defined further in the following kinds of questions. How can incentives be designed to promote a more cost-effective delivery system? What is the proper mix of market and non-market forces? How can physicians and other health professionals be motivated to locate and stay in underserved areas? What factors influence people's health-seeking and illness behavior? What factors influence patients' adherence to medical advice? Can health care organizations be better designed and managed to meet the needs of professionals working in them as well as the needs of the patients they serve? How do health care organizations adapt to new technology and regulations and what effects do they have on management practices, patient care practices, access, cost and quality of care? How are health care organizations affected by the larger political economy?

Health services research provides a key linkage between the basic social science disciplines and the above-mentioned concerns of health consumers, professionals and policy makers. This chapter examines the contribution and relevance of one of these disciplines, sociology, to health services research. Considerable attention is given to sociological concepts, theories and paradigms and their relationship to HSR. This focusing is intended to provide greater understanding of the sociologist's perspective in performing health services research, but not to be a comprehensive review of sociological contributions to such research, either across areas or within selected areas of emphasis such as health, illness, sick role behavior, or organizational analysis. The *Handbook of Medical Sociology* (Freeman, Levine and Reeder 1979) as well as several texts exist for that purpose.

It must be recognized that the boundaries within the social sciences (anthropology, economics, political science, psychology, sociology, etc.) are becoming increasingly blurred, both theoretically and empirically. Therefore, the present discussion of sociological perspectives and contributions will, of necessity, draw on closely related disciplines as well. While there is not yet a commonly used set of analytic concepts or assumptions for the social sciences, Kuhn has provided a general systems theory basis for such development in his book, *The Logic of Social Systems* (1974). Given the range and complexity of problems encountered in the delivery of health services, attempts toward greater unification of the social sciences are to be encouraged. This can be accomplished without sacrificing the basic integrity of the individual discipline. It must be recognized that sociological approaches frequently offer partial explanations at best, and can be fruitfully combined with economic, psychological, epidemiological and other approaches in the interest of a broader examination. Some of these linkages are suggested.

In order to discuss the contribution of sociology to the field, it is first necessary to establish a definition of health services research. It is also necessary to provide more background on the development of sociology as a discipline, particularly for the uninitiated. These tasks are taken up in the following section. With the background laid, the major concepts, theories and paradigms of sociology relevant to HSR are then discussed, followed by selective, focused reviews of relevant literature pertaining to health and illness behavior, and the structure, functioning and effects of health care organizations. The area of health and illness behavior is selected because it is moderately well developed and illustrates a range of sociological perspectives and contributions. The organization area is selected because, although less well developed, it illustrates a number of challenging issues and problems for future investigation. Space precludes documentation of the many important contributions which have been made in other areas such as mental health, social disability, the health professions, and related areas of medical sociological inquiry. For those with particular interest in these areas, several excellent review chapters by Graham and Reeder, Clausen, Kaplan, Mechanic and others can be found in the recent edition of *The Handbook of Medical Sociology* (1979). A brief section is also devoted to methodological advances, and the chapter concludes with an examination of future directions involving sociology and health services research with particular attention given to the contribution of sociology to the development of health policy.

DEFINITIONS AND BACKGROUND

HEALTH SERVICES RESEARCH: AN APPLIED AREA OF INVESTIGATION

Health services research has been defined as "inquiry to produce knowledge about features of the structure, processes or effects of the provision of personal health services" (Bice et al. 1979, p. 14). It focuses on "the dynamic relationships involving the process by which consumers seek health services, the patterns of patient flow through the system, and the cost, quality, and equity consequences of both health care seeking behavior and health care receiving and providing behavior" (Shortell and LoGerfo 1978, p. 230). Health services research is an applied and inherently inter- and multidisciplinary field of investigation. As an organized endeavor, it originated in the mid-1950s and was stimulated in the late 1960s by the development of the National Center for Health Services Research. Optimists claim that HSR has contributed important knowledge and understanding of how the health care system works and has been drawn upon, at least indirectly, in the development of a number of national health policies. Conversely, pessimists claim that HSR has yielded little cumulative knowledge or understanding, is overly fragmented, and is seldom considered in the development of health policy. The truth, undoubtedly, lies somewhere between. Debate concerning the quality, coherence and relevance of health services research will continue, and it is within this context that sociology's particular contributions must be considered.

SOCIOLOGY AS A DISCIPLINE

As an organized intellectual discipline, sociology is barely over 100 years old, and medical sociology is one of the youngest specialties, having been formally recognized as a section of the American Sociological Association in 1959. Indicative of the interest in the area, it is also the largest section of the Association, with well over 1,000 members. From its early beginnings, there has been a close link between the development of sociology as a discipline and its specific application to issues of health and illness. With the 1951 publication of his book *Suicide* which presented the seminal examination and explanation of the varying rates of suicide across different countries, Durkheim might well be considered the first "medical sociologist." Additionally, a number of major thinkers who have helped shape the discipline have used the medical arena in formulating their theories, e.g., Parsons' *The Social System* (1951).

The discipline contains a number of competing concepts, hypotheses, theories and paradigms. Nevertheless, as Twaddle and Hessler (1972) suggest, most sociologists would agree to the following propositions: (1) there exists a social structure; thus, human activities follow a pattern and are not random; (2) the most useful explanations of human behavior lie in the study of collectivities, not individual behavior; and (3) the social structure imposes a set of behavioral constraints on individuals and groups; therefore, people must take into account existing constraints and patterns of social relationships. As previously noted, however, medical sociologists working in the health field find that such basic propositions offer only partial explanations of behavior.

Economic and psychological factors also play important roles in the decision to seek medical advice. Likewise, sociological factors alone may not explain all the variations in the decision to seek a health career, choice of specialty within the health professions, and choice of practice setting. As Mechanic (1978) notes, medical sociology has become an interdisciplinary field in itself, drawing frequently on economics, psychology, anthropology, epidemiology and related areas. This is increasingly so, given the emergence of chronic illness, soaring costs, and the development of larger and more complex organizational settings for the delivery of health services.

In the process, the traditional distinction between sociology *in* medicine (Strauss 1957) (study of factors influencing the disease process which might produce knowledge directly relevant to clinical work) and the sociology *of* medicine (study of the profession of medicine itself and the settings in which it is practiced) has become blurred and less relevant. This is because it is increasingly evident that health professions and health organizations can be changed in ways which impact on clinical work while at the same time studies of the social-psychological factors which influence disease processes shed light on how professional work is conducted and its variability across different organizational settings. A prime example is the research on patient adherence or compliance with medical advice in which changes in organization structure designed to improve continuity of care have been associated with greater patient adherence to medical regimens. Similarly, microstudies of provider-patient communication designed to improve patient adherence have resulted in greater knowledge about the organizational and professional contexts in which such communications take place.

The vast research on utilization of health services also provides testimony to the diminishing distinction between the sociology in medicine and the sociology of medicine. This is evidenced by its focus on both physiological (e.g., health status) and social-psychological (e.g., health beliefs) predispositions of people to seek care, along with medically evaluated symptom severity (sociology in medicine concerns), as well as its focus on regular sources of care, the nature of different organizational settings for care, provider and facility/population ratios, and degree of third-party insurance coverage (sociology of medicine concerns). The important distinction is whether or not the variables are responsive to public policy and/or administrative intervention.

MAJOR CONCEPTS, THEORIES, AND PARADIGMS

CONCEPTS

There are a number of key concepts central to the sociological perspective which also hold meaning for health services research. Many of these are shared with the closely related disciplines of anthropology and psychology, and are briefly noted below along with a health services application.

1. Culture—a system of socially acquired and socially transmitted standards of judgment, belief and conduct transmitted from one generation to another

   Good health is highly valued in almost all cultures. The ways in which people attempt to maintain their health, however, will vary from culture to culture; for example, the health behavior and care-seeking practices of American Indians, Chicanos, Blacks and Anglo-Saxons differ widely.

2. Values—underlying motives or preferences that provide legitimacy for social arrangements and social behavior

   Physicians (particularly in the U.S.) place a high value on professional autonomy.

3. Norms—expectations, standards and rules that regulate interaction among persons and groups

   A part of Parsons' (1951) "sick role" concept is the norm that people desire to seek appropriate sources of medical care for purposes of getting well.

   Note: A norm often reflects an underlying value(s); for example, the norm that administrators should not interfere in the decision making of physicians is a reflection of the underlying values regarding the need for professional autonomy.

4. Role—collectively held expectations which define appropriate behavior for persons in a given social position

   The generic role of the health services administrator is to acquire and then coordinate human and capital resources in a fashion which will increase the probability of effective patient care.

5. Socialization—the transmittal of culture, norms, values, roles, ideas (etc.) from one group to another and one person to another

   Physicians and other health professionals are exposed to intensive periods of socialization during their training (regarding the "appropriate" values, norms and roles of their profession).

6. Social status—relative degree of prestige or honor accorded to given positions within a social system

   Differences in social status between health professionals and patients can create problems in provider-patient relationships.

7. Social structure—relationship patterns between and among people, groups and organizations—features of these patterns which are most

salient include the demographic characteristics of participants (age, sex, race, etc.) and the socioeconomic class characteristics of participants (occupation, education and income)

Some people believe the social structure of medical care to be quite diverse considering the different types of health professionals involved and the often loose linkages among them.

8. Social stratification—systematic differences in values and status among individuals, social positions or groups

It is generally believed that those involved in the delivery of health services constitute a highly stratified system with an extensive degree of specialization and subspecialization.

9. Social control—influence exerted on individuals by social groups, norms, values and sanctions

Health professionals are influenced by a number of groups (professional societies, consumer groups, etc.), norms (e.g., treat all patients alike), values (e.g., belief in autonomy over one's work), and sanctions (legal suits, etc.). These forces of social control, however, are not particularly well-articulated and, in fact, are frequently at odds with each other.

10. Deviance—departure from a given society's and culture's commonly accepted and shared norms, values and roles

Patients who are not interested in getting well are often referred to as "malingerers" and are viewed as deviant members of society.

11. Relative deprivation—perceived inequality in relation to certain individuals or groups which one chooses for comparison

In the United States, there no longer exists income differences in volume of ambulatory visits, but the poor may still feel relatively deprived of access to health services because they have larger perceived or actual need for care. In brief, they ought to experience significantly more visits because of their greater relative need for services. Relative deprivation may also exist among health providers as they perceive the inequities and rewards of one profession versus another.

The above are not all of the significant sociological concepts relevant to health services research but do constitute a representative set of building blocks. Further, the definitions represent the more commonly used interpretation of each term, although variations of each exist in the literature. In general, these concepts and their definitions constitute a relatively common language which sociologists use in the development of theoretical perspectives and paradigms, and which are found in the HSR literature.

THEORETICAL APPROACHES

More so than other disciplines, sociology lacks a single integrated view of the world; rather, it encompasses a large number of competing theories and paradigms. While this makes the discipline less parsimonious than, for example, economics, it also offers wider choice of explanation both within and across different levels of analysis (individual, group, organization, larger society).

Three major theoretical perspectives which have dominated sociological thinking are structural-functionalism, conflict theory, and symbolic interactionism. Structural-functionalism has its origins in analogies to biological organisms based on: (1) bounded systems which are self-regulating and maintain equilibrium; (2) basic societal need which, like the human body, must be met for the society to survive; (3) various parts which play key functions for the survival and equilibrium of the society; and (4) certain structures which must exist to ensure survival and homeostasis of the system (Maykovich 1980). The focus is on the functional unity of society brought about by a consensus of values which link people together and by certain functional prerequisites including goal attainment, adaptation, integration and latency (Parsons and Smelser 1956, p. 16). Goal attainment refers to establishing priorities among goals and mobilizing resources to achieve them. Adaptation refers to actually obtaining the necessary resources from the environment and making use of them to the system's benefit. Integration is concerned with the maintenance of social and emotional solidarity among members of a social group to ensure cooperation in attaining goals (one means of social control), while latency means maintaining within the individual the internal motives and values of the society. Linking all of the above is the notion of automatic feedback by which a system can regulate itself, undisturbed by external influences.

Structural-functionalism has been criticized on a number of grounds including its lack of empirical referents, its tautological reasoning (e.g., inequality exists because it is functional for society) and its inherent conservatism (e.g., basically ignores the phenomena of change and conflict). Nevertheless, it provides a useful, if partial, way of thinking about the health care system. For example, Parsons (1951) describes the sick role as one in which patients have certain obligations (seek competent help and desire to get well) in return for being exempted or absolved from certain responsibilities (that one is responsible for one's illness and is exempt from normal responsibilities). Such a portrayal helps to draw attention to how behavior is influenced by values and beliefs, and not solely by physical or psychological symptoms (Levine 1977), although the strict applicability of the sick role concept has been questioned by a number of investigators (Gordon 1966; Twaddle 1969; Segall 1976). A functionalist perspective is also useful in thinking of the social control and gatekeeper role which the health services systems play for the larger society.

The conflict theory, the second of the three major perspectives, developed in part as a reaction against the conservatism of the structural-function-alist approach. Its focus is on conflict, deviance and change. In *A Contribution to the Critique of Political Economy* (1911), Marx specified the conditions under which conflict will be violent. Coser goes on to indicate conditions under which conflict will be considered as well as how it can provide a positive integrative force in society in his *Continuities in the Study of Social Conflict* (1967). While functionalists like Parsons view the doctor-patient relationship as an asymmetric equilibrium in which patients are willingly subordinate, conflict theorists like Freidson (1970*a*; 1970*b*) posit a clash of interests be-tween doctors and patients. The conflict perspective is also relevant to the study of the health professions, analysis of professional behavior within health care organizations, and competition of professional groups and organizations for scarce resources.

Symbolic interactionism focuses on the processes of social interaction and the meaning which individuals attach to them. Unlike the structural-functionalist school, behavior is not assumed to be merely a function of ad-herence to normative standards. Rather, behavior is perceived as being di-rectly influenced by the interpretation of the situation. Symbolic interaction draws on the early work of Mead (1934) and the more recent work of Goffman (1961), and has found wide applicability in health services investigations. This is particularly so in the area of illness behavior where Gove (1975) and others have developed the labeling theory perspective in regard to mental illness, and Mechanic (1976), among others, has emphasized the attribution processes by which patients and providers attach meaning to symptoms. Others (e.g., Shortell 1973; 1974) have used concepts derived from symbolic interactionism in the form of social exchange theory to explain rates and patterns of patient referral among physicians.

PARADIGMS

The above mentioned theories constitute building blocks in the development of several major paradigms currently guiding sociological research and which, in turn, are pertinent to health services research. The major paradigms, as articulated by Ritzer (1975), are the social facts approach, the social definition approach, and the social behavior approach. The social facts approach em-phasizes the importance of social structures and institutions in shaping indi-vidual behavior. Values, roles, groups, norms and institutions have a reality of their own. Both structural-functionalism theories and conflict theories rep-resent examples of the social facts approach. Methodologically, emphasis is given to interview and questionnaire data. Within medical sociology, the structural-functionalism approach is best represented by Parsons and the con-flict perspective by Freidson. Within health services research, the social facts paradigm is found most frequently in studies of health care organization and responses to regulation and other external environmental factors.

The social definition paradigm focuses on human meaning and perception. Unlike the social facts paradigm, social structures and institutions are viewed as more than mere social facts. Situations are personally defined and acted upon. Symbolic interactionist theories represent examples of the social definition paradigm. Within medical sociology, the work of Mechanic and others concerned with perception of symptoms in relation to health seeking behavior constitutes an application of the social definition paradigm. In health services research, the social definition paradigm is most frequently drawn upon in studies of health services utilization and adherence to medical regimens. While questionnaires and interviews tend to be used, data collection also encompasses field observations and case studies.

The social behavior paradigm emphasizes the relationship between the individual's behavior and how the environment shapes that behavior. The difference between the social factist and the social behaviorist is that the social factist emphasizes macrostructures and institutions as forces of control while the social behaviorist focuses on individual contingencies of reinforcement— the rewards and costs resulting from individuals' interactions with their environment. Within medical sociology, the work of Levine and White (1961) represents one example of the social behavior paradigm. Within health services research, examples include studies of physician referral patterns, prospective reimbursement of hospitals, and capitation reimbursement of physicians and other health providers. While interviews, questionnaires and secondary data are all drawn upon, those working within the social behavior paradigm are also more inclined to direct interventions and social experiments to evaluate the impact of incentives designed to change behavior.

It should be recognized that considerable overlap exists among the social facts, social definition and social behavior paradigms. For example, while studies of patient adherence to medical regimen may emphasize individual meanings and perceptions in the symbolic-interactionist-social definition tradition, they also frequently take into account various rewards and costs (social behavior tradition) of individual adherence to medical advice and this, in turn, is frequently influenced by the realities of the larger social/organizational settings (social facts tradition) of medical practice. As will be seen in subsequent sections, health services research frequently draws upon all three paradigms in combination. Unfortunately, many investigators seem unaware of their orientation, which results in critical assumptions being left unstated or hidden, leading to unnecessary confusion. Thus, an understanding of the major concepts, theories and paradigms is important for sociologists and other social scientists engaging or about to engage in health services research. Figure 2.1 provides a framework for considering sociological contributions to health services research, while table 2.1 summarizes and provides some examples of the major paradigms, theories and concepts that have been discussed.

HEALTH, ILLNESS, AND SICK ROLE BEHAVIOR

HEALTH AND ILLNESS BEHAVIOR

Who uses health services? With what frequency? Of what sort, and with what cost and quality outcomes? These are some of the focal questions faced by health policy makers, and answers to them represent a central area of health services research. Along with anthropologists, economists and social psychologists, sociologists have made important contributions to the understanding of health services utilization, but much remains to be done.

Several reviews of the literature on utilization exist (e.g., Aday and Eichhorn 1972; McKinley 1972; Anderson 1973; Andersen and Anderson 1979; Shortell 1980). These identify a number of relatively distinct approaches to studying utilization behavior. They include the demographic approach, emphasizing variables such as age, sex and family size; the social-structural approach, emphasizing variables such as education, occupation, social class and ethnicity; the social-psychological approach, emphasizing people's values, attitudes, norms and cultures; the economic approach, focusing on variables such as price and income related to demand and supply factors; the organizational approach, emphasizing the organization of provider practices, referral patterns and interorganizational linkages; and the systems approach, which suggests that all of the above factors need to be taken into account in explaining differences in utilization. The demographic and social-structural approaches have basically followed the social facts paradigm, arguing that "facts" of demography and social class are important correlates of illness and utilization behavior. With the exception of the increased interest in the impact of sex on utilization (Nathanson 1975), the demographic approach has not been widely used in studies of health services utilization. More frequently, it is used in combination with other approaches. Social-structural approaches have been heavily influenced by the work of Zborowski (1952) and Zola (1966) concerning ethnic differences in the perception of pain and subsequent illness behavior, and by Suchman (1965) and Geersten et al. (1975), who have studied the influence of family and kin relations on health care seeking behavior.

The social-psychological approach derives from the social definition paradigm and is best represented by the health belief model (Rosenstock 1966). According to this model, the probability of engaging in health or illness behavior is a function of (1) the individual's perceived susceptibility to the particular illness; (2) the individual's perception of the severity of the illness; (3)

FIGURE 2.1: Framework for Considering Sociological Contributions to Health Services Research

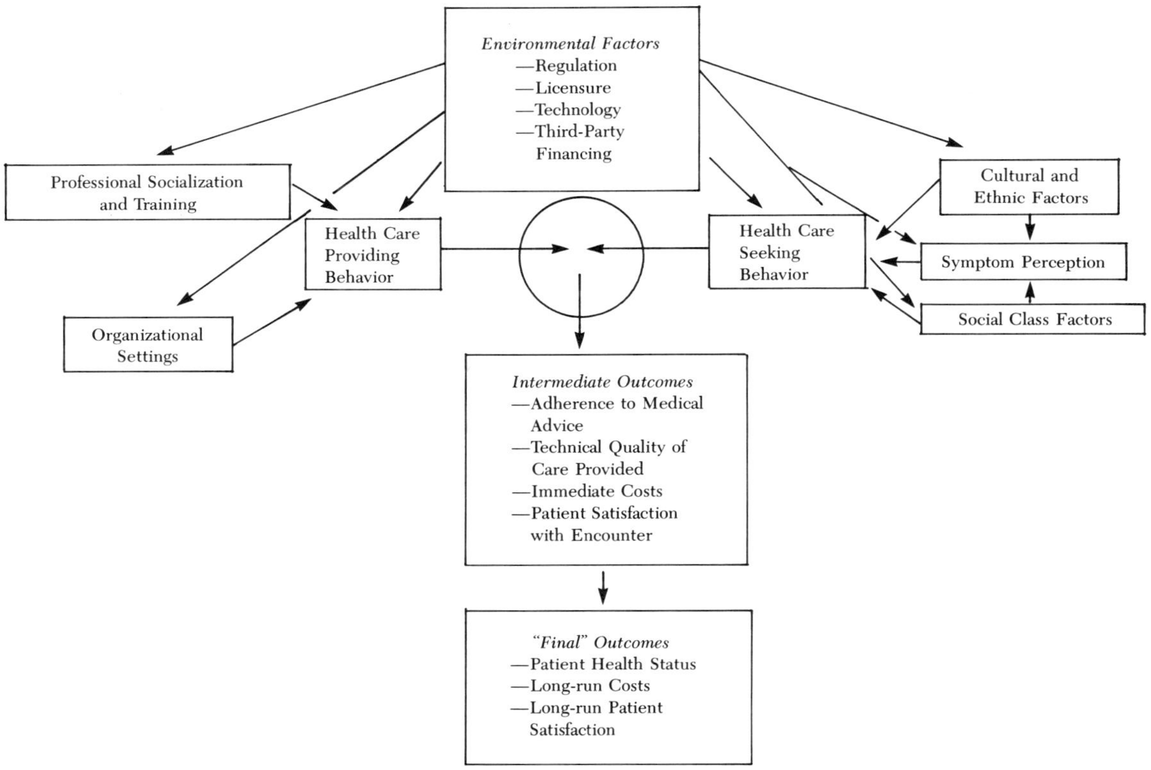

TABLE 2.1: Applications and Examples of Paradigms Relevant to Health Services Research

Paradigm	Health Issue Area	Relevant Models	Frequently Used Concepts	Examples of Empirical/Conceptual Work*
Social Facts (e.g., Structural Functionalism vs. Conflict Theory)	Health Care Seeking Behavior	Social Network Model	Social Role, Culture, Socialization, Social Structure, Social System, Lay Referral System	Parsons (1951) (Functionalist Perspective), Freidson (1970a; 1970b) (Conflict Perspective), Suchman (1965), Segall (1976), Geersten et al. (1975), Twaddle (1969)
	Health Care Providing Behavior	Bureaucratic vs. Open Systems	Same as above	Coser (1958), Goss (1961), Reeder (1972) } All Functionalist Perspective; Freidson (1970a; 1970b) (1975), Waitzkin and Waterman (1974) } Conflict Perspective
Social Definition (e.g., Symbolic Interactionism)	Health Care Seeking Behavior	Health Belief Model, Attribution Models	Values, Attitudes, Perceptions, Culture, Norms, Relative Deprivation, Deviance	Rosenstock (1966), Becker (1974), Kirscht (1974), Mechanic (1976), Zola (1966)
	Health Care Providing Behavior	Attribution Models	Same as above	Mechanic (1972), Greenley and Mechanic (1976)

	Health Care Seeking Behavior	Behavioral Model	Rewards Costs Social Status Social Stratification Social Control Norms Sanctions	Andersen (1968) Bice, Eichhorn and Fox (1973) Wan and Soifer (1974) Andersen et al. (1975)
Social Behavior (e.g., Social Exchange Theory)	Health Care Providing Behavior	Social Exchange	Same as above	Levine and White (1961) Elling and Halebsky (1961) Bucher and Stelling (1969) Shortell (1972) Fox and Swazey (1975) Freidson (1975) Rhee (1976; 1978)

If one were to include the study of the health professions, social disability, social epidemiology, mental illness and other areas of inquiry, a number of other investigators would be indicated. The above simply represent some examples of relevant work in the health services utilization and organizational research areas. Further, placement in any particular cell is governed by the main orientation of the particular work in question; several of the works cited actually draw to some extent from all three paradigms.

the individual's evaluation of the costs and benefits of engaging in the behavior; and (4) a cue to action, either within the individual as in the experience of symptoms or through interactions with others or mass media messages. While retaining its cognitive basis, in recent years health belief model research has incorporated social network and organizationally related variables in more refined explanations of health services utilization (Langlie 1977). It has also become more social behaviorist in its attempts to change health behavior through application of behavioral modification and related theories. Recent reviews of health belief model findings (Becker 1979; Kirscht 1974) indicate modest but relatively consistent support for the importance of perceptions and motivations in explaining differences in preventive health behavior and in health services utilization. This is particularly true for perceived susceptibility to illness and the perceived costs and benefits of engaging in health or illness behavior.

The economic and organizational approaches essentially follow the social behavior paradigm focusing on incentives and disincentives for engaging in behavior. Examples of the economic approach include the work of Grossman (1972), Phelps (1975) and Feldstein (1977), all focusing on determinants of the demand for health services, and Benham and Benham (1975), dealing with the effects of increased access to medical care on health status. Examples of the organizational approach include a number of emerging investigations dealing with the effects of alternative organizational models for care (Hetherington et al. 1975; Shortell et al. 1977; Meyers et al. 1977; Gaus 1976; Dutton 1979).

Finally, the systems approach attempts to integrate the above perspectives. Andersen's "behavioral model" (1968) represents a partial attempt toward a more integrated framework for explaining differences in use. This model posits a set of predisposing variables comprised of demographic social-structural, and social-psychological variables; a set of enabling variables comprised of economic and quasi-organizational factors; and a set of medical need variables determined both by patient perception and physician evaluations. The model has been tested using national data over three different time periods with recent results indicating that when other factors such as health status are controlled, nonwhites have fewer physician and dental visits than whites; dental visits are positively associated with income; having a regular source of care influences both contact and volume of services received; and degree of insurance coverage is positively associated with both hospital and physician utilization (Andersen 1975). However, most of the variation in different types of utilization is explained by medical need for care. A number of these factors have also been studied in other countries (e.g., Bice and White 1969).

From a health policy perspective, the results suggest that utilization of hospital care is remarkably well distributed with regard to equity since the primary determinants of use are illness and illness-related factors such as age. To a lesser extent, use of physician services is equitably distributed. Diagnostic severity is the best predictor of differences in use, but other factors (such as the existence of a regular source of care, degree of insurance coverage, and number of providers available) are also important. Dental care is least equitably distributed, since differences in use are more highly related to education, income, social class, and ethnic differences.

At the present time, there appears to be a convergence of the various approaches to the study of health services utilization and the underlying social factist, social definition, and social behavior paradigms from which they derive. A good example is a recent study of delay factors in emergency room use by Schwartz (1975) who analyzes the meanings which different social groups attach to delay (social definition approach), organizational responses to triage (social factist approach), and how these factors determine the length of delay (social behavior approach) experienced. Schwartz shows how these perspectives supplement the purely economic explanation based on supply and demand.

In part, such convergence may be due to the fact that a large amount of unexplained variation in health services utilization exists (typically 75–80 percent), suggesting the need to reformulate current models and consider the possible advantages of more integrative approaches. The convergence may also be due to the emergence over the past ten years of a relatively new group of medical sociologists trained in inter- and multidisciplinary academic settings with early exposure to health services issues and some of the theories and methodologies of other disciplines, including economics and, to a lesser extent, epidemiology, psychology and anthropology. These investigators may be somewhat more inclined to take a broader perspective on issues and recognize the potential utility of incorporating different paradigms and perspectives, at least within the discipline if not across disciplines. While this convergence may be desirable, there is continued need for improvement in measurement and study design methodology (particularly the need for more longitudinal studies) cutting across the various perspectives. There is also the need for further incorporation of decision theory approaches, and to consider issues of utilization in relation to other key issues and components of the system, including continuity, quality and cost of care. In the future, less emphasis is likely to be placed on access per se and more on the measurement of cost-effective utilization patterns and associated factors.

SICK ROLE BEHAVIOR

Kasl and Cobb (1966) have defined sick role behavior as "activity undertaken by those who consider themselves ill for the purpose of getting well." Inherent in the definition is the structural-functionalist perspective involving the restoration of an individual's health to a previously existing equilibrium state. Parsons' delineation of the sick role is also reflective of this orientation. Twaddle (1969), Segall (1976), Gordon (1966), Kassebaum and Baumann (1965) and others have called into question the strict applicability of Parsons' formulation, particularly for chronic illnesses and such conditions as alcohol and drug addiction. Freidson (1970a; 1970b), in particular, has criticized the structural-functional approach to provider-patient behavior by emphasizing how professional and client orientations and motivations differ, pointing out some of the consequences for sick role behavior. Most of the empirical work on sick role behavior has used the health belief model and focused on adherence with medical advice. Becker (1979), and Becker and Maiman (1975) have summarized most of this literature which generally suggests that perceived susceptibility, perceived severity, and perceived benefits and costs are positively related to compliance or adherence with medical regimen. Reflecting the convergence of perspectives noted above, this area suggests that the above factors can be influenced by structural and organizational changes in health care delivery as well as by direct behavioral interventions. Future research questions center on the further specification of the organizational/individual change relationships as they affect patient and provider behavior.

ORGANIZATIONAL BEHAVIOR

Of the various approaches to the study of organizations, the bureaucratic approach derived primarily from Weber (1947) and the open-systems perspective developed primarily by Katz and Kahn (1966) have been most frequently used in studies of health care organizations. More recently, contingency perspectives emerging from open-systems theory have received attention. The bureaucratic and open-systems perspectives are probably best illustrated by stating their position on key organizational issues as shown in table 2.2.

The bureaucratic approach (basically a social factist paradigm) has typically been limited by its neglect of individual motivation, environmental considerations, and its suggestion that there is "one best way" to manage an organization. The open-systems approach (which incorporates elements from social definition and social behavior paradigms) has remedied the latter two shortcomings, but still tends to neglect individual motivation considerations. Further, the theoretical and empirical linkages between environment, structure, process and outcome variables have yet to be clearly delineated. Using primarily the bureaucratic and open-systems perspectives, the following paragraphs briefly highlight some of the contributions of organizational studies to health care issues. A comprehensive review of all hospital organizational

TABLE 2.2: Comparison of Bureaucratic and Open-Systems Positions on Key Organizational Issues

Organizational Issues	Bureaucratic Position	Open-Systems Position
Efficiency	Maximized through a hierarchically ordered chain of positions and specified procedures for operation	May be attained in several ways depending on the nature of the tasks involved, the people involved, and external environmental circumstances.
Effectiveness (Goal Attainment)	As above	Above, plus expanding or changing goals to meet new demands from the environment.
Conflict	Minimize potential for conflict by having a "rule or procedure for everything"	Not necessarily dysfunctional. Can be promotive of creativity and innovation. The problem is to minimize "disruptive" conflict.
Change (Innovation)	Handle through rational accommodation and intervention. Establishment of new rules and procedures	Can occur either from within or without the organization. Again, depends on nature of tasks, people and environment. Some evidence to indicate that more loosely structured organizations are more innovative in an "invention" sense but that more tightly structured organizations are better at implementing and diffusing the innovation.
Social Integration	Basically not considered	May be achieved in a variety of ways including both intrinsic and extrinsic factors contributing to job satisfaction. The emphasis is on *roles*—getting people to function in their roles and understanding the roles of others.
Coordination	Activities coordinated through the establishment of a hierarchy and a specification of rules and procedures	The more specialized the organization the greater the need for coordination. May be achieved through committees and establishing coordinative departments as well as informal organization.
Maintenance (Interaction with Environment)	Basically not considered	Crucial to understanding organizational behavior. The organization must accommodate itself to its environment. "Environment" includes competing organizations, regulatory bodies, clients, customers, suppliers, labor markets, and related factors.

research in the 1960s is provided by Georgopoulos (1975) and more recent work by Shortell and Brown (1976).

Much of the research to date has focused on hospitals and most of the early studies concentrated on hospitals as bureaucratic organizations (Smith 1955; Anderson and Warkov 1961; Perrow 1965). These studies dealt with dual lines of authority and control, the effect of size on administrative components, and the bureaucratizing influences of technology. More recent work by Starkweather (1970) and Heydebrand (1973) on hospitals, as well as Roemer and Friedman (1971) and Shortell and Getzen (1979) on medical staff organization, has continued to delineate relationships involving organizational size, centralization/decentralization, formalization, coordination and control, and related factors. In general, as hospital size and complexity increase greater numbers of coordination mechanisms are necessary, both bureaucratic and nonbureaucratic. Among the nonbureaucratic mechanisms are specialization and professionalization itself. In fact, medical staff studies indicate that a more formalized degree of professionalization is taking place in terms of greater numbers of physicians on contract, as well as more formal physician participation in hospital decision making.

Research based on the open-systems perspective has probably made an even more important contribution to the understanding of how health care organizations function. The early work of Levine and White (1961) and Elling and Halbesky (1961) called attention to environmental factors and their impact on hospital structure and performance. Georgopoulos and Mann's (1962) early study of community general hospitals is a classic open-systems example of organizational research and helped lay the groundwork for a number of subsequent studies. In more recent years, the works of Becker and Neuhauser (1975), Pfeffer (1973), Roos et al. (1974), Morse et al. (1974), Rushing (1974), Shortell et al. (1976), Flood and Scott (1978) and Kimberly (1978), among others have contributed additional knowledge about factors influencing hospital performance. A common thread in all of these studies is the examination of the impact of the environmental and/or work technology factors on hospital structure and performance. There is increasing evidence that organizational and managerial variables explain more of the variability in cost and quality performance measures than such factors as medical staff composition or percentage of board-certified physicians. These findings have important implications for health policy makers because they suggest that the success of regulatory policies (certificate of need, prospective reimbursement, professional standards review organizations) will depend on how they impact on variables under managerial and medical staff control, as well as on the differential responses of these groups and the adaptability of organizational structure to the regulations. In brief, organizational research can begin to fill in major knowledge gaps concerning program and policy implementation issues.

As hospitals become more of an organized industry (for example, the growth of multihospital systems) and are increasingly vertically integrated with ambulatory care and long-term care services, the developing work of sociologists in the area of interorganizational relationships will become particularly important. The above developments are also likely to lead to further strains between organizational needs and the needs of professionals working in them. The organization needs predictability while the profession requires freedom to operate in the face of uncertainty. There must be a certain amount of commitment to organizational goals, while the professional's commitment is primarily to the profession and the development of one's work within the profession. Organizations require coordination and integration across departments while professionals need the freedom to operate within specialized interests. Organizations must have control and feedback to meet increased demands for public accountability while professionals are primarily interested in personal accountability to individual patients or to one's profession. Finally, specialization is necessary in order to accomplish certain organizational tasks, while for professionals, specialization is more likely to focus on personal goals not necessarily compatible with organizational needs. In sum, from the organization's viewpoint, professionals are a vehicle to achieve organizational goals, while from the professional's viewpoint, the organization is a vehicle to achieve one's professional goals. Examining these divergent forces under an increased regulatory environment will be an important area of research for sociologists and all social scientists in the coming years. Goss (1977) stated the case well: ". . . in realms bearing on physician organization and the review and control of medical work, U.S. policy decisions made within the past decade and presently pending have outpaced available sociological research."

METHODOLOGICAL ADVANCES

By its very nature health services research is essentially problem solving, dealing with issues of access, cost, quality and equity of health services. The social sciences' contribution to such problem solving lies in both its theories and methods. In the past decade there has been a somewhat closer integration between theory and method in health services research than previously. Within sociology, this development is characterized by the remarkable eclecticism with which medical sociologists freely draw on econometric and epidemiological methodologies, as well as place greater emphasis on experimental and quasi-experimental designs. In fact, while theoretical and paradigmatic differences among the disciplines continue to exist, a common methodological language and set of investigative tools are beginning to develop which both facilitate interdisciplinary collaboration and are a result of such collaboration.

The net result is that a greater number of ideas and verbal theories about access, cost, quality and equity issues have been subjected to increasingly rigorous empirical testing.

The literature on prepaid group practices represents a good example of methodological advances in health services research. The early studies descriptively documented the relationship between prepaid group practice and lower hospital use. These studies were, in turn, extended to prepaid groups with different characteristics (e.g, those owning their own hospital versus those contracting with other hospitals). Research then progressed to testing in a multivariate fashion an even greater number of alternative explanations for the lower use of hospitals by prepaid groups (e.g., differences in patient mix and differences in scope of benefits). Studies which analyzed such factors over time began to appear along with examination of possible causal relationships among the variables. Most recently, studies involving true experiments or approximations to true experiments have begun to appear, providing a more rigorous test of causal relationships. In brief, inquiry has progressed from purely descriptive examination of a few cases to additional settings involving a greater number of variables, to examination of relationships over time, and, eventually, to delineation of cause and effect relationships. Research involving the health belief model has followed a similar progression.

From a data analysis viewpoint, perhaps the single major methodological advance of sociologists doing health services research has been in the application of increasingly sophisticated econometric methods. While ordinary least-squares regression continues to be appropriate for many studies, increasing reliance is being placed on two-stage least-squares regression, development of structural equation models, path analysis, logit analysis, probit analysis, and time series analysis. The need for such analyses is due to the increased complexity of health phenomena being examined (e.g., the increase in health care costs) with the associated difficulty in determining which variables are endogenous and which exogenous. As previously noted, those working in the social behavior paradigm are particularly likely to be involved in some of the more refined multivariate methods.

There have also been significant advances in social survey research methodology, especially in questionnaire design, testing for reliability and validity of measures, and measuring survey response errors. Of particular note has been the use of the telephone in conducting interviews. Existing evidence suggests that data collected by telephone are as reliable and valid as data collected in face-to-face interviews and, furthermore, use of the telephone is usually less costly (Horton and Duncan 1978).

The trend toward increased methodological rigor is likely to continue (and in a more multidisciplinary fashion) as sociologists continue to work more closely with economists and epidemiologists, among others. Further, there are likely to be more combinations of methods employed within studies, using case study and qualitative methods with multivariate analyses and experimentation. This is due to the increased public policy nature of health services research which demands answers to both why a given program or policy worked (assessed through experimentation and multivariate analysis which rules out alternative explanations), and how it worked (addressed through case studies and related qualitative methods focusing on implementation issues). As Patrick and Elinson (1979) note, "To measure is to point the way to policy"; the final section of this chapter is devoted to policy implications.

FUTURE DIRECTIONS AND HEALTH POLICY CONTRIBUTIONS

FUTURE DIRECTIONS

Undoubtedly there will be further refinements to existing models of health, illness, and sick role behavior, new approaches and insights into the functioning of health care organizations, and significant advances in areas of mental illness, social disability, social epidemiology, the professions and related contemporary areas of sociological investigation. Without minimizing these potential accomplishments, the major contribution of sociology to health services research and health policy in the next decade lies in other areas, although not unrelated to the issues noted above.

First, sociologically oriented health services research can help provide consumers, providers and policy makers with a broader view of the issues and problems. Most of the issues facing the health care system involve a complex web of economic, cultural, social, political and organizational factors. For example, consumers complain about bureaucratically organized impersonal care while health providers complain about lack of compliance or adherence with their advice. The sociological perspective draws attention not only to the association between these two phenomena but to the fact that both may be the result of a common third factor—namely, the attempt by health care organizations and the professionals working in them to adjust to a more complex environment caused by increased regulation. Such regulation stems, in part, from increased public concern about the rising costs of health care.

Second, health services are becoming increasingly population-based within the context of larger and more organized systems of care. The study of large social systems and organized social structures is a comparative advantage of sociology, and thus the sociological perspective is likely to become an increasingly important component of health services research.

Third, the health system is faced with a number of new issues raised by technological advances and changes in social values and norms regarding issues such as death and dying. Again, sociologists have experience in considering such issues beginning with the early work of Blauner (1966) and Sudnow (1967) and continuing with the recent work of Fox and Swazey (1975) and Kimberly (1978).

Fourth, the trend for sociologists to work more closely with economists will continue at an accelerated pace, and three developments will encourage this collaboration. The first is the increased interest in regulation. The work by Salkever (an economist) and Bice (a sociologist) on the impact of certificate of need is a recent example. Secondly, as noted in the previous section, advances in sociological methodology drawing on econometrics (for example, path analysis and related structural equation models) have enabled a number of sociologists and economists to speak a relatively common modeling and data analysis language. It might be that continued collaboration of sociologists and economists could lead to better integrated socioeconomic models of medical practice. The third development is the increased sociological interest in the larger political economy affecting the delivery of health care as represented by the work of Krause (1977). The central question of economists and of increasing interest to growing numbers of sociologists is "Who benefits?"

There will also be growing collaboration with epidemiologists due to the increased importance of chronic illness, the growth in addictive disorders, and the increased emphasis, noted earlier, on population-based delivery systems.

Finally, with the greater demand for public accountability has come a significant increase in health programs which are required to be formally evaluated. Sociologists and other social scientists will ride the wave of the increased interest in evaluation research. In such research, sociology enjoys a comparative advantage over economics in that sociologists have given much more attention to variables involved in process evaluations (for example, organizational structures and processes, goal conflict, role conflict). On the other hand, economists, particularly those involved with cost-benefit and cost-effectiveness analysis, have had somewhat more experience in conducting impact or outcome evaluations. Again, collaboration between the two disciplines is likely to lead to important contributions to our understanding of new health programs and policies.

PUBLIC POLICY IMPLICATIONS

Current health policy is dominated by the social behaviorist paradigm (emphasis on incentives and disincentives to shape behavior) to the relative neglect of social definition and social facts perspectives. Regulatory and payment mechanisms fail to take into account the perceptions and meanings which consumers, providers and administrators attach to them or which assume that these meanings are the same as those of the policy maker. Implementation problems associated with rate review programs and health systems agencies serve as two examples. In like fashion, policies are frequently implemented without taking into account the realities of existing social structures and role relationships. It is precisely in these areas that sociology as a discipline can contribute to better health policy. As Luft (1976) has noted, economists have generally ended their policy efforts with the submission of their cost-benefit studies to the policy maker. There have been no attempts to go further and deal with the implementation issues involving interest group analysis and the calculation of what amounts to the utility functions of the major parties involved with the new policy. While more economists should get involved in such issues (as Luft suggests), sociologists and political scientists have been the prime movers in developing many of the concepts, perspectives and methodologies to best deal with these issues.

In addition, as health care organizations become increasingly interdependent, sociologists can begin pointing out the nature of these interdependencies in a way which lends itself to more realistic and enlightened health policy. Because the health industry is increasingly interdependent, regulatory controls on one part of the industry (e.g., hospitals) are likely to have ripple effects on other parts (such as physician practices and ambulatory care). Recent experiences with certificate of need legislation and prospective reimbursement experiments illustrate this effect. Sociologists, particularly those working at the macroindustrial level, can provide insights into such interdependencies and second-order consequences which can have a general enlightening effect on future policies.

Furthermore, sociologists can contribute to public policy in a general sense by further theoretical development of independent variables like culture, ethnicity, social norms, social sanctions, relative deprivation, social conflict, status inconsistency, socialization and organizational structure, among others. In the process, it is important for sociologists to distinguish between those factors potentially susceptible to public policy or administrative intervention (such as rewards and sanctions, socialization experiences, and organizational structure) and those more resistant to such change (e.g., culture, ethnicity, and long-standing social norms). Coleman (1972) discusses these in terms of policy variables subject to change and situational variables not subject to change, both of which are needed to predict the impact on policy outcome variables such as access to care, cost of care, or quality of care. The situational variables help to identify the target groups for change, and shed light on how specific policy or programmatic changes may exert differential effects across different cultural or ethnic groups or groups with different social norms.

Eichhorn and Bice (1973) have also noted the distinction between the disciplines which tend to focus on independent variables and then search for dependent variables to be explained, compared to health services research which begins with dependent variables (access, costs, quality, etc.) and then searches for explanatory independent variables. While one is left with the implication that this creates a problem for sociologists and other social scientists working in health services research, it also represents an excellent opportunity for collaboration. The key lies in the willingness of the sociologist to invest enough time to understand the nature of the health problem or issue (the dependent variable) and the willingness of the health care decision maker to work through the implications of the explanations (the policy and situational variables) offered by social scientists. The latter is the more difficult problem, given the acute time demands faced by most decision makers. Much of the burden must remain with the social scientist to conceive of the problem in realistic terms and to offer explanations in terms understandable and relevant to decision makers.

While the above represent potential areas of impact, actual impact will depend on three additional factors. First is the ability of sociologists to get close to the issues. This will depend on greater numbers of sociologists working in governmental agencies at national, state and local levels and on the interface between universities and governmental agencies. In brief, sociologists willing to influence policy need to become "reality oriented" about the issues and their short-run and long-run implications. Second is the need for better research itself with clearer, more reliable and more valid concept measurement, better articulated theories, more rigorous research designs and more careful data analysis. Third is the need for sociologists and other social scientists to do a much better job of research brokerage and dissemination of findings. This involves personal face-to-face interaction with policy makers, continual reinforcement, keeping issues before the key parties involved, writing in language understandable to the policy makers, and publishing in forums which attract the attention of the mass media, such as *The New York Times* coverage of the *New England Journal of Medicine*.

The above is not meant to suggest that all sociologists can or should influence public policy. Neither is it meant to suggest that sociology's main contribution as a discipline is to influence public policy. On the contrary, sociology's main contribution will continue to be the exploration of humanity's relationships with society which only from time to time may be explicated in the form of specific social policies. Rather, what is intended is to note that there are some interesting and important health policy issues facing the country, such as access-cost-quality of care trade-offs, incorporation of new technology, ethical issues of death and dying, and development and deployment of new types of health professionals—all of which represent more or less natural opportunities for explanation by social scientists and which, in turn, can advance social science theory. However, Gibson (1971), Mechanic (1974) and others have wisely cautioned against expecting too much. The social sciences' impact on public policy will continue to remain largely indirect, more often providing an information base and climate for shaping issues rather than tracing specific new programs or policies to single, discrete pieces of social science research. In the health services area one must keep in mind that, unlike most of the biomedical sciences, the findings of sociologists and other social scientists often pose a direct threat to the existing autonomy, organizations, and relationships of health professionals and not infrequently to the policy makers themselves.

REFERENCES

Aday, L., and Eichhorn, R. 1972. *The utilization of health services: Indices and correlates.* Publication no. (HSM)73-3003, Department of Health, Education, and Welfare. Rockville, Maryland.

Andersen, R. 1968. *A behavioral model of families' use of health services.* Research Series 25, Chicago: Center for Health Administration Studies.

Andersen, R., and Anderson, O. W. 1979. Trends in the use of health services. In *Handbook of medical sociology*, 3rd ed., ed. H. E. Freeman, S. Levine, and L. G. Reeder, pp. 371-91. Englewood Cliffs, NJ: Prentice-Hall Inc.

Andersen, R., Kravits, J., and Anderson, O. W. 1975. *Equity in health services.* Cambridge: Ballinger Publishing Co.

Anderson, J. G. 1973. Health services utilization: Framework and review. *Health Services Research* 8:184-99.

Anderson, J. and Warkov, S. 1961. Organizational size and functional complexity. *American Sociological Review* 26(February):25.

Becker, M. H. 1979. Psychosocial aspects of health-related behavior. In *Handbook of medical sociology*, 3rd. ed., eds. H. E. Freeman, S. Levine, and L. G. Reeder, pp. 253-74. Englewood Cliffs, NJ: Prentice-Hall Inc.

Becker, M., and Maiman, L. 1975. Sociobehavioral determinants of compliance with health and medical care recommendations. *Medical Care* 13(January):10-25.

Becker, S., and Neuhauser, D. 1975. *Organization efficiency.* New York: Elsevier Press.

Benham, L., and Benham, A. 1975. Impact of incremental medical services on health status, 1963-1970. In *Equity in health services*, eds. R. Andersen, J. Kravits, and O. W. Anderson, pp. 217-28. Cambridge: Ballinger Press.

Bice, T. et al. 1979. *Report of a study–health services research.* Washington, D.C.: National Academy of Sciences, Institute of Medicine, Division of Health Care Services.

Bice, T., Eichhorn, R., and Fox, P. 1973. Economic class and use of physician services. *Medical Care* 11(July–August):287-96.

Bice, T., and White, K. 1969. Factors related to the use of health services: An international comparative study. *Medical Care* 7(March–April):124-33.

Blauner, R. 1966. Death and social structure. *Psychiatry* 29(November):383-87.

Bucher, R. and Stelling, J. 1969. Characteristics of professional organizations. *Journal of Health and Social Behavior* 10:3-15.

Clausen, J. A. 1979. Mental disorder. In *Handbook of medical sociology*, 3rd ed., eds. H. E. Freeman, S. Levine, and L. G. Reeder, pp. 97-112. Englewood Cliffs, NJ: Prentice-Hall Inc.

Coleman, J. 1972. *Policy research in the social sciences*, pp. 1-23. Morristown, NJ: General Learning Press.

Coser, L. A. 1967. *Continuities in the study of social conflict.* New York: Free Press.

Coser, R. 1958. Authority and decision making in a hospital. *American Sociological Review* 23(February):36-63.

Durkheim, E. 1951. *Suicide.* New York: Free Press.

Dutton, D. 1979. Patterns of ambulatory care in five different delivery systems. *Medical Care* 17(March):221-43.

Eichhorn, R., and Bice, T. 1973. Academic disciplines and health services research. In *Health services research and R&D in perspective*, eds. E. E. Flook and P. J. Sanazaro. Ann Arbor: Health Administration Press.

Elling, R., and Halebsky, S. 1961. Organizational differentiation and support: A conceptual framework. *Administrative Science Quarterly* 6:185-209.

Farris, R. 1964. The discipline of sociology. In *Handbook of modern sociology*, ed. R. Farris, pp. 1-36. Chicago: Rand McNally.

Feldstein, M. 1977. Quality change and the demand for hospital care. *Econometrica* 45(October):1681-1702.

Flood, A., and Scott, W. R. 1978. Professional power and professional effectiveness: The power of the surgical staff and the quality of surgical care in hospitals. *Journal of Health and Social Behavior* 19(September):240-54.

Fox, R. and Swazey, J. 1975. *The courage to fail: A social view of organ transplants and dialysis.* Chicago: University of Chicago Press.

Freeman, H. E., Levine, S., and Reeder, L. G., eds. 1979. *Handbook of medical sociology*, 3rd ed. Englewood Cliffs, NJ: Prentice-Hall Inc.

Freidson, E. 1970a. *The profession of medicine.* New York: Dodd, Mead, and Co.

———. 1970b. *Professional dominance: The social structure of medical care.* New York: Atherton Press Inc.

———. 1975. *Doctoring together: A study of professional social control.* New York: Elsevier Scientific Publishing Co. Inc.

Gaus, C. et al. 1976. Contrasts in HMO and fee-for-service performance. *Social Security Bulletin* 3(May):3-14.

Geersten, R. et al. 1975. A reexamination of Suchman's views on social factors and health care utilization. *Journal of Health and Social Behavior* 16(June):226-37.

Georgopoulos, B. F. 1975. *Hospital organizational research: Review and source book.* Philadelphia: W. B. Saunders.

Georgopoulos, B. F., and Mann, F. C. 1962. *The community general hospital.* New York: MacMillan.

Gibson, G. 1971. Explanatory models and strategies for social change in health care behavior. *Social Science and Medicine* 6:635-39.

Goffman, E. 1961. *Asylums.* Garden City, NJ: Doubleday.

Gordon, G. 1966. *Role theory and illness.* New Haven, CT: College and University Press.

Goss, M. 1963. Patterns of bureaucracy among hospital staff physicians. In *The hospital in modern society*, ed. E. Freidson, pp. 170-94. New York: The Free Press.

_____, et al. 1977. Social organization and control in medical work: A call for research. *Medical Care*, Supplement. 15(May):1-10.

Gove, W. R. 1975. Labeling and mental illness: A critique. In *The labeling of deviants: Evaluating a perspective*, ed. W. R. Gove. New York: John Wiley & Sons.

Graham, F., and Reeder, L. G. 1979. Social epidemiology of chronic diseases. In *Handbook of medical sociology*, 3rd ed., eds. H. E. Freeman, S. Levine, and L. G. Reeder, pp. 71-96. Englewood Cliffs, NJ: Prentice-Hall Inc.

Greenley, J., and Mechanic, D. 1976. Social selection in seeking help for psychological problems. *Journal of Health and Social Behavior* 17(September):249-62.

Grossman, M. 1972. The demand for health: A theoretical and empirical investigation. National Bureau of Economic Research, Occasional Paper No. 119. New York: Columbia University Press.

Hetherington, R. W., Hopkins, C. E., and Roemer, M. I. 1975. *Health insurance plans: Promise and performance*. New York: John Wiley & Sons.

Heydebrand, W. 1973. *Hospital bureaucracy: A comparative study of organizations*. New York: Dunellen Press.

Horton, R. L., and Duncan, D. J. 1978. A new look at telephone interviewing methodology. *Pacific Sociological Review* 21(July):259-74.

Kaplan, H. B. 1979. Social psychology of disease. In *Handbook of medical sociology*, 3rd ed., eds. H. E. Freeman, S. Levine, and L. G. Reeder, pp. 53-70. Englewood Cliffs, NJ: Prentice-Hall Inc.

Kasl, S. B., and Cobb, S. 1966. Health behavior, illness behavior, and sick role behavior: I. health and illness behavior. *Archives of Environmental Health* 12(February):246-66.

Kassebaum, G. G., and Baumann, B. O. 1965. Dimensions of the sick role in chronic illness. *Journal of Health and Human Behavior* 6(Spring):16-27.

Katz, D., and Kahn, R. 1966. *The social psychology of organizations*, 2nd ed. New York: John Wiley & Sons.

Kimberly, J. 1978. Hospital adoption of innovation. *Journal of Health and Social Behavior* 19(December):361-74.

Kirscht, J. P. 1974. The health belief model and illness behavior. *Health Education Monographs* 2(Winter):387-408.

Krausse, E. 1977. *Power and illness: The political sociology of health and medical care*. New York: Elsevier Press.

Kuhn, A. 1974. *The logic of social systems*. San Francisco: Jossey-Bass.

Langlie, J. K. 1977. Social networks, health beliefs, and preventive health behavior. *Journal of Health and Social Behavior* 18:244-60.

Levine, S. 1977. Medical sociology—Part 1. Paper prepared for the Behavioral Science–Health Science Task Force, Association of University Programs in Health Administration.

_____, and White, P. 1961. Exchange as a conceptual framework for the study of interorganizational relationships. *Administrative Science Quarterly* 5:583-601.

Luft, H. 1976. Benefit-cost analysis and public policy implementation: From normative to positive analysis. *Public Policy* 24(Fall):437-62.

Marx, K. 1911. *A contribution to the critique of political economy.* Chicago: C. H. Kerr.

Maykovich, M. 1980. *Medical sociology.* Palo Alto, CA: Mayfield Publishing Co.

McKinley, J. B. 1972. Some approaches and problems in the study in the use of services—An overview. *Journal of Health and Social Behavior* 13:115-52.

Mead, G. H. 1934. *Mind, self, and society from the standpoint of a social behaviorist.* Chicago: University of Chicago Press.

Mechanic, D. 1972. *Public expectations and health care: Essays on the changing organization of health services.* New York: Wiley-Interscience.

————. 1974. *Politics, medicine, and social science.* New York: Wiley-Interscience.

————. 1976. Illness, illness behavior, and help seeking: Implications for increasing the responsiveness of health services. In *The growth of bureaucratic medicine,* D. Mechanic, pp. 161-76. New York: John Wiley & Sons.

————. 1978. *Medical sociology,* 2nd ed. New York: Free Press.

————. 1979. Physicians. In *Handbook of medical sociology,* 3rd ed., ed. H. E. Freeman, S. Levine, and L. G. Reeder, pp. 177-92. Englewood Cliffs, NJ: Prentice-Hall Inc.

Meyers, S. M., Hirshfeld, S. B., Walden, D. C., et al. 1977. Ambulatory and medical use by federal employees: Experience of members in a service benefit plan and in a prepaid group practice plan. Paper presented at the 105th Annual Meeting of the American Public Health Association, Nov. 1, Washington, D.C.

Morse, E. V., Gordon, G., and Tanon, C. 1974. Hospital costs and quality of care: An organizational perspective. *Milbank Memorial Fund Quarterly* 52 (Summer):315-45.

Nathanson, C. A. 1975. Illness and the feminine role: A theoretical view. *Social Science and Medicine* 9:57-62.

Parsons, T. 1951. *The social system.* New York: Free Press.

————, and Smelser, N. J. 1956. *Economy and society,* p. 16. Glencoe, IL: Free Press.

Patrick, D., and Elinson, J. 1979. Methods of sociomedical research. In *Handbook of medical sociology,* 3rd ed., ed. H. E. Freeman, S. Levine, and L. G. Reeder, p. 438. Englewood Cliffs, NJ: Prentice-Hall Inc.

Perrow, C. 1965. Hospitals: Technology, structure, and goals. In *Handbook of organizations,* ed. J. G. March. Skokie, IL: Rand-McNally and Co.

Pfeffer, J. 1973. Size, composition, and function of hospital boards of directors: A study of organization-environment linkage. *Administrative Science Quarterly* 18(September):349.

Phelps, S. 1975. Effects of insurance on demand for medical care. In *Equity in health services,* eds. R. Andersen, J. Kravits, and O. W. Anderson, pp. 105-30. Cambridge: Ballinger Press.

Reeder, L. G. 1972. The patient–client as a consumer: Some observations on the changing professional–client relationship. *Journal of Health and Social Behavior* 13:406-12.

Rhee, S. O. 1976. Factors determining the quality of physician performance and patient care. *Medical Care* 14:733.

Ritzer, G. 1975. Sociology: A multiple paradigm science. *The American Sociologist* 10(August):156-67.

Roemer, M. I., and Friedman, J. 1971. *Doctors in hospitals*. Baltimore: Johns Hopkins University Press.

Roos, N. P., Schermerhorn, J. R. and Roos, L. L., Jr. 1974. Hospital performance: Analyzing power and goals. *Journal of Health and Social Behavior* 15(June):78.

Rosenstock, I. M. 1966. Why people use health services (Part 2). *Milbank Memorial Fund Quarterly* 44(July):94-127.

Rushing. W. 1974. Differences in profit and nonprofit organizations: A study of effectiveness and efficiency in general short-stay hospitals. *Administrative Science Quarterly* 19(December):473-84.

Salkever, D., and Bice, T. 1976. The impact of certificate-of-need controls on hospital investment. *Milbank Memorial Fund Quarterly/Health and Society* 54(Spring):185-214.

Schwartz, B. 1975. *Queuing and waiting: Studies in the social organization of access and delay*. Chicago: University of Chicago Press.

Segall, A. 1976. The sick role concept: Understanding illness behavior. *Journal of Health and Social Behavior* 17(June)162-69.

Shortell, S. M. 1972. *A model of physician referral behavior: A test of exchange theory in medical practice*. Research Series 31. Chicago: Center for Health Administration Studies.

_____. 1973. Patterns of referral among internists in private practice: A social exchange model. *Journal of Health and Social Behavior* 14(December):335-48.

_____. 1974. Determinants of physician referral rates: An exchange theory approach. *Medical Care* 12(January):13-31.

_____. 1980. Factors associated with the utilization of health services. In *Introduction to health services*, eds. P. Torrens and S. Williams, pp. 48-90. New York: John Wiley & Sons.

_____, Becker, S. W., and Neuhauser, D. 1976. The effects of management practices on hospital efficiency and quality of care. In *Organizational research in hospitals*, eds. S. M. Shortell and M. Brown, pp. 90-106. Chicago: Blue Cross Association.

_____, and Brown, M., eds. 1976. *Organizational research in hospitals*. Chicago: Blue Cross Association.

_____, and Getzen, T. 1979. Measuring hospital medical staff organization structure. *Health Services Research* 14(Summer):97-110.

_____, and LoGerfo, J. 1978. Health services research and public policy: Definitions, accomplishments, and potential. *Health Services Research* 13(Fall):230-31.

_____, Richardson, W. C., and LoGerfo, J. P., et al. 1977. The relationship among dimensions of health services in two provider systems: A causal model approach. *Journal of Health and Social Behavior* 18(June):139-59.

Smith, H. L. 1955. Two lines of authority: The hospital's dilemma. *The Modern Hospital* 84(March):59-64.

Starkweather, D. 1970. Hospital size, complexity, and formalization. *Health Services Research* 5(Winter):330.

Strauss, R. 1957. The nature and status of medical sociology. *American Sociological Review* 22:200.

Suchman, E. 1965. Social patterns of illness and medical care. *Journal of Health and Human Behavior* 5(Spring):2-16.

Sudnow, D. 1967. Dead on arrival. Transaction 5, 1967; also in 1978. *Dominant issues in medical sociology*, ed. H. B. Schwartz and C. S. Kart, pp. 173-80. Reading, MA: Addison-Wesley.

Twaddle, A. C. 1969. Health decisions and sick role variations: An exploration. *Journal of Health and Social Behavior* 10(June):105-15.

―――――, and Hessler, R. 1977. *A sociology of health*, p. 32. St. Louis, MO: The C. V. Mosby Co.

Waitzkin, H. B., and Waterman, B. 1974. *The exploitation of illness in capitalist society*. Indianapolis: Bobbs-Merrill.

Wan, T. and Soifer, S. J. 1974. Determinants of physician utilization: A causal analysis. *Journal of Health and Social Behavior* 15:100-108.

Weber, M. 1947. *The theory of social and economic organization*, trans. A. M. Henderson and T. Parsons. New York: Oxford University Press.

Zborowski, M. 1952. Cultural components in responses to pain. *Journal of Social Issues* 8:16-30.

Zola, I. 1966. Culture in symptoms: An analysis of patients presenting complaints. *American Sociological Review* 31(October):615-30.

Three

Political Science and Health

THEODORE R. MARMOR and
ANDREW B. DUNHAM

INTRODUCTION

The substantial extension and expansion of public government programs in health and medicine since 1965 have augmented the importance of political analysis to health services research. Comprehending governmental actions and the responses they generate are subjects of considerable contemporary importance for government itself, patients and professionals, and social science research.

This chapter introduces the political science approach and its analytical tools through a presentation of various political science concepts, perspectives, and a brief outline of the American governmental system. It examines in detail the conceptual models that analysts and practitioners use in assessing political activity in both governmental and nongovernmental settings, and summarizes the major explanatory paradigms in political science. The chapter concludes with an evaluation of politics in the health industry, depicting the varied nature of its political conflicts and typical patterns of American health policy. Our goal is to answer a question posed by students of health and medicine: "What should we know about the use and limits of political science for understanding medical care and health?"

CONCEPTIONS OF POLITICAL SCIENCE

Political science is the study of how men are governed. Standard professional definitions of the subject range from the "authoritative allocation of values" (Easton 1953) to "who gets what, when and how" (Lasswell 1936). The focus is on social choices concerning the distribution of benefits and burdens within society. These benefits and burdens are not only material, but also involve power, status, and symbolic and psychological factors.

CONTEMPORARY APPROACHES

The Life of Politics

The narrowest and most common approach to political science concentrates on conflict and decision making in government: who gets what and how in the public arena. Such analysis emphasizes the direct influences on government (inputs), how governmental institutions convert (process) those influences into decisions or actions (outputs), and the impacts of actions (outcomes). Outputs and outcomes exert influence on government (feedback), and thus the circuit is completed.

This approach has spawned a substantial literature on public opinion, the role of parties, voting and other forms of political participation. Political scientists who work from this perspective emphasize the importance of interest groups in politics, not just in elections or the passing (or blocking) of legislation, but also in the administrative implementation of programs. They also argue that the internal organization and processes of government themselves have a profound effect on decisions and actions.

Simply discerning what the government is actually doing, moreover, is not easy. Indeed, a major function of political science has been a descriptive one, devoted to identifying and clarifying government action. Such efforts have yielded numerous studies on governmental structure, legislative arrangements and rules, public administration and bureaucratic behavior, and judicial process. This conception of political analysis, concerned with what one might term the "life of politics"—the activities in the governmental or public sector—is now the conventional approach of American political scientists.

The Politics of Life

A broader but less frequently exercised approach to political science examines the "politics of life"—conflict and collective, authoritative decision making in general, not just governmental, settings. This approach recognizes that politics occurs everywhere: hospitals, universities, private organizations, and offices. The politics of life approach deals with the micropolitics of everyday life.

Social Structure and Political Settings

The broadest approach to political science begins with social structure, political culture, and ideology. This perspective emphasizes the context within which the life of politics and the politics of life take place. The values and social arrangements of every society create systematic biases that favor some interests, promote certain types of action, and affect whether some issues and policies are even placed on the political agenda. Studies that include cross-cultural and cross-national comparisons often embody this approach. Such comparative studies (e.g, Altenstetter 1974; Heidenheimer 1973) can be valuable in showing new alternatives, the probable consequences of choices, and the limits of effective choice.

Nondecisions and the Political Agenda Many important issues do not reach the level of collective choice, but are settled outside the public realm by what have been termed *nondecisions* (Bachrach and Baratz 1962). The fact that national health insurance proposals never received serious attention during the Depression of the 1930s reflects a nondecision. In 1935 President Roosevelt excluded national health insurance from his Social Security proposals because he feared vitriolic and powerful political opposition. There was virtually no serious congressional consideration of health insurance because individual decisions on the political agenda tacitly determined the extent of public consideration of the issue.

There are innumerable instances of prolonged lack of recognition of issues by decision makers. Such issues are outside the contemporary politics of life or the life of governmental politics, and yet they are significant both because the biases of a system are revealed as much by what is not done as by what is done and because they may become politically salient. Politics may well be the "art of the possible," but it is important to understand what makes something possible, and how and why circumstances change. There have been few political and sociological analyses of the important subject of how, when and why political "possibilities" change over time.

The Social Setting of Politics The social system places limits not only on what is seriously considered, but also on what can be accomplished. The structural approach to political science locates health (or any other sector) within the larger society, focuses on the incentives for coherence and compatibility with society, and assesses the impact of society on the behavior of the health care system. Consider, for example, a society with a barter economy contemplating a national health insurance program that includes deductibles payable in cash. Such a policy is simply incompatible with the social system. Though simplistic, the example draws attention to the fact that every society has limits that are vitally important for the formation and implementation of social policies.

A more realistic example is the constraint on egalitarian policies in a society based on individual material incentives. It is obvious that the basic problem of the poor in America is that they do not have enough money. But massive redistribution of cash in an economic system based on wage labor would weaken the incentive to work. Even public services—education, public housing, food stamps, medical care—if provided at "too high" a level, might diminish such incentive. This is not to say that such a limit is approached in America today, but that there is a ball park within which social welfare policy is played. The ball park perimeter, of course, can and does change; every industrialized nation has developed a variation of the welfare state over the last 50 years. The structural approach in political science tries to understand, explain and predict such basic societal changes (Wilensky 1975).

Politics as Channeled Social Behavior The social structure not only sets boundaries for social behavior, but also directly affects that behavior. Characteristic incentives, constraints and possibilities in a society channel behavior in predictable directions. For example, the undersupply of physicians serving poor or isolated areas is part of larger social processes. Merely increasing the number of physicians will do little to bring medical care to these areas because existing incentives and other social and medical opportunities continue to channel most physicians elsewhere. This example stresses the importance of the structural approach. It indicates that many health services problems are part of larger social problems and effective attempts to deal with them must consider the social context. This context, too, changes over time. Thus a political analyst must be concerned not only with feasible short-run solutions to immediate problems, but also the long-term impacts—how such solutions will interact with and possibly alter basic social features.

Appraising Alternative Approaches

Obviously political science encompasses a vast range of behavior, from conflict over minor, day-to-day, collective decision making to major governmental actions and ultimately to social structure and values. There are disadvantages to this broad range of subject matter. A field that covers everything from office politics to the Marxist theory of historical development of course appears (and sometimes is) unfocused or contradictory. But there are major advantages to be gained from this wide scope.

On the primary level, all of us face the politics of life in the course of our daily work. We are constantly embroiled in issues of conflict and power, both with other organizations (Elling 1973) and within our own (Perrow 1963). While effectiveness in such situations is to some extent an art—to be truly mastered only through experience—political science can help to sensitize workers, administrators, clients and citizens to typical inter- and intraorganizational political problems and processes. Merely alerting people to the fact that most problems they face are partly political is an important first step. By explaining what is typical and why, political science can provide the methodology to achieve desirable but untypical results.

On the secondary level, increased governmental involvement in medical care means that health care actors are affected more significantly by government. They must, in short, be able to predict governmental behavior and impact, foresee uncontrollable factors, and act more efficiently within imposed constraints. Political activity often becomes desirable, necessary or both in order to achieve goals, and political science can promote efficiency and effectiveness in dealing with government.

On the final level, political science is a consumer—and, at its best, a synthesizer—of the full range of social sciences. It is concerned not merely with governmental affairs, but with the distribution of all types of social benefits and burdens. For example, perceptive and sensitive work on the development of Medicare would include a variety of approaches: sociological analysis of the changing role of the family and the plight of the elderly in industrial societies; psychological discussion of the needs and fears of the elderly and the response of the rest of the population; historical study of events and processes that led to the current situation; economic breakdown of the supply, demand, cost and benefit distribution of services under alternative health insurance programs; consideration of the political struggle and the organizational character of the various proponents and the bureaucracies that would administer the program; and description of the stakes and personalities involved in decision making and implementation.

GENERAL APPLICATIONS OF POLITICAL SCIENCE

THE AMERICAN GOVERNMENTAL SYSTEM

Branches of Government

It is important to understand the governmental structure within which political activity takes place. The American system is sometimes inaccurately described as incorporating a separation of powers; actually, its central feature is a sharing of authority. Rather than distinct arenas of legitimate power, the executive, legislative and judicial branches are overlapping jurisdictions. The bureaucracy has grown so large and influential that it is now often considered a fourth branch of government that also shares power. (According to Graham Allison (1975), the bureaucracy has become so important that about 50 percent—and sometimes as much as 90 percent—of what we call policy occurs after legislative decision making.)

The budget process is a good example of how power is shared among the branches. Although the Constitution grants Congress the "power of the purse," the budget is actually determined through a long, complicated, interorganizational process: executive agencies make requests for what they need (want, hope) to get; this is modified by the President's Office of Management and Budget before the budget message is sent to Congress, though presidential involvement continues after submission; the various committees again change it and the Senate and House as a whole may have to compromise on its terms; Congress sends the appropriation back to the President who may veto it; the courts may force the President to spend money, if any is impounded, or may forbid certain expenditures; and finally, the bureaucracy administers—and often alters—expenditures. Thus, the executive, legislative, judicial and bureaucratic branches are all involved in important, inter-mingled ways.

Federalism

The federal nature of the American system also produces a substantial degree of shared, overlapping authority. Though federal, state and local governments are often viewed as hierarchical and separate, as in a layer cake, they are more accurately regarded as a marble cake, mixed and swirled together (Grod-zins 1966). This is partly because federal legislators have strong regional ties. More important, most programs are a complex mixture of federal, state and local action.

The federal government provides categorical grants for a vast number of specific projects and sets standards for state and local governments. Many federal programs, such as neighborhood health centers, are administered ex-clusively by local units and are altered significantly to fit the political and social features of the area. Conversely, even a basically local function such as elementary education is strongly influenced by federal grants and regulations.

This sharing of and struggling over authority—both horizontally among the branches and vertically among the units of the federal system—means that most governmental activity involves complex interaction among the com-ponents of the system. The complexity is magnified because of the overlapping responsibilities and programs of the agencies involved. Legal structures, pro-grams and political settings vary widely among the 50 states, 3,000 counties, and tens of thousands of local governments and special districts. Despite the complexity, those interested in the health industry should have an under-standing of at least the basic components of the American governmental sys-tem, information that can be acquired from an introductory political science course or textbook. A more thorough knowledge of the governmental agencies and programs that directly affect the health care industry can only be learned on the job and must be augmented in each new position. The wealth of specific information—personalities, past histories, programs, legal rules—re-quired to operate effectively cannot be taught in a classroom, but a recognition of the importance of learning these facts can be gained there.

Certain aspects of politics, such as basic ways of looking at political activity, the key determinants of political behavior, and typical patterns of results, are universal and ever useful. The greatest contributions of political science are analytic models and explanatory paradigms that can be applied in both governmental and nongovernmental settings.

THE POLITICS OF HEALTH: HOW DISTINCTIVE?

The politics of health depends not so much on the substantive sector, the medical care industry, as on political factors that also commonly affect other sectors. Many of the specific issues and actors are, of course, unique to the field of health, but the nature of the politics of health is not obviously distinctive. This can be most simply explained by the fact that the health industry faces the same governmental arrangements as most other industries. There is the same mixing and balancing between public and private responsibility, the same marble cake of local, state and federal authorities, the same voting alignments and party systems, the same federal legislature representing local interests and divided into contained committees, the same political culture and social structure. This subject will be covered in more detail below, the underlying premise being that the political arena of health fits into the general pattern of American politics.

PERSPECTIVES OF POLITICAL ANALYSIS

Before we turn to the current state of political science, it will be helpful to look at the current state of political scientists. Allison (1971) has persuasively argued that analysts—and practitioners—tend to use one or more of three conceptual models in thinking about the actions of government and other political actors. The models are usually implicit, but each focuses attention, often unconsciously, on different facets of a situation and accentuates different problems and facts. The models are not so much theories of how or why events occur as they are conceptual "lenses" that direct our search to derive theory. Because perspectives vary, it is important to be aware of three distinguishable models, or lenses: rational actor, political bargaining and organizational process. Each has an important but dissimilar focus, and each can be used to answer the question: "Why did or why will the government (or hospital or planning agency) take a particular action?"

Rational Actor

This model examines governmental action as the product of the rational choice of a single policy-making center. It assumes that government acts as a single unit that faces problems and works toward their resolution. In using this model, one focuses on the goals and objectives of government, looks at possible alternative means to achieve those ends, analyzes their probable consequences, and then identifies the optimal solution as the predicted action (or explains an action as being a solution to a particular problem). A statement such as "the Hill-Burton hospital construction program was instituted because there was a shortage of hospital beds in the United States" is a good example of an application of this mode of analysis. A problem is identified—here, a shortage of beds—and governmental action is explained as a rational response to that problem.

Political Bargaining

An analyst using this model perceives governmental policy as a result—not necessarily rational—of bargaining among various actors with individual interests, stakes, resources and political skills. The model recognizes that "the government," and groups trying to affect policy, consist of many different agencies, groups and individuals almost never sharing exactly the same goals and priorities. Analysis focuses on the players or actors in various positions and the rules of the game that order the process. Actors have their own parochial perceptions and priorities, for it is recognized that people's positions affect their viewpoint—"where you stand depends on where you sit." This is true both horizontally (the secretary of HEW has different concerns from those of the secretary of HUD) and vertically (the President's perspective on matters concerning health differs from that of the secretary of HEW).

There is, thus, not one set of problems but many, and the players bargain, compromise, compete and form coalitions with others to try to achieve their ends. The result of this maneuvering is determined by the political skill of the players, the resources they command (money, time, staff help, information, access to or personal ties with other players, official authority), and their stake in the outcome. Often the result satisfies no one. According to this model, the characteristics of the Hill-Burton program would be viewed as the product of many different forces: hospitals seeking money, but only for non-profit hospitals; sponsors in the Senate seeking political recognition; states struggling over the formula to apportion money; planners and state health officials attempting to acquire and control their part of the largess from Washington.

Organizational Process Model

This model interprets governmental action primarily as the output of large organizations. What is termed governmental action is mostly what goes on in such large bureaucracies as the Social Security Administration and the Internal Revenue Service. In order to deal methodically with the myriad assignments faced, the personnel of such organizations must adopt rules, repertoires, and standard operating procedures (SOPs). Such SOPs contribute, no doubt, to the organization's ability to function smoothly and perform its normal tasks, but they are often neither particularly innovative nor adaptable to new or unusual circumstances or changes in goals and responsibilities. They are systematic and can be analyzed rigorously with fair predictability.

A central assumption is that large organizations change slowly and incrementally. If the government is doing something today, it usually means that the output was already in the bureaucracy's repertoire, and that the government was behaving similarly yesterday. However innovative a plan may have been when it was conceived, it is usually implemented by a bureaucracy that continues to operate as in the past, at least in the short run. (This is part of the rationale for creating new agencies to administer new programs.) In complex programs involving more than one agency, problems of coordination become immense. Each agency follows its own SOPs and deals with its own area of jurisdiction, often leaving no one responsible for the overall result.

The organizational process model, then, incorporates a triple restriction on governmental behavior. First, recognition and definition of problems and suggested solutions often reach a top decision maker from within a bureaucracy, and so are shaped and altered by the way a bureaucracy typically processes information. Moreover, the bureaucracy, in performing its normal functions, has often helped to create the very problem the decision maker faces, and its behavior has foreclosed alternatives. Second, there is a gap between "choice" at the top and actual implementation by an organization. The decision maker's real options are, as a result, still further constrained. Third, the decision maker is faced with a problem of coordination among different branches of the organization, each doing its own task in its own way.

The interpretation of the Hill-Burton program from an organizational perspective highlights factors that are subordinate in the other models. Organizational analysts emphasize that the problem of inadequate health care for many Americans, especially in rural areas, was redefined and generalized as inadequate medical facilities and, in particular, as a shortage of hospital beds. They stress that the Hill-Burton program was not novel, but was similar to other categorical grants to states. In evaluating the program, one is not surprised to find that because at first the critical shortage was in rural areas, bureaucratic rules were established to channel funds there. But, when central cities demonstrated the most pressing need for modernized hospitals, partly because of the success of the program, the bureaucracy continued to channel funds to rural areas until a 1964 amendment.

Directed by the model to look for gaps between policy decisions at the top and actual organizational behavior, the analyst finds that, although hospitals receiving Hill-Burton funds were required to devote five percent of their resources to charity cases, this provision was simply not enforced by the bureaucracy. Finally, an analyst using this model looks for evidence of poor coordination; e.g., one may discover that the Small Business Administration has granted loans to new proprietary hospitals, which were not included in the Hill-Burton Program, to build in the same areas as established hospitals receiving Hill-Burton funds (Lave and Lave 1974).

It should be reemphasized that these models apply to nongovernmental as well as governmental behavior. An action of a large hospital can be seen as a rational adaptation to the problems it faces, as the result of the procedures and bureaucratic rules of internal departments, or as the outcome of bargaining or adjustment among trustees, medical staff and administrators (Perrow 1963).

Conceptual models emphasize that what one sees depends partly on how one looks at political actions. The central task is to use them systematically and consciously, and not to allow one model to dominate. Using only one lens can give an incomplete and inaccurate picture; some combination of all three models is usually necessary to understand an organization's behavior. In this context, the organizational process model should be emphasized since there is a tendency to assume that once a decision is made—whether through struggle and compromise or some "rational" choice—the issue is resolved. Use of this model ensures that the problems and distortions of implementation will be anticipated.

TYPES OF EXPLANATIONS: SOURCES OF INFLUENCE AND WHO BENEFITS

It is helpful to follow a discussion of how political scientists and political actors view the world with one concerning the ways in which political scientists attempt to explain its features. To understand who gets what and how, political scientists have offered several broad theories about the relationship between political systems and their social settings. Political science paradigms locate power in a variety of sources and regard governmental action as dominated by distinct actors and processes and benefiting different interests. While these paradigms are not mutually exclusive, they do rest on divergent assumptions about government and society.

Popular Rule through Elections

The first paradigm emphasizes the role of elections in public policy, focusing on the ultimate formal power of the American electorate to select and discard top officials. Because these leaders themselves choose a considerable proportion of the nonelected officials, it can be argued that government is ultimately accountable and responsive to the needs and desires of the citizens. Governmental policies are thus understood as expressing the "will of the people."

Any simple version of democratic theory applied to American government, however, encounters grave difficulties. In the first place, voting for a candidate does not imply that the voter is making a statement of policy on each of the many issues of the day, especially when candidates are ambiguous about their positions. Respected public opinion surveys indicate that a majority of the American population does not consider politics to be particularly important and that the general public is uninformed about most political issues, personalities and facts (Campbell 1964).

When politics and government are especially salient, for example, during the upheavals of the 1960s and the Vietnam War, citizens become more knowledgeable. Most citizens, however, because of their sense of powerlessness in relation to government, do not consider it worthwhile to understand the government's actions unless direct impacts are perceived. It is hard enough, for, say, nursing home operators to keep abreast of governmental programs and regulations that affect their livelihood, much less ordinary citizens who usually have little obvious stake in the issues.

Between a quarter and a third of the adult American population never engages in political activity, while another quarter does nothing but vote every two years. Perhaps ten percent of the population can be considered aware and deeply involved in political activity. It should be noted that those who do vote or are active tend to be wealthier, with views that are not representative of the whole population (Verba and Nie 1972). It is still possible, however, that the general public influences the tone or direction of governmental policy, if not the specifics, by not voting for officials when "things go badly."

Most voters identify themselves as either Democrats or Republicans, and that identification, rather than issues or personalities, is the strongest determinant of how they cast their votes. To the extent that parties formulate different programs, the public, though unaware of specific political issues, may exercise some choice and control over policy by voting for the party whose basic stance they prefer. Still, it is certain that governmental policies are not a direct expression of popular views and that what government does and will do cannot be explained or predicted simply by public opinion and the electoral will of the citizenry.

Interest Groups

The group process model, probably the dominant paradigm in political science, claims that large organizations, not individual citizens, are the vital force in American politics. These organizations raise issues, lobby for positions, help select officials, and influence the administration of governmental programs (Banfield 1961; Dahl 1961). The vital importance of organizations stems from their possession of the resources—time, information and expertise—necessary for effectiveness in the political process.

One version of this approach holds that organizations, not the electoral system, reinforce our democracy because, even though individual workers or doctors may not be politically active, the union or the AMA represents their position and promotes their interests. But not all voters are members of organizations, professional or otherwise, and many members themselves disagree with their organization's political positions (Colombotos 1975). There are also problems in assuming that the individual's interests and opinions are independent of the issues. Changes in public opinion often follow events or official statements; perhaps governmental action creates public opinion, not vice versa (Edelman 1964). Interest groups expend much of their political efforts in convincing their own members; thus, it is possible that unions create labor opinion as much as they express it (Bauer et al. 1963). Regardless of these qualifications, the paradigm centers on the influence of interest groups, not on their democratic nature.

Use of Pressure   Pressure on governmental officials is one of the least used and least effective means of influence despite the common usage of the term pressure group to denote organizational participants in the political process. Interest groups are not in a position to pressure officials except in rare circumstances. Few groups control enough votes to threaten a recalcitrant official with electoral defeat, and their use of money or other resources is not consistently adequate to impose their will. The influence of interest groups comes, therefore, partly from the good relations they maintain with officials. For example, since members of Congress simply cannot keep abreast of all issues, interest groups provide information, write speeches, and even help draft bills. Interest groups usually work at helping their supporters rather than converting their opponents.

It is difficult for elected officials to ascertain their constituents' or the public's thoughts. If, however, those views seen most often are vehemently opposed to a particular policy, it is likely that elected officials will also have doubts about it. Officials, like the rest of us, want to work in an environment that is pleasant, nonconflictual and secure. They prefer to avoid decisions that offend major groups with whom they must work and that generate political controversy, but trying to control their environment through conciliation leads to an orientation toward the status quo and implies a pattern of policies that typically benefits, or at least does not harm, the most active interest groups. Thus, mutually beneficial relations and extensive contacts are the typical basis of an interest group's influence.

To the extent that the influence of an interest group rests on its good relations with officials, its power is problematic. Marmor (1973) has pointed out that much of the AMA's reputed power and ability to block Medicare rested upon the large number in Congress who agreed with the AMA and were themselves opposed to a major new governmental health insurance program. When Johnson's election landslide in 1964 brought new members and different beliefs to Congress, the power of the AMA was revealed in a different light. The AMA was unable to pressure the new members into opposing Medicare. It is obvious that the AMA has influence on policy, but its form is dictated by an ideology that favors such groups and the private control of health care; it does not depend on pressure.

Bias of Group Organization   Even if organized groups seldom have the political power to force a favorable outcome, they are nonetheless deeply involved and influential in the political process. But all interests are not equally well organized; hence groups have unequal access to political influence. First, because money is required to organize and engage in political activity, there is a bias in favor of wealthy organizations. Schattschneider (1960) concluded in his classic study of interest politics that "the business or upper-class bias of the pressure system shows up everywhere." Second, a bias exists against large groups with relatively diffuse interests and small stakes, especially those whose interests relate to public goods, such as clean air or conservation. Public goods are essentially available to all, so that beneficiaries cannot be adequately charged for activity on their behalf.

Assume, for example, that Americans could save an average of five dollars a year if drugs were prescribed by generic name only. While this implies a total saving of over $1 billion a year, few individuals have a large stake in the issue. Since most individuals have little to gain, few are likely to campaign for or contribute money to a group advocating mandatory dispensing of generic drugs. In addition, if such a group were organized, noncontributors would gain as much as contributors; even though they might favor the law there is no economic incentive for people to join or to help. This dilemma is called the "free rider" problem. Mancur Olson (1965) has shown, in fact, that under some conditions groups will not form and policies will not be promoted even where the policy is in everyone's interest.

To carry the example further, let us assume that the drug companies oppose the plan. They are already organized, both as individual firms and as an industry. Because of their large financial stake in the outcome, they have considerable economic incentive to be actively opposed. They also have the resources to employ skilled personnel for full-time lobbying. Their expertise is hard to challenge; indeed, they often have a virtual monopoly on data. Few people can dispute a drug company official who testifies that, "our figures show that the law would cut profits 8.2 percent, reduce the amount of research on new drugs 22 percent, and so retard the discovery and production of 17 new lifesaving drugs each year." A member of Congress or a governmental bureaucrat who aims to serve the wider public interest might find it difficult to advocate a law with such economic consequences, especially in the absence of reliable countervailing information.

American Political Culture

A variant of the group process model emphasizes the distinctiveness of American political culture (Hartz 1955). Americans tend to distrust power, particularly governmental power and compulsion, and prefer voluntarism and self-rule in small homogeneous groups with limited purposes. But the problem of compulsion and dominance is not overcome by voluntarism; it is simply overlooked. Distrust and avoidance of governmental power typically lead to the capture of public authority by private groups (McConnell 1966). In many states, for example, doctors themselves establish the standards for licensing physicians; public authority is, in effect, wielded by a private group.

There is an implicit American assumption that self-rule in small groups maximizes freedom. The importance of this ideology is both expressed in and reinforced by the federal nature of American politics. Even programs initiated and financed largely by the national government are often run by state and local interests. The belief in self-rule is not, of course, restricted to the medical field. Agricultural policy, for example, is made by congressional committees composed of members of agricultural districts working in close collaboration with representatives of the Farm Bureau. Self-rule is a cherished American belief, but when hospitals make hospital policy and wheat farmers make wheat policy, their particular interests are represented at the expense of others.

American distrust of power produces a general opposition to increases in the scope of governmental authority. Efforts by American government in the area of social welfare have been much more limited than those in other industrialized democracies, and they have tended to be decentralized and piecemeal (Heidenheimer 1973). American politics has been characterized as incremental, with programs growing only slowly through time. Lindblom (1959) argues that policy is more the result of accretion than of broad decisions; it is not made as much as it evolves. Wildavsky (1964) found this same incrementalism in the budgetary process, arguing that programs typically receive the funding of previous years with only marginal changes. Lindblom, in particular, asserts that incremental policy making is ideal in a pluralist democracy, ensuring mutual adjustment and restraining authoritatively imposed policies in situations of uncertainty and conflicts of values.

Elite Rule

Elite theory is the most common of the paradigms discussed. Its advocates stress that there are relatively few large and immensely powerful institutions in this country and that these institutions are controlled by a few men in top positions. C. Wright Mills has most forcefully presented this view, arguing that there is a power elite in the commanding positions of society that controls vast resources and makes decisions that dominate the country's activities. Mills (1956) maintains that the few hundred who run the key institutions— such as the President of the United States, the heads of General Motors, Exxon, CBS, and the Joint Chiefs of Staff—in effect run the country. While most political scientists are skeptical of Mills' extreme formulation, there is no denying the immense importance of a relatively few public and private institutions.

Most of the debate in political science over the role of elites has centered on studies of community power. Elitists have argued that there are only a small number of powerful people in each community or city. Pluralists agree that there is an iron law of oligarchy—that relatively few actors are directly involved in public decision making—but they disagree with the elite theorists on the size of this oligarchy, its homogeneity, and its openness to citizens' pressures. It is obvious, for example, that not all of the six million people in Chicago participate in decision making; the real question concerns the responsiveness and accountability of the few who do.

In his classic study of New Haven, Robert Dahl (1961) argued that different leaders are influential on different issues; that is, there is not one power elite, but different elites in school policy, urban renewal, and so on. Further, the actual decision makers are responsive to and influenced by a larger public, partly through anticipated reactions, especially of election results, and it is possible for newcomers to become influential and affect decisions. Dahl also argued that these elites are not restricted to the rich, but extend to middle- and even lower-income groups.

The debate about the role of elites is still unresolved among political scientists, partly because different cities have different power structures, but mostly because methodological and ideological issues seem to dominate the arguments.

Marxism

A Marxist variant of elite theory asserts that key decision makers are either wealthy themselves or make decisions for the benefit of the capitalist class. On a more general level, Marxists see government in capitalist countries as serving the interests of capitalism, sometimes muting conflict but primarily perpetuating the dominance of the propertied classes. This dominance is maintained in part by meliorative programs for the lower classes that reduce the most disrupting consequences of capitalism without eliminating its basically unequal class structure. Thus, for example, the elderly are not discharged from hospitals just because they have no money, and unemployed workers are "bought off" by subsistence allowances. Other governmental programs socialize costs so that the government pays for the education or health programs required by capitalism for greater productivity and profits (Miliband 1969; O'Connor 1973; Navarro 1975).

At its strongest, this paradigm attempts to explain why the needs of capitalist development have led all industrial democracies to some form of welfare state and why this trend seems to be inevitable. In this connection, it is noteworthy that education is seen not simply as an individual right but as a social duty. The young are required by law to attend school because society needs educated citizens. Some of the arguments in favor of national health insurance are also based on this line of reasoning, stressing the social more than the individual benefits of improved health.

Public Finance

It is interesting to compare Marxist paradigms with a traditional theory of public finance. There are striking similarities, except, of course, for the final evaluation. Theorists in public finance argue that the state should provide certain key services that cannot be, or are not, provided efficiently by the private sector. Defense and environmental protection are obvious examples, but so are education and vocational training programs. An individual firm may not provide the latter two because workers are mobile, and citizens may not provide them for themselves because of the expense. Since such services ultimately benefit the whole society, the government should intercede. Government, then, augments or corrects the private sector's services (Musgrave 1959).

Statist Theory

A small but growing body of literature deals with "corporatist" or "statist" theory. The state itself and its top governmental functionaries are seen as the source of the majority of decisions and as the most powerful influence on public policy. Reacting to the greatly increased role of the government, particularly at the federal level, and the shift in power from the legislative to the executive branch, several theorists have pointed out that the government now has far more resources at its command and a much wider sphere of influence than any other sector. The secretary of defense, after all, is the head of a far larger enterprise than is the chairman of General Motors, and many governmental officials control more resources than the individuals or nongovernmental organizations with which they deal. Much public policy originates with these officials, who reflect their own views of the public interest or meet their own personal or organizational needs. While statist theory was developed in studies of authoritarian governments, it is also increasingly recognized as relevant to the United States and other democratic countries (Navarro 1975; Lowi 1969).

PARADIGMS AND THE 1965 MEDICARE BILL

The above paradigms are useful in explaining and predicting what the government has done or might do because they help identify the forces that shape and influence governmental behavior. While they do not allow analysts to predict with great certainty, they can at least direct attention to the right issues and the right questions. They should also help analysts avoid surprise at governmental behavior or concern over unlikely events. Table 3.1 applies these paradigms to the 1965 Medicare Bill.

The paradigms give different interpretations of the reasons for the passage of Medicare and the impacts of the legislation. Their relative value depends somewhat on the level of generality desired. For example, the actual passage of Medicare cannot be fully explained without reference to the Democratic election landslide of 1964, and yet elections and party ideology give

TABLE 3.1: Political Science Paradigms and the 1965 Medicare Bill

Paradigm	Application
Public Rule through Elections	The public was "permissive," not directive: it favored "action," but did not specify what action or when. There was no public agreement on provisions. Public views did not determine when Medicare passed; there had been general support for several years with no legislative enactment. The Democratic party, loosely allied with labor in ways similar to the social democratic parties of Europe, scored large gains in the 1964 election and passed social welfare legislation.
Interest Groups	There were many bills before Congress, but most had no chance of passage. The "serious" bills had strong backing of important groups: labor, AMA, AHA. These groups had a significant effect on specific provisions of bills. In particular, efforts were made to ensure the participation of providers by including provisions such as noninterference with the practice of medicine and payment of usual and customary fees.
American Political Culture	There is minimal governmental involvement in the medical industry, and it is largely restricted to finance. The program is developed through accretion: beneficiaries are the same as in other programs; the program is run through existing structures, such as Blue Cross and the Social Security Administration; and existing methods are retained, e.g., payment by usual and customary fees.
Elite Rule	The President gave vital support and worked for the passage of a bill, and he and the majority of Congress belonged to the same party. One individual, Wilbur Mills, played a crucial role, such as expanding coverage of doctors, with the inadvertent assistance of committee Republicans. There was a change in elites because the electoral landslide eliminated many opponents and added many supporters. Even though there was no change in public opinion, a changed elite led to passage.
Marxism	Medicare socializes the cost of labor and lessens pressure on corporations for retirement benefits. It shifts costs to a regressive Social Security tax and widens the gap in disposable income. Some benefits go to the aged and the poor, but the major benefits go to providers.
Public Finance	The private system was not providing the desired care to the elderly and the poor. Government acted to correct this. The poor and aged are rational target groups since they have high medical costs and little income. The private system works for other groups.
Statist Theory	Strategy is developed largely by governmental officials in the executive branch, who decided to devise a limited program, to use the Social Security System, and to focus on the aged.

little insight into the specific provisions of the bill. If one is concerned with why the United States lagged behind Western Europe in initiating a major governmental health care program, then the political culture paradigm is very useful. But that paradigm does not explain why a program was finally enacted in 1965. Thus, the aspects of governmental behavior in which one is interested affect what paradigms seem most useful.

EMERGING AREAS OF POLITICAL SCIENCE RELEVANT TO THE HEALTH SECTOR

Domestic public policy has only recently become a popular field within political science. Three areas of study, in particular, should be especially useful to practitioners: (1) implementation of programs, (2) "correlates of policy" studies, and (3) modeling.

IMPLEMENTATION

With the realization that policy goals and legislation can be greatly altered upon administration, political scientists have sharpened their focus on implementation of programs. Most work in this area to date has merely confirmed and documented this realization by revealing differences between programs as conceived and as carried out (see Pressman and Wildavsky 1973; Derthick 1972; Foltz 1975). It is now clear, for example, that establishing commissions to regulate industries will not alone achieve the desired public goals and that much closer attention to the practices of regulators is required. Allison (1975) makes an excellent first step in this direction, but such research is still largely in the future. We can expect a clearer understanding of the key variables in implementation and, hopefully, look forward to a better understanding of alternatives on the part of policy makers.

CORRELATES OF POLICY

Correlates of policy studies have been conducted on both American state/ local programs and on international programs to analyze the factors associated with the existence and success of different kinds of public programs. The early studies on American programs indicated the importance of socioeconomic variables in determining policy. For example, the wealth of a state has been found to be the best predictor of the extent of its welfare program. It can also be shown that there is often no clear relationship between inputs into programs and outcomes, e.g., money spent on education does not necessarily affect its quality. Preliminary studies have often been crude (Jacob and Lipsky 1968), but more sophisticated, detailed, reliable and useful information is emerging.

The expansion from American cases to international comparisons is a fairly new but important development in correlates of policy studies. Some have examined the correlates of social welfare policy by comparing nation-states throughout the world. Others (e.g., Altenstetter 1974; Heidenheimer 1973) have looked at only a few nations to investigate in depth their similarities and differences. International comparisons of this sort can adopt the natural science experiment approach to analyze and predict in some detail the consequences and impacts of specific policy options (Andreopoulos 1975).

FORMAL MODELS OF POLITICAL BEHAVIOR

Modeling is a rapidly growing method that differs significantly from the two areas of study just described. Researchers employ rigorously constructed theories of behavior, draw predictions from these assumptions, and test them against data. Modeling has been used with remarkable success in studies of voting and electoral behavior, and proponents have begun to extend the method to other areas, such as public policy. When coupled with empirical work, modeling can prove valuable in generating explanations of governmental behavior and the impact of programs.

AN APPLICATION OF POLITICAL SCIENCE
TO THE FIELD OF HEALTH

How can one apply the political science paradigms to governmental behavior in the field of health? As mentioned earlier, there is no single "politics of health," but rather a politics throughout the health industry whose character depends on the particular policy arena in question. Lowi (1964) has argued that each policy-related issue exhibits singular political processes, actors, styles, locations of conflict, and outcomes. Disputes in any single substantive area, such as health, vary and fall into what can be termed the "redistributive," "regulatory" or "distributive" arenas of American politics.

REDISTRIBUTIVE ARENA

Redistributive programs have broad impacts on economic classes or large demographic units of the population. However, because participant perception determines the nature of the political arena, a proposal or program can be classified as redistributive even though, objectively, it is not redistributive in impact. For example, what matters is not so much whether Medicare actually redistributed medical care or income as whether it was depicted as redistributive and "socialistic."

In the field of health, redistributive politics confronts such issues as the proper role of government in organizing, financing and redistributing health services. While government involvement is often perceived to restrict private initiative, it actually can and often does increase private authority. The creation of professional standards and review organizations (PSROs), for example, led to increased authority for private medical organizations.

Certain variables of political conflict, e.g., site, contestants and argument, are common to redistributive policies regardless of the substantive field. Large national organizations tend to oppose one another, sides are relatively stable over time, disputes are normally ideological in nature, and political battle is centralized, usually in the federal legislature. The struggle over Social Security, the long dispute over federal aid to education, the fight over Medicare, and now the debate over national health insurance exemplify the redistributive political arena.

The scope of conflict—or who is involved—has been called the "most important strategy of politics" (Schattschneider 1960, p. 31). It is obvious that the arena of dispute has a major impact on what kinds of policies emerge and whom they benefit. Redistributive political conflict takes place on the state and local levels, but because of larger constituencies, it is more salient and more common at the national level. McConnell (1966) and Madison (1961) argued that the larger the constituency actively involved in conflict, the closer the result will be to the interests of the mass public. Accordingly, small constituencies enable private power to appropriate public authority for its own interests. Federal programs, according to McConnell, tend to favor private interest less and are more progressive than state programs.

Resolutions of national redistributive conflicts do appear to extend benefits to groups that seemingly derive little from American politics and society. And yet clear decisions about redistributive conflicts are relatively rare. The politics of Medicare was battled, with varying intensity, from Truman's administration until passage in 1965. Because of the stable cleavages associated with redistributive policies, an unusual or dramatic event is normally necessary for political resolution. In this case, the Johnson landslide in 1964 created the conditions for the immediate passage of Medicare, as well as Medicaid and federal aid to education. Stable cleavages associated with redistributive politics contribute to the cyclical nature of American politics—periods of relative stability followed by periods of major innovation in programs.

REGULATIVE ARENA

When decisions are finally made about the proper scope and role of government, new conflicts emerge over the administration and financing of programs and their effects on the industries involved. Most political controversies over finance and administration conform to the pattern Lowi (1964) terms "regulative politics." Regulative politics does not involve broad social groups, but a sector, industry or organized set of producers or consumers. The groups are not class-based. Conflict is less ideological and tends to center in the executive branch. Regulative politics is not confined to what are officially called regulatory commissions or agencies, but is a factor in any decision that changes the burdens or benefits of an industry or sector.

Producer groups, with relatively strong organizations, substantial resources, and high stakes in the outcome, typically dominate struggles in the regulative arena. For example, whereas the general public was very concerned about the enactment of Medicare in 1965, it was much less actively interested in the program's mode of payment to hospitals and physicians. While the overall impact of a program may be large, each individual may have only a small stake in the outcome; regarding the payment issue, the public did not perceive direct impact. On the other hand, the Medicare payment question was of vital importance to hospitals and doctors. In such cases of "unbalanced interests," the stakes are weighted to the side of producer groups that have the resources with which to fight and normally to achieve their ends (Marmor 1973).

The regulative policy arena is often characterized by what Edelman (1964) has called symbolic politics: "the rhetoric to one side and the decision to the other." For example, in response to popular demand to control the rising costs of medical services, a regulative commission might be created to mediate rate increases. Such action satisfies the public that "something is being done," but the commission may actually have little control over the industry and may even assist it. In the political market of unbalanced interests, the public may receive symbolic benefits, while the producers gain material benefits.

DISTRIBUTIVE ARENA

Distributive arena issues can be divided into small units and decisions, independent of the general rules that apply to a whole sector or industry. Questions about the supply of services—where to build a new hospital, how to divide the funds for a program between different localities or functions—typically fall into this arena. The key characteristics are that beneficiaries are separated from those who bear the burdens; decisions are discrete and can be made with little obvious relation to other decisions. This is not to say that there is no relationship; e.g., because of finite resources, a research grant to one medical center means that another will get less. However, because decisions can be made on a case-by-case basis after which the affected parties may never have to face each other, one group's winning does not obviously point to another group's losing.

Rules need not apply universally. An overall policy emerges, of course, but it is the aggregate of a large number of discrete decisions, not a consciously planned and coherent policy. Decisions are often arrived at through logrolling, a process through which all participants gain. Actors in this arena are usually individuals, committees and planning commissions, rather than classes, national organizations, or large groups of producers or consumers. Struggle tends to be nonideological, and results depend on the specific circumstances of each case.

When distributive arena issues are decided at the local level, the outcome depends on the local power structure, the importance of the issue, and the attitudes and skills of the individuals involved. Outcomes vary by community and may change with time, but the dominant local elites and notables usually win. Robert Alford (1975) gives an insightful and stimulating analysis of such conflict in New York City. He describes the health policies of the city as largely the result of decisions made by the professional monopolists, although those he calls the "corporate rationalizers" are beginning to challenge established medical powers and privileges. He feels that "equal health advocates" are not, at this time, a significant factor in urban health policy, and concludes that "dominant, challenging, and repressed structural interests" are not restricted to either local politics or even to health, but are representative of American politics in general.

ON THE JUDICIAL PROCESS

Most political science research on the judicial process is not directly relevant to this discussion. The courts certainly do not easily fit any of Lowi's three arenas of politics. Robert Dahl (1970), in his study of the Supreme Court, pointed out that since justices are appointed by the President with the consent of the Senate, they tend to be part of the dominant electoral coalition. He went on to show that only rarely have court rulings thwarted the strong desires of the other branches. In an intensive study of a single judicial doctrine, Sorauf found wide local variations in the impact of a ruling of the Supreme Court and concluded: "To rephrase the old saw, . . . the Constitution in reality consists of what influential partisans and decision makers say the Supreme Court says it is (Sorauf 1970, p. 225). These studies seem to indicate that the effects of legal struggles will usually not be markedly different from the results of other political conflicts, but exactly when and how the results do differ is simply not known.

CONCLUSION

Political science is concerned with conflict, influence and authoritative decision making in both private and public settings. Superior political analysis reflects this broad subject matter. While political expertise is largely acquired through experience, skillful political analysis is central to accurate description, explanation and prediction of operational health policies. As such, political studies constitute a share of areas known as social science and health services research.

REFERENCES

Alford, R. 1975. *Health care politics*. Chicago: University of Chicago Press.

Allison, G. 1971. *Essence of decision*. Boston: Little, Brown.

————. 1975. Implementation analysis. In *Benefit cost and policy analysis, 1974*, ed. R. E. Zeckhauser et al. Chicago: Aldine.

Altenstetter, K. 1974. Medical interests and the public interest: West Germany and USA. *International Journal of Health Services* 4:29-48.

Andreopoulos, S. 1975. *National health insurance: Can we learn from Canada?* New York: John Wiley & Sons.

Bachrach, P., and Baratz, M. 1962. Two faces of power. *American Political Science Review* 59:947-52.

Banfield, E. 1961. *Political influence*. New York: Alfred A. Knopf.

Bauer, R. A., Pool, I. S., Dexter, L. A. and Dexter, L. A. 1963. *American business and public policy*. New York: Altherton.

Campbell, A. 1964. *The American voter*. New York: John Wiley & Sons.

Colombotos, J., Kirchner, C. and Millman, M. 1975. Physicians view national health insurance. *Medical Care* 13(5):369-96.

Dahl, R. 1961. *Who governs?* New Haven, CT: Yale University Press.

————. 1970. Decision-making in a democracy: The role of the Supreme Court as a national policy-maker. In *Readings in American political behavior*, ed. R. Wolfinger, pp. 165-81. Englewood Cliffs, NJ: Prentice-Hall.

Derthick, M. 1972. *New towns in town*. Washington, D.C.: Urban Institute.

Easton, D. 1953. *The political system*. New York: Alfred A. Knopf.

Edelman, M. 1964. *The symbolic uses of politics*. Urbana: University of Illinois Press.

Elling, R. 1973. The shifting power structure in health. In *Politics and law in health care policy*, ed. J. McKinley. New York: Prodist.

Foltz, A. 1975. The development of ambiguous federal policy: Early and periodic screening, diagnosis and treatment (EPSDT). *Milbank Memorial Fund Quarterly* 53:35-64.

Grodzins, M. 1966. *The American system*. Chicago: Rand McNally.

Hartz, L. 1955. *The liberal tradition in America.* New York: Harcourt, Brace and World.

Heidenheimer, A. 1973. The politics of public education and welfare in the USA and Western Europe. *British Journal of Political Science* 3:315-40.

Jacob, H., and Lipsky, M. 1968. Outputs, structure, and power: An assessment. *Journal of Politics* 30:510-39.

Lasswell, H. 1936. *Politics: Who gets what, when, and how.* New York: McGraw-Hill.

Lave, J., and Lave, J. 1974. *The hospital construction act.* Washington, D.C.: American Enterprise Institute.

Lindblom, C. 1959. The science of muddling through. *Public Administration Review* 19:79-88.

Lowi, T. 1964. American business, public policy, case studies, and political theory. *World Politics* 16:677-715.

————. 1969. *The end of liberalism.* New York: W. W. Norton.

Madison, J. 1961. Federalist 10. In *The federalist papers*, A. Hamilton, J. Madison, and J. Jay. New York: New American Library.

Marmor, T. 1973. *The politics of Medicare.* Chicago: Aldine.

McConnell, G. 1966. *Private power and American democracy.* New York: Alfred A. Knopf.

Miliband, R. 1969. *The state in capitalist society.* New York: Basic Books.

Mills, C. W. 1956. *The power elite.* New York: Oxford University Press.

Musgrave, R. 1959. *The theory of public finance.* New York: McGraw-Hill.

Navarro, V. 1975. Health and the corporate society. *Social Policy* 5:41-49.

O'Connor, J. 1973. *The fiscal crisis of the state.* New York: St. Martin's Press.

Olson, M. Jr. 1965. *The logic of collective action.* Cambridge: Harvard University Press.

Perrow, C. 1963. Goals and power structures: A historical case study. In *The hospital in modern society*, ed. E. Freidson. Glencoe, IL: Free Press.

Pressman, J. and Wildavsky, A. 1973. *Implementation.* Berkeley: University of California Press.

Schattschneider, E. 1960. *The semi-sovereign people.* New York: Holt, Rinehart and Winston, p. 31.

Sorauf, F. 1970. Aorach versus Clauson: The impact of a Supreme Court decision. In *Readings in American political behavior*, ed. R. Wolfinger, p. 225. Englewood Cliffs, NJ: Prentice-Hall.

Stevens, R., and Stevens, R. 1974. *Welfare medicine in America.* New York: Free Press.

Verba, S., and Nie, N. 1972. *Participation in America.* New York: Harper & Row.

Wildavsky, A. 1964. *The politics of the budgetary process.* Boston: Little, Brown.

Wilensky, H. 1975. *The welfare state and equality.* Berkeley: University of California Press.

SUGGESTED READINGS

Alford, R. 1975. *Health care politics.* Chicago: University of Chicago Press. A provocative critique of current medical care organization in terms of structural power arrangements: dominant (professional monopolists), challenging (bureaucratic reformers), and repressed (equal health advocates). Author uses New York City as a case study to illustrate his contention that the current structural interests in the medical system effectively prevent any significant change or improvement in the delivery of health care.

Allison, G. 1971. *Essence of decision*. Boston: Little, Brown. Shows that analysts have certain conceptual lenses through which they look at the world, and that these lenses significantly affect what is seen and what is considered important. The three lenses—termed rational actor, political bargainings and organizational process models—are then applied to the Cuban missile crisis to produce three alternative but overlapping interpretations.

Allison, G. 1975. Implementation analysis. In *Benefit cost and policy analysis, 1974*, ed. R. E. Zeckhauser et al. Chicago: Aldine. A first step at helping administrators include political cost benefits and problems of implementation in their decision making. Presented as a classroom exercise, it uses the building of the Massachusetts Medical School as a case study of political decision making.

Anderson, O. 1968. *The uneasy equilibrium: Private and public financing of health services in the United States, 1875-1965*. New Haven, CT: College and University Press. Examines the historical development of American health services up to 1965. Contends that the health services system was essentially nongovernmental, and so the account of the government's role is quite lean.

Banfield, E. 1961. Political influence. New York: Alfred A. Knopf. A classic political science "pluralist" community power study that examines six important decisions in Chicago. The case of Cook County Hospital is an especially insightful and relevant study.

Bardach, E. 1972. *The skill factor in politics*. Berkeley: University of California Press. An attempt to study systematically political leadership and skill by examining several medical issues in California.

Campbell, A. 1964. *The American voter*. New York: John Wiley & Sons. The classic study of voting, stressing the insignificance of politics to the American voter and the importance of party identification.

Ehrenreich, B. 1970. *The American health empire*. New York: Random House. A strong radical critique of the American medical system. Has some interesting points for those not distracted by the strident rhetoric.

Elling, R. 1973. The shifting power structure in health. In *Politics and law in health care policy*, ed. J. McKinley. New York: Prodist. Provides a thoughtful, if preliminary, discussion of "power relations" in health. Sees a fluid system rather than a stable power structure. The other articles in this book (all from the *Milbank Memorial Fund Quarterly*) are also interesting.

Feingold, E. 1966. *Medicare, policy and politics*. San Francisco: Chandler. A selection of articles and comments that reveal both the issues and the climate of the Medicare controversy.

Lowi, T. 1964. American business, public policy, case studies, and political theory. *World Politics* 16:677–715. A "seminal" article in political science for interest group studies and policy analysis. Argues that the type of policy affects the political process and then describes three major policy types or "arenas": redistributive, distributive, and regulatory.

Marmor, T. 1973. *The politics of Medicare.* Chicago: Aldine. A case study of the development of the Medicare issue up to enactment in 1965. A concluding chapter analyzes Medicare in the larger context of social policy and politics in America.

McConnell, G. 1966. *Private power and American democracy.* New York: Alfred A. Knopf. An extended and insightful examination of private power both within organizations and in relation to the general public interest. Argues that the size of the real constituency is a central political issue: small constituencies are homogeneous with limited goals and tactics, but they allow the weak to be excluded and lead to private appropriation of public authority.

Navarro, V. 1975. Health and the corporate society. *Social Policy* 5:41–49. Analyzes how the U.S. economic structure influences the health sector. Argues that the control of providers is only secondary to control of classes by corporate elites.

Perrow, C. 1963. Goals and power structures: A historical case study. In *The Hospital in modern society*, ed. E. Freidson. Glencoe, IL: Free Press. An excellent discussion of internal power relations in a hospital. Argues that an organization will be controlled by the groups that perform the most difficult or critical tasks and that these groups will determine the organization's policies. Discusses how these groups have changed through time (from trustees to medical staff to multiple leadership) and the effect this has had on hospital policy. Also contains a good account by Elling of the relation of hospitals to the power structure of the community.

Redman, E. 1973. The dance of legislation. New York: Simon and Schuster. A light and interesting personal account of the legislative process leading to the passage of the Emergency Health Personnel Act of 1970 (PL 91-623).

Skidmore, M. 1970. *Medicare and the American rhetoric of conciliation.* Birmingham: University of Alabama. Examines redistributive politics in the context of an American ideological structure that is hostile to redistribution and welfare policies.

Stevens, R. and Stevens, R. 1974. *Welfare medicine in America.* New York: Free Press. An excellent political history of Medicaid with extensive documentation and wide-ranging discussion. Particularly strong on legislative history and implementation problems, but lacks a clear perspective and real political analysis.

Verba, S., and Nie, N. 1972. *Participation in America.* New York: Harper and Row. A basic source book for information on who participates, how they participate, and why. Using data from a nationwide survey, authors study the socioeconomic bias of political participation (voting, campaigning, contacting officials, and so on). Book ends with an attempt to discover what difference participation makes on leaders' responsiveness.

Wildavsky, A. 1964. *The politics of the budgetary process.* Boston: Little, Brown. A classic study of the federal budgetary process. Argues and attempts to explain why budget changes are only incremental since agencies receive basically what they received in the previous year with only slight adjustments.

Four

A Legal Perspective on Health Care Services

CARL J. SCHRAMM

INTRODUCTION

Many of the issues subjected to research by persons concerned with the delivery of health services clearly involve legislative initiatives in the area of health care. Indeed, positive health policy has increasingly been made in federal and state legislative forums. Yet, despite the evident importance of legal process in modern health policy making, a systematic view of the legal paradigm and how it affects social and economic change evades researchers who are critically analyzing programs and who would actively apply their labor in attempting to produce a new organization of health care delivery. As a result, the rigid means of reordering health care organizations and delivery imposed by the legal process does not respond well to the quantum of research findings from which it could benefit. In large measure, the blame for this state of affairs rests with researchers seeking organizational change, but whose view of the process of health care policy making and administration is incomplete in that it fails to include an understanding of the process of legal decision making.

This chapter sets out the basic assumptions on which the legal organization of health care services is founded. These legal assumptions are contrasted with the rational-patient and scientific-provider models which direct health care research today. Second, the process of rule making is examined in the context of changing existing health care policy. Finally, a systematic view of health policy making is presented which relies on the legal paradigm. The legal paradigm, it is argued, should prove useful in understanding why our society's legal mechanism hinders, perhaps appropriately in light of our experience, the development of a national health care policy.

PREVAILING ASSUMPTIONS REGARDING HEALTH SERVICES

Existing research on health services implicitly assumes one of two models of how man will attain the highest level of health. The first, characterized here as the rational-patient model, does not adopt an absolute "best" level. Rather, the rational-patient model envisions man as presented with a series of potential goods. Within a context of limited resources, including both time and money, he will choose among them in some manner which is rational. His "rationalness" generally is seen as behavior which optimizes his enjoyment of life within his operating constraints in a consistent manner, such that, faced with similar resources, the choice pattern will be roughly consistent through time. Thus, the rational view assumes a model of man which can assign health care or medical attention a subordinate place relative to other goods, so that one reaches an optimum level of happiness, given a set of personal tastes, or, stated differently, some psychological predisposition to a certain mix of goods.

An example of the rational-patient approach in contemporary health services research is Enthoven's (1978b) recent articulation of a "consumer choice" plan for national health insurance. Under this scheme, incentives are structured so that the individual will behave in a rational way, i.e., take only that health care which will improve his physical state while doing the least damage to his financial position. The current movement to make the individual increasingly responsible for the cost of curative medicine resulting from "irrational" risk taking, such as smoking and drinking, represents a second example of the attempt to reaffirm rational decision making in the individual (see, e.g., Knowles 1977). Similarly, health education programs, which attempt to enlighten the individual about personal health care and the appropriate use of available health care facilities, with the avowed purpose of modifying consumer behavior, rely on a rational-patient approach. Finally, at the macropolicy level, programs designed to elicit consumer participation in the process of planning new health care resources in the community, as provided for in the national health planning program, assume that more rational outcomes regarding the location and construction of health facilities will result if consumers, acting in their own interest, have input into the planning process.[1]

The scientific-provider model assumes that to maximize the health status of the population, the most intensive levels of health care and medical attention must be available to the population as needed. The focus of this approach is on the individual patient in need of therapeutic intervention. In the here and now of patient demand, resources must expand to the limits of science and practice. While some will find such a statement jarring at a time when the joint concerns of efficiency and efficacy in health services are high, it cannot be disputed that many adhere to a model of health care delivery which implicitly assumes that for medical attention to be optimal, the available resources must expand to accommodate any demand the patient's condition might require. The scientific-provider model emphasizes the medical or health needs of the individual as they are determined objectively or externally, and requires that the patient be subject. Here, medicine is thought of as the artful application of science to the prevention of physical deterioration of the individual.

Much current health care research and program development reflects the predominance of the scientific-provider model. The kidney dialysis effort, whereby the federal government underwrites the total cost of dialysis, thus ensuring access for all chronic renal patients, represents one example of the model.[2] The proliferation of CT scanners in the absence of any efficacy research which, at the very least, would establish an appropriate ratio of scanners to population (Abrams and McNeil 1978), is another example of how technological advances will be called for in what seems to be an unnecessarily high number of cases. Finally, the established rate of excessive and unnecessary surgery offers evidence that at least a significant portion of practitioners and medical researchers believe that surgical intervention is an optimal means of handling any number of clinical conditions.[3]

It would seem evident that the rational-patient and the scientific-provider models are fundamentally irreconcilable. The former relies on the patient as the primary controller of the expenditure of medical resources and as the auditor of his or her health status, while the latter assumes that an external, "scientific" norm of health exists to which the patient can be made to conform with intervention. The rational-patient school is based on the idea that various incentives can be structured so that the individual both engages in a lower-risk, more healthful lifestyle and demands less costly attention from the health care delivery system. The scientific-provider model is concerned almost solely with maximizing the health status of the patient demanding care. While the provider-centric model is individualistic in its perspective, the patient-oriented model attempts a systematic view of the health of the society, and thus is more concerned with optimizing the deployment of the resources society has dedicated to health care. As a result, the rational-patient model is more amenable to the concerns of preventive health measures and to controlling inflation of health costs. Indeed, the scientific-provider model is little concerned with either, focusing instead on curative steps to affect the individual.

Whether true or not, contemporary commentary indicates that the rational-patient view is ascending in influence relative to the scientific-provider model, and that such a shift is normatively positive. From a legal perspective, such a shift is unguided by cultural imperatives which direct legal thinking regardless of which model is dominant. While legislatures have increasingly become the battlegrounds between the two models, with various statutory enactments adding the force of law to one side or the other, the law makes several basic assumptions which are unaffected by statutory efforts to guide the mode of delivering health services. Moreover, while new health programs may be established by statutes which would change one or more of these fundamental legal tenets, such laws seldom attempt to effect changes in legal process, which, in the area of health policy, is at least as important as the legal principles at issue.

THE LEGAL PERSPECTIVE ON HEALTH SERVICES RESEARCH

As will be seen momentarily, several legal tenets are universally applied in evaluating any problem raised by the individual's interaction with the health care delivery system or by any proposed change in the structure of the system. Above all of these assumptions, which are divided into substantive and procedural groupings, stands a critical operating premise—namely, that the law is the proper, if not the exclusively appropriate, means for bringing about social change. The law, in the eyes of lawyers, is always able to accommodate change, whether through case-by-case determinations or through statutory enactments.

The first of the substantive assumptions is that a contractual approach to ordering human affairs is to be preferred to all others. Affirming the free market ordering of society, the contract is seen as the way in which private agreements are enforced by the courts, generally without inquiry into the terms of the underlying transaction. By so ordering the exchange of health care services between provider and consumer, the lawyer as policy maker confines the transaction to a familiar paradigm with long established and well understood boundaries. This contractual approach requires that a health care exchange be analyzed like any other transaction between buyer and seller, and enforced without question by the courts unless a fundamental contractual rule has been violated. As a result, the medical care transaction, when subjected to legal analysis, loses its character as a fight for life over death and appears as a more prosaic exchange of services for money.[4]

The second assumption is that certain fundamental rights of the individual must be preserved. These rights, based on the guarantees assured by the Constitution, encompass the American vision of being able to do with one's body what one wants, from purchasing excessive medical attention to completely neglecting one's physical condition altogether. The preservation of the individual's freedom to choose what attention his body will receive is regarded by legislators and judges as sacred and will not be examined except in the most extreme cases. Thus, a court will interfere with an individual's exercise of his or her will regarding health care only if the intervention is well established as necessary for continued life. The clearest examples of judicial interference, which are equally helpful in illustrating the reluctance of the law to intervene, are cases involving refusal of blood transfusions based on religious grounds and those involving the decision to withdraw mechanical life support for terminally ill persons without conscious faculties.[5]

The third assumption is that institutions, such as hospitals, must be preserved in their procedural rights. Thus, while the individual's protection is centered around substantive rights,[6] institutions, which do not enjoy many of the privileges of citizens, must be similarly protected from the arbitrary use of government power against them. While the government may regulate nearly any phase of an institution's activity in which a rational governmental interest can be shown,[7] in the process of applying such regulation, the government is restrained by a concept of fundamental fairness. It cannot, for example, set limitations on the operations of an organization without showing the need for government presence and without adhering to the due process route which must be followed any time there is an arguable taking of life, liberty, or, more germane in the case of an affected institution, property.

The institution's right to due process requires an adversarial hearing, with the attendant right of access to the opponent's case prior to hearing; a neutral hearing procedure, including an unbiased administrative decision maker; and the right of appeal (Davis 1972). Notwithstanding the long established presumption that interference by the government in the decisions of an institution or organization, when done in good faith, is legitimate, the guarantee of legal procedure, principally access to a hearing where the issue is decided on the merits, has proven to be the fundamental safeguard for the institution (see Davis 1977). Indeed, procedure is the protection which permits the institution to resist government incursions into its discretionary authority by using empirical evidence and logical argument.

The superordination of individual rights over the rights vested in institutions is the fourth assumption imposed by the legal paradigm. This assumption seems evident from the preceding two postulates. Again, the need to protect the personal freedom of the natural person to act in any manner he chooses, short of narrowly proscribed behaviors, is paramount to the rights which private institutions enjoy. Thus, while a hospital's decision to move to a new neighborhood might be examined by a government agency with authority to grant operating licenses applying location as one criterion in its decision, the citizen has an unqualified, constitutionally specified right to move anywhere he or she chooses. Because of the perceived harm which might result from qualifying the citizen's freedom relative to the institution's, and which ultimately might threaten the nature of our society, the discretion granted to organizations and institutions, particularly chartered bodies,[8] will always be accorded a lesser degree of due process protection.

The fifth element of the legal approach to public policy is that ultimately the advancement of social goals prevails over the protection of most individual rights. Throughout our history, both the substantive and procedural rights enjoyed by citizens and organizations have been tempered by the need to advance the society through means essentially inimical to the complete freedom of the individual. While this concept was early recognized as the social contract by which individuals submit to behavioral rules in return for the benefits of society (Locke 1960), in the history of American law, the rights of the individual have been tempered by government, or at least this is a widespread perception. Certainly, since the 16th Amendment, one can no longer control all of one's income with total freedom (U.S. Constitution, Amendment XVI). Nor, subsequent to the ruling in *National Macaroni Manufacturers' Association* v. *FTC*, 345 F.2d 421 (7th Cir. 1965), may one engage in a price conspiracy not contemplated when the Sherman Act was passed. Similarly, while *Griswold* v. *Connecticut*[9] makes it clear that the bedroom is a sanctum beyond the reach of the government and thus nearly any object may be lawfully possessed therein, one may not legally purchase or even privately transport certain prohibited materials for use in the bedroom.[10] The Controlled Substances Act[11] makes the possession or use of many chemical substances illegal. A firm can no longer violate reasonable safety standards for its work force without exposure to criminal sanctions[12] any more than a chemical plant can discharge materials described by the law as environmentally offensive into the water or atmosphere.[13] It seems obvious that progressive collective initiatives, made via Congress and the courts, have circumscribed the discretion of the individual.

The apparent relativism of absolute rights around which policy is built suggests that the legal approach is more flexible than many researchers would initially think. While it is certain that there are absolutes which will always be held sacred by the law, it is impossible to predict how legislatures and courts will articulate and interpret these principles. Mr. Dooley's observation, that "th' supreme court follows th' iliction returns" (Dunne 1901), is still a useful, albeit particularly cynical, reminder that health proposals which the law presently regards as unthinkable may someday be embraced as the fundamental elements of the American health care system.

The remaining two characteristics of the legal approach are methodological in nature. The law represents an unflinching commitment to the position that social progress arises from conflict, and that the legal process is the most constructive means of resolving this conflict. Out of this assumption grows the adversarial system, whereby each of the parties to a dispute makes no pretense regarding his antagonism toward the other. They battle out their positions applying the rules of law which are announced in the statutes and cases, with a neutral tribunal deciding the issue by applying the rules to the facts in dispute. At its most elementary level, the tribunal process is a balancing of particular rules, such as those set out above, within a context allowing the decision maker some discretion in order that a more fair or just outcome can be had in the particular case.[14]

The final characteristic of the legal approach is the assumption, again more easily thought of as methodological, that the law is the proper, if not the exclusive, vehicle for social change. To the lawyer, equipped with the rules of law, the adversarial method and the tribunal system, the legal approach to social change is the most appropriate. To the lay person thinking over his or her last encounter with an attorney, it may be hard to believe that the lawyer's self-image is one of social policy maker. Nevertheless, the educational process in modern law schools, professional literature at all levels, and the common organizational form of practice (the multiple-member firm) itself, all conspire to enforce the lawyer's notion that he or she is a member of a group whose experience and social function both suggest that policy making is its special preserve.

THE COMPETING HEALTH MODELS AND THE LEGAL PROCESS

Quite obviously, while the rational-patient and the scientific-provider models provide a way of thinking of how we will attain some optimal health status as a population, the legal perspective is concerned more with process, provided certain fundamentals are preserved. While the rationalist and provider models are in tension, the legal perspective is theoretically neutral. Because it focuses primarily on the preservation of individual rights and established procedure, the law is indifferent as to which side prevails in serving as the model. The law cannot resolve a scientific question, and most lawyers would feel incompetent to judge which approach would optimize the health status of the population. Indeed, despite the predominantly positivist view of American jurisprudence, the law is reluctant to choose sides in an area where little in the way of absolute principles can be stated.

In reality, however, the law is shaped and constrained by human experience. Thus, while shrouded in impartiality, the legal system harbors inherent biases. The most important is that the law is more comfortable with what exists by way of precedent than with new and untried things. The culture of the law is the application of past experience to current dilemmas. Both approaches to health care research, on the other hand, take their self-identity from the physical sciences. The approach used in each is based on the method of scientific inquiry, which in turn rests on the assumption that phenomena exist and humanity must discover and describe their behavior. The scientific approach is, by its very nature, oriented to the future, to pursuing the discovery process so that various phenomena can be made to conform to a human standard of satisfaction. The distinction between the legal and the scientific approaches as they relate to health care research is that the former looks to culturally agreed upon rules for structuring health services, while the scientific approach appears to pursue absolute or physically determined rules and structure health care to accommodate them.

A second distinction which may be drawn between the two approaches, and one bearing on the question of the law's neutrality, is the value each attaches to experience. The law plainly reveres the concept of wisdom, as might be imagined from its methodological concern with precedent. As a result, the legal influence on the structuring or restructuring of health care services will reflect an assumption that the existing system has some inherent and useful rationale, and that any change should be adopted only if certain improvement will result. In the approach of the physical sciences the importance of subjectively derived knowledge, or wisdom, is, properly, much less important. Both of the prevailing models of delivery are, like the scientific method, oriented to the future. To the advocate of either the rational-patient or scientific-provider perspective, it is certain that the future must bring better medical care and that the received model must be changed. Indeed, while a familiar legal maxim states that "The law hateth invention and innovation,"[15] being content to accept existing institutions as legitimate, the scientifically inclined health care delivery models anticipate fundamental structural change as a natural and desired aspect of the passage of time.

The final bias of the legal approach, which to a large extent is shared by the scientific approach, is that it serves the purposes of certain groups in society better than it serves others (see Truman 1971). The law has often been seen as enforcing the ruling elite (Mills 1956). Certainly, the corpus of statutory and case law reflects the concerns and conflicts of wealthier citizens wishing to protect or increase their financial position. Because the interests of various elites are better represented in legislatures and courts, it is certain that a systematic bias is reflected in the way the law relates to questions regarding health care delivery. The practice of medicine is dominated by a highly visible elite, and, as a result, the view of medicine embraced by the law will tend to gravitate to the view held by the medical establishment, and any movement toward a contrary position will be resisted by both the personal inclination of members of the legal elite and by the legal process itself.

In sum, it appears that the legal approach to questions involving the reordering or changing of the manner in which our nation's health care is provided is not indifferent, as might be assumed because of the absence of a scientific disposition toward one side or the other in the health services debate. Rather, because of its commitment to a highly stylized method of procedure, its inherent comfort with precedent, and its inclination to affirm the ruling elites, the law must be assumed to be a force in support of the status quo, which will actively resist any proposed changing of the existing institutional arrangements for providing care.

RULE MAKING

By far the most important aspect of the legal approach to health care organization from the perspective of one seeking to effect change is the process by which the legal system makes decisions. These decisions can be thought of as the rules which govern the behavior of all pertinent actors on the health care scene. There are three principal deposits of these rules. The first, of course, is the aggregation of laws passed by legislatures, both the Congress and state assemblies. The second, as mentioned above, is the body of interpretive decisions rendered by courts. Because our system of jurisprudence accords great weight to the rulings of courts by using them as precedents in subsequent controversies, judges have a major hand in rule making. But, in terms of modern health policy making, increasingly the most important sources of rules are administrative agencies (Rosenblatt 1978). For example, at the federal level, the Food and Drug Administration (FDA), Environmental Protection Agency (EPA) and Consumer Protection Agency (CPA) and, at the state level, professional licensing agencies,[16] health planning and development agencies[17] and hospital rate-setting commissions[18] have increasingly influenced the daily management of health care institutions. The importance of these agencies is witnessed by the current concern over governmental interference with the discretionary authority of health providers in the name of "deregulation."[19] In any event, the administrative agency has emerged as a principal rule maker from the perspective of the health policy maker.

The administrative agency is essentially different from the other two rule makers because of its composition and authority. The power of the administrative agency is not inherently granted by constitutional sources nor is its jurisdiction established by tradition. Rather, the authority of the administrative body is delegated by the legislature which established the body in the first place.

A second critical difference between the administrative agency and other rule makers is that rule making is only one of the tasks performed by the agency. While the legislature and the courts are exclusively concerned with rule making, either through initiating statutory rules or adjudicating contests by interpreting and announcing new rules, the administrative body is vested with all three traditional functions of government: legislative, which it carries out by making regulations; judicial, which it performs by sitting as a court to decide conflicts arising under its regulations; and executive, which it executes when it enforces its regulations, whether by conducting hearings, or carrying on investigations, or levying fines against violators of the agency's regulations. The administrative agency thus functions in a much different environment than either the legislature or the courts, since it makes rules, enforces them and adjudicates disputes arising under them. The agency lives with the rules it makes and theoretically benefits from its experience in administering regulations when it establishes new rules. Of course, this "closed system" in rule making is subject to criticism. The principal problem cited is that the key members of regulatory bodies, as appointees of the chief executive, are not as responsive to public interests as are legislative rule makers (Leiserson 1942;

Stewart 1975). It is also observed that administrative bodies eventually become too responsive to special interests, that agencies often become "captive" or "clientele" regulators (see, e.g., Herring 1936; Truman 1971; Sabatier 1975). In any event, it is certain that the administrative agency is of increasing importance as a source of rules in our society and that in the future it will be as important in the daily operating decisions of various health delivery institutions in our society as are the Congress, state legislatures, and courts.

THE PROCESS OF HEALTH POLICY MAKING— A LEGAL PERSPECTIVE

As noted above, people engage in the exercise of research in health services with a view toward restructuring the existing system. This approach is compelled by the logic of the physical sciences employed by both of the competing approaches to health services research and reflects the predisposition of most, if not all, of the persons so engaged. Essentially, of course, such research is part of the larger process of policy making, which necessarily takes change as its raison d'être.

The strategy for bringing about change in health care policy is much like that used by groups with other concerns in our society, with some significant idiosyncracies. The policy-making strategy in health care generally involves five steps. The first, common to all policy strategies regardless of the substance involved, is problem recognition. Here some unmet need is identified as significant enough to be the object of a campaign to change social, economic or political rules which relate to the problem. The second step is a determination of where the rules which govern the phenomenon are made and what rule-making body is the proper target for a campaign to bring about change. Sometimes problems are easily resolved by changing operating rules within an organization (Thompson 1967). However, in the case of problems observed in the society at large, policy must be made to apply society-wide and be implemented, most likely, by a government body. If an existing rule-making body has authority sufficient to establish new rules, the policy drive may be targeted here. However, if a problem is either new or of particular significance, such as a cancer epidemic, then a new set of rules, including an agency to adminster them, may have to be established. If the latter option is the desired outcome for the policy drive, then a legislative body must be the maker of the new rules.

Once the appropriate rule-making body is identified, those with the power to make the necessary new rules must be made to appreciate and internalize the underlying problem and the need for changing the applicable rules. In the case of health policy this task falls primarily on the academic health establishment. While the academic establishment is not universally included in or required as part of the policy process, e.g., its role is nearly nonexistent in developing defense strategy, in health matters the scientific community is critical in raising consciousness on issues and in making the call for change legitimate. Implicit in this step is the assumption that the relevant rule makers must perceive the identified problem as having sufficient political importance to be a subject of action. Be it a legislative or executive agency, the rule maker must be convinced that action is necessary to satisfy the demand for new rules. Because of the complex nature of health issues, scientific-academic groups must translate the issues into social realities and persuade rule makers that the matter merits consideration and, ultimately, action.

The fourth step in the process is the decision to make new rules itself. This step is the point at which the rule maker must accommodate the interests of groups with divergent expectations of how the new rules will work. As anyone who has observed a legislative or administrative body in its rule-making function knows, if there are one or more groups which perceive that the proposed rules will affect them adversely, the rule maker will compromise the proposed rule reflecting a positive correlation between the manner in which the rules are adjusted and the quantum of political power of the adversely affected group(s).

The fifth step in the process is administering and carrying out the rules once established. This is often the most difficult phase of the process, as the rules are often inadequate or poorly adopted to the central task for which they were conceived. (For a discussion of the failures of regulatory programs, see Breyer 1979.) It often occurs that the problem which was the focus of the rule-making process in the first place is substantially different in nature than originally thought. When this happens, changes in the rules are sought, or else various modifications of the rules are developed by way of routine interpretations or regulations. Another administrative problem, albeit of a more prosaic nature, is that the carrying out of a set of administrative rules often requires resources greatly in excess of the budgeted funds available. Further, once new rules are made, i.e., the process is completed through step four, the political force for change in the underlying problem may be satisfied and no political support for an adequate budget may be forthcoming (Edelman 1964; Downs 1972). Finally, during the administrative step, the rule-making process falls on a different group of persons than those who recognized the initial problem and who agitated for new rules. Administrative personnel generally have a different, perhaps more neutral, perspective on the issue in question and hence emphasize certain rules at the expense of others. Thus, the administration of a regulatory mandate may fundamentally change the way in which the problem is dealt with as compared to the way its solution was conceived by the rule-making body. Not infrequently, the approach used in the administration of the rules eventually reshapes the entire manner in which the underlying problem is thought about and what its real nature is (Schramm 1976). And, of course, in the case of *de novo* initiatives, such as the Hill-Burton provisions as they applied during the 1950s, the underlying phenomenon is completely shaped by the administrative rules.

From this process-oriented view of rule making, one develops a sense of the importance of its temporal dimensions. Because of the time lag imposed by the hearing process required in the consideration of new rules, those finally promulgated may be so out of date that they have no effective impact on the problem as originally perceived. However, the passage of time influences the rule-making process in a second more significant way. As the political need for attention to a given problem wanes, the resources devoted to the administration of the rules invariably decrease relative to the necessary commitment needed to carry out the task envisioned by the rules themselves. As already mentioned, this dissipation of interest, often set in motion by the mere enactment of the rules, occurs as the society allows its interest to shift to some newly identified problem, content that the previous problem has been settled with the establishment of rules. The administration of the National Environmental Policy Act, which contemplated a much stricter ban on atmospheric contaminants than was authorized under the program, is a good example of this phenomenon (Downs 1972). The Occupational Safety and Health Act[20] also predicted a much greater impact on our occupational fatality experience than has occurred, in part because the issue of work-related health hazards is politically much less important now than it was in the late 1960s (Schramm 1976).

Overlooking the inherent substantive biases of legal procedure outlined above, the rule-making process seems to underscore the neutrality of the law in policy making. The constraints of administrative law are concerned with process more than substance. Moreover, the legal constraints on the way in which policy is developed apply universally, shaping securities-trading regulations in the same fashion that new drug approvals are granted. As a result of the dominance of legal procedure over the policy process, the lawyer's role is critical in the development of policy. Only the lawyer can authoritatively speak to the conflict between proposed and existing rules, and only the lawyer can make informed judgments about whether new rules, once adopted, will stand up to scrutiny in appellate courts. These two skills are essentially general in nature, and the lawyer participating in the formulation of health policy need bring no specific health training or experience to bear. The lawyer will be concerned above all with ensuring the preservation of individual rights and procedural safeguards. Beyond these objectives, the law is no more or less concerned with whether a particular rule will in fact deal with the problem in question in the manner hoped for than is any other discipline, nor is the law particularly concerned with advancing some larger view of social equity. Nevertheless, in our society, legal process, however neutral, clearly influences substantive outcomes. While the application of legal constraints is accepted with indifference as a given, legal process shapes rather significantly the very essence of the rules which emerge.

APPLYING THE PERSPECTIVE TO POLICY REFORM—TWO CASES

To better appreciate the utility and application of the legal perspective on health policy research, two case studies may be useful. One of the most significant and controversial areas of policy activity in recent years, namely health planning, is a good subject for analysis because it represents a program where commitment to the underlying objectives remains relatively strong, while the impact of policy on the perceived problem is a matter of dispute. In addition, there is growing evidence that the rules which embody the policy may soon be the subject of pressure for significant change (Iglehart 1978).

The story of health planning is familiar. The first efforts at stimulating some national facilities planning process were embodied in the Hill-Burton Act.[21] Through successive legislative experiments and with an evolving position among health care elites that a rationalized system of providers would render better quality care more efficiently, the drive to a fully developed health planning program culminated in 1974 in the National Health Planning and Resources Development Act.[22] Under the Act, the fifth generation[23] of a federally designed planning process was born which established a two-tier planning apparatus. The first level of planning was assigned to newly formed, locally oriented health systems agencies (HSAs). The second planning level is statewide, with review power over decisions of the HSAs vested in the state health planning and development agencies (SHPDAs) and the state health care coordinating councils (SHCCCs), agencies which are usually established by state legislatures to comply with the federal mandate.[24]

The policy embodied in the Act emphasizes the work of the HSAs. This reflects primarily the philosophy that the locality knows best how its health delivery system should be structured. A critical feature of the HSA, mandated by the Act, is that its governing body, which typically numbers in excess of 100 members, be composed of a majority of "consumers." The balance, but not less than 40 percent, is made up of providers.[25]

The philosophy underlying the planning process is that participation by citizens can make the delivery system function more responsively. In many respects, the composition of the HSA governing bodies represents the high water mark of what has been termed interest-group liberalism (Lowi 1969).

In practice, the roughly 60 consumer members represent formalized constituencies, and the constituencies are generally represented even though particular members come and go. Thus, labor, organized charities, various influential religious bodies, local governments, and voluntary health associations will always be represented. Similarly, on the provider side, professional associations, local hospital associations, and insurers are represented. This attempt at making government more responsive by ensuring consumer participation in various administrative agencies was a hallmark of the Great Society legislation and was mandated by the presence of particularly vocal and alienated populations within the larger society (Lowi 1969).

The National Health Planning and Resources Development Act also represents one of the clearest legislative enactments based on the rational-consumer model. By statute, the role of consumers in approving and designing new health facilities and services is established, and providers are required to respond to the input of potential patients. It must be noted, however, that the Act involves the consumer only in facilities management at the macrolevel, and does nothing to increase the individual patient's control or interest in any actual encounter with the medical system.

The Act does little to challenge the traditional concerns of the law. No individual rights or liberties are affected and procedural safeguards, by way of appeal to state-level bodies, are available to those aggrieved by HSA decisions. The law continues to vest facilities-licensure power in state health commissioners where it has traditionally rested, and, because it does not provide for any sanctions in the HSAs, due process concerns are minimal.

Essentially, because of its extraordinary concern with form and procedure in place of real substantive control over decisions to capitalize new facilities and to redirect existing provider resources, the planning law represents an example of how health policy making may produce unsatisfactory solutions. One reason the law has performed poorly,[26] and I believe it has, is that it is much too concerned with imitating legal process without paying sufficient attention to the real concerns of the legal perspective. Thus, given the rational-consumer assumption on which the law is based, it cannot work effectively because its "legal concerns" are misdirected. This result obtains both because the Act includes unnecessary structure to accommodate the need for an appellate option and because consumer influence is minimized due, in part, to the Act's intimidating and cumbersome legalism.

Several aspects of the planning process as it is crystallized in the Act exemplify these problems. The composition of the governing body may accommodate the needs of a liberal participatory theory, but the members are hardly representative. As mentioned, vested "consumer" groups have taken over the planning bodies, and their interests, because they represent other elites, are often no different from the interests of providers. Moreover, by essentially requiring an interest group identity of each member of a very large board, the HSAs have become particularly unsuited to representing the larger public interest. This is most evident in cases involving the approval of new capital construction in areas which are already recognized as overserved. Imagine a typical case of a request to build a new hospital in a service area which all agree is currently served by several hundred excess beds. In the face of such a decision, HSA delegates, perceiving that such a project is in their constituents' interest, vote for the project. When widely diverse delegates such as consumers, providers, labor unionists, bankers, politicians and community activists see a new hospital as increasing the welfare of their constituent group, the project in question is approved, because some combination of these groups invariably constitutes a majority. This outcome obtains despite the fact that each delegate is cognizant of the existing excess supply of hospital resources and the worsening impact that the instant decision will have on what is universally seen as a situation in need of solution. Given that most of the decisions of the HSAs focus on the question of capital construction, the impotence of the planning bodies to really rationalize the delivery system becomes painfully evident.

Second, the appeals mechanism envisioned by the Act, and regarded by persons working with the Act as critical, is illusory. Almost no incentive exists for HSAs to make negative determinations on significant projects; hence, there is little of substance which is appealed. Moreover, since HSAs are without power to close either beds or hospitals, truly appealable decisions never come from the HSAs. Finally, because HSAs cannot levy fines or take other punitive steps, hospitals and providers seldom seek redress in higher forums.

A third criticism of the Act is that it has no authority over the question of financing the providers which it regulates. It is widely accepted that the financing of systems determines their behavior (Enthoven 1978a). An agency designed to control hospital service delivery without power over how such care is financed is somewhat like the draft system after 1972, a bureaucracy with a clear mission but no tools to carry it out.

In sum, the National Health Planning and Resources Development Act represents a case where concern over legal formality may have run wild. The Act is filled with legal process but provides for little authority over the actual restructuring of the health care system, contrary to the purpose stated in the Act's preamble.[27]

The second case demonstrates an even more direct relationship between legal constraints and health policy outcomes. As new health care provider occupations were purposefully developed in the 1960s and 1970s,[28] the importance of professional licensure laws to the success of the policy became clear. The new occupations, chiefly characterized as requiring fewer skills than physicians but more skills than traditional nurses, were developed as a substitute for physician providers. While physicians' assistants, nurse extenders, and midwives were trained to handle many clinical situations traditionally dealt with only by physicians, state laws governing the practice of medicine severely constrained the utilization of these new "subphysician" occupations. Here the focus of rule making has been in the state legislatures, which have shown varying degrees of solicitude to the interests of these new groups.[29] Indeed, in some states, persons trained as alternate providers of care cannot be employed, as the traditional physician and nurse licensing acts have not been significantly modified (Forgotson and Cook 1967). It is interesting to note that the policy approach to the licensing of new occupations has assumed the course of original physician and nurse licensing legislation by seeking a separate statutory statement for each new occupation setting forth what members can and cannot do relative (whether articulated or not) to the physician's unlimited powers to practice. This represents, again, a negative outcome of the legal perspective. A more efficient policy approach would be the simple revision of the state's physician licensing law so that it describes those functions reserved to physicians. All unspecified functions could be performed by any other skilled person working in a health care institution, shifting the burden for limiting entry to the field to the providing institution and away from the state. The fact that the question of permitting skilled subphysician personnel to practice has been solved by licensing each separate occupation reflects an imprudent adaptation of a legal solution devised decades ago. Its application in the 1970s seems an example of how adherence to a precedent, with which lawyers are comfortable, has produced a cumbersome and complicated solution to a relatively simple problem, and a solution which engenders further segmentation in our nation's labor market and which may also stimulate inflation of health care costs.

CONCLUSION

Health care research has been concerned with the development of change in the operation of our health care system. While two schools of thought guide the process of change and attempt to design the new system, the process of change is essentially one of rule making. As such, it is, in turn, guided by several elemental legal precepts and by our society's concern for due process. To overlook individual rights or the safeguards of legal procedure, with which the individual is empowered any time an attempt is made to alter his or her freedom to live as he or she chooses, is to make policy which will not survive no matter how altruistic its claims or how universal its support. In the past, health policy has been frustrated by the existence of legal procedure in its drive to bring about new mechanisms of service delivery. Too much can be made of legal procedure, such that policy goals are completely swallowed up by process. Our national health planning program offers an example of this result, as does our experience with licensing new health occupations. Hence, the proper legal perspective on health policy making should be respect for the goals of the legal system, both the preservation of individual rights and the procedural system used in their protection, but with an awareness that the law exists to serve and not to be served. With this in mind, the headlong rush to educate students in health policy programs and in many health delivery disciplines in the complexities of the law, in large part to satisfy a contemporary and passing fascination with legalism in our society, is to potentially produce persons whose creativity in developing new methods and modes of health delivery may be overly inhibited by fears of doing something "illegal." Mere familiarity with law breeds conservatism, which is the last outcome that the educational process should promote.

NOTES

1. National Health Planning and Resources Development Act of 1974, Public Law 93-641, Jan. 4, 1975, codified at 42 U.S.C. sections 300k *et seq.* (Supp. V 1975). *See* Senate Report No. 1285, reprinted in *U.S. Code Congressional and Administrative News* (1974), pp. 7885-86, for a statement of this assumption.
2. Kidney Disease Amendments of 1970, Public Law 91-515, October 30, 1970, codified at 42 U.S.C. sections 299 *et seq.* (Supp. V 1975).
3. Carl P. Schlicke, "Doctor, is this operation necessary?" *American Journal of Surgery* 134(1977):3-12. The Subcommittee on Oversight and Investigations of the House Committee on Interstate and Foreign Commerce (chaired by Congressman John E. Moss) estimated that 2.38 million Americans were subjected to unnecessary operations in 1974, at a cost of $3.92 billion, and with 11,900 resulting unnecessary deaths. Subcommittee on Oversight and Investigations of the House Committee on Interstate and Foreign Commerce. *Report on the cost and quality of health care: Unnecessary surgery.* Washington, D.C.: Government Printing Office, 1976, pp. 30-31, 34.
4. *See, e.g.,* Sullivan v. O'Connor, 296 N.E.2d 183 (Mass. 1973); Gault v. Sideman, 42 Ill.App.2d 96, 191 N.E.2d 436 (1963); Hawkins v. McGee, 84 N.H. 114, 146 A. 641 (1929).

5. *See, e.g.*, Harley v. Oliver, 404 F.Supp 450 (D. Ark. 1975), blood transfusion; In re Quinlan, 70 N.J. 10, 355 A.2d 647 (1976), withdrawal of mechanical life support.

6. Some examples of these substantive rights include the right to vote, Strauder v. West Virginia, 100 U.S. 303 (1880); freedom of travel, Crandall v. Nevada, 73 U.S. (6 Wall.) 35 (1868); freedom of expression, Abrams v. United States, 250 U.S. 616 (1919), (Holmes, J., dissenting), Whitney v. California, 274 U.S. 355 (1927), (Brandeis, J., dissenting); and freedom of association, NAACP v. Alabama, 357 U.S. 449 (1958).

7. Munn v. Illinois, 94 U.S. 113 (1877), sustaining an Illinois law regulating the maximum charges of grain warehousemen, as being businesses "affected with the public interest"; Lochner v. New York, 198 U.S. 45 (1905), stating the general test while invalidating a New York law fixing maximum hours of employment, as lacking a rational government interest; Nebbia v. New York, 291 U.S. 502 (1934), upholding the New York Milk Control Board's power to regulate the prices charged by retail stores; and Williamson v. Lee Optical Co., 348 U.S. 483 (1955), sustaining an Oklahoma law regulating the business of opticians.

8. Corporations, as entities created and chartered by the law, do not enjoy coextensive protection of the full catalog of substantive rights which is afforded the individual. For example, in the Privileges and Immunities Clause of the Constitution (U.S. Constitution, art. IV, section 2), the word "citizen" does not include corporations and aliens. Similarly, in the Fifth Amendment, the privilege against self-incrimination does not extend to corporations and institutions. In a different vein, it is apparent that the very nature of the substantive rights which are enjoyed by an individual takes on less importance vis-à-vis an institution. The right of interstate travel, the right to vote, and the right of privacy have little meaning for an institution. Likewise, the First Amendment guarantees of freedom of expression and freedom of religion mean less to an institution. While a corporation may engage in political speech and be protected from governmental interference to the same degree as an individual, corporations are generally more concerned with commercial speech, which is subject to a much greater amount of governmental regulation. Consequently, an institution will place more emphasis on, and value more, relatively speaking, the amount of procedural due process protection it receives, rather than the degree of protection of its substantive rights.

9. 381 U.S. 479 (1965). The court in Griswold found an implicit right of privacy in the Constitution, although unsure of its exact source, and held that a Connecticut statute forbidding the use of contraceptives was an unconstitutional infringement upon privacy right. The Griswold rationale was extended in Stanley v. Georgia, 394 U.S. 557 (1969), where the court held that the private possession of pornographic material could not, constitutionally, be made a crime, and in Eisenstadt v. Baird, 405 U.S. 438 (1972), where the court held that the decision to use contraceptives was one of individual privacy, and hence belonged to single as well as married adults.

10. U.S. v. Reidel, 402 U.S. 351 (1971), upholding federal statute banning the distribution of pornographic materials through the mails; Miller v. California, 413 U.S. 15 (1973), upholding state statute prohibiting the sale or exhibition of

pornography; and U.S. v. Orito, 413 U.S. 439 (1973), upholding federal statute prohibiting the interstate transportation of pornographic materials, even where the transportation is by private vehicle and for the private use of the transporter.

11. Public Law 91-513, Oct. 27, 1970, codified at 21 U.S.C. sections 801 *et seq.* (Supp. V 1975).

12. Occupational Safety and Health Act of 1970, Public Law 91-190, Jan. 1, 1970, codified at 42 U.S.C. sections 651 *et seq.* (Supp. V 1975).

13. National Environmental Policy Act of 1969, Public Law 91-190, Jan. 1, 1970, codified at 42 U.S.C. sections 4321 *et seq.* (Supp. V 1975).

14. Not every dispute brought before a court can be decided by using rules of law which were previously laid down, as the appropriate rules may not quite fit the instant case, or may be nonexistent, or may even produce an unjust result in the case at hand. This inability of the courts of law to provide a remedy for every injury was recognized early in the history of Anglo-American law, and led to the development of a separate, coexistent system of "equity," whereby justice could be done in those cases where the common law would provide no or inadequate redress. While equity and law are no longer bifurcated but are today merged in nearly all jurisdictions, the concept of allowing a judge to exercise his discretion in the light of reason and conscience still remains viable. For a modern exposition of this thesis, see K. C. Davis, *Discretionary Justice*, Baton Rouge: Louisiana State University Press, 1969, pp. 17-20.

15. *Wingate's Maxims*, p. 756, maxim 204, as cited in Henry Campbell Black, *Black's Law Dictionary*, 4th ed., St. Paul: West, 1968, at p. 1029.

16. In Maryland, "practitioners of medicine" must be licensed by the Board of Medical Examiners, a part of the State Department of Health and Mental Hygiene. Md. Ann. Code, art. 43, sections 119 *et seq.* (1976). Nurses are licensed by the State Board of Examiners of Nurses. Md. Ann. Code, art. 43, sections 290 *et seq.* (1976).

17. Maryland has, for example, several state-level administrative agencies: the Maryland Health Planning and Resources Development Agency, the Maryland Planning and Development Agency, and the State Health Coordinating Council.

18. In Maryland, the Health Services Cost Review Commission was created in 1971, with jurisdiction over the costs and rates of hospitals and health care institutions in the state. Md. Ann. Code, art. 43, sections 568H-568Y (1976).

19. A typical example of this is the study done by the Maryland Hospital Association, which found that Maryland hospitals are subject to the regulations of 108 different agencies in 1078 different capacities, resulting in duplication of regulations, conflicting regulations, and unnecessary costs. Maryland Hospital Association, "Duplication of regulation study," December 1978, pp. 6-8. More generally, and with greater and more far-reaching implications, is the Supreme Court's apparent change in attitude toward regulatory agencies: specifically, a more constricted view of the agencies' discretionary authority. L. Greenhouse, "Riding shotgun on the bureaucratic herd," *The New York Times*, April 22, 1979, Section 4, p. E4.

20. Public Law 91-190, Jan. 1, 1970, codified at 42 U.S.C. sections 651 *et seq.* (Supp. V 1975).

21. Hospital Survey and Construction Act, Public Law 79-725, Aug. 13, 1946, cod-

ified at 42 U.S.C. sections 291 *et seq.* (Supp. V 1975). Not only did the Hill-Burton program provide funds for the construction of needed hospitals, but it also clearly contemplated that the states that received those funds would use them in accordance with a planning process.

22. Public Law 93-641, Jan. 4, 1975, codified at 42 U.S.C. sections 300k *et seq.* (Supp. V 1975).

23. The second of the major federally designed planning programs began in 1964, when Congress amended the Hill-Burton Act to provide for federal funding for private, nonprofit groups (sometimes called "318 agencies" after the section of the Public Health Act under which they were authorized) for areawide planning. This effort was followed by the establishment of the Regional Medical Program (RMP) (authorized under the Heart Disease, Cancer, and Stroke Amendments of 1965, Public Law 89-239), which encouraged regional planning and the co-operation and transfer of technology between health care providers. A year later the Comprehensive Health Planning and Public Health Services Amendments of 1966 were enacted (Public Law 89-749), which set up Comprehensive Health Planning (CHP) agencies responsible for planning for regional needs.

24. In Maryland, for example, the General Assembly enacted the Joint Comprehensive Health Planning Agencies Act, Md. Ann. Code, art. 43, sections 871-877 (1976), in response to the National Health Planning and Resources Development Act of 1974.

25. National Health Planning and Resources Development Act of 1974, Public Law 93-641, Jan. 4, 1975, section 1512b(3)(c), codified at 42 U.S.C. section 300 1-1(c) (Supp. V 1975).

26. Typical of evidence to the "contrary" is the 1978 survey conducted by the American Health Planning Association, which examined the amount of capital investment proposals which were reviewed by local health planning agencies (HSAs and SHPDAs) pursuant to either state certificate of need (CON) programs which were required to be developed under Public Law 93-641, or "1122 agreements" (agreements between state planning agencies and DHEW providing for state review of capital investment proposals to ensure that federal funds appropriated for Medicare and Medicaid would not be used to reimburse hospital providers for unnecessary capital expenditures). The survey concluded that, of the $12 billion in capital investment proposals which were reviewed by the reporting agencies, over $3.4 billion of the proposed investments were disapproved. This approach, emphasizing the amount of money turned down, but not questioning the necessity of the $8.6 billion in approved proposals, speaks for itself. American Health Planning Association, "Second Report on the 1978 Survey of Health Planning Agencies," February 1979, p. 1.

27. Several "National Health Priorities" are enumerated in the beginning of the Act, namely: "(2) The development of multi-institutional systems for coordination or consolidation of institutional health services (including obstetric, pediatric, emergency medical, intensive and coronary care and radiation therapy services) . . . (5) The development of multi-institutional arrangements for the sharing of support services necessary to all health service institutions." National Planning and Resources Development Act of 1974, Public Law 93-641, section

1502, codified at 42 U.S.C. sections 8300k-2 (Supp. V 1975). While the Act clearly contemplates a restructuring of the health care system, to be accomplished in part by combining separate institutional systems into a multi-institutional arrangement, nowhere in the remainder of the Act is there specific authority as to how this reorganization is to be carried out.

28. Comprehensive Health Manpower Training Act of 1971, Public Law 92-157, Nov. 18, 1971, codified at 42 U.S.C. sections 292-295h (Supp. V 1975).

29. The Washington State legislature, for example, after prohibiting the practice of medicine without a license, specifically lists an exemption for "the practice of medicine by a registered physician's assistant which practice is performed under the supervision and control of a person licensed pursuant to this chapter." Wash. Rev. Code, section 18.71.030. Maryland, on the other hand, does not carve out an exception for the practice of medicine by physicians' assistants. Md. Ann. Code, art. 43, sections 119-123A (1976).

REFERENCES

Abrams, H. L., and McNeil, B. J. 1978. Medical implications of computed tomography ('CAT scanning'), Parts I and II. *New England Journal of Medicine* 298:255-61, 310-18.

Breyer, S. 1979. Analyzing regulatory failure: Mismatches, less restrictive alternatives, and reform. *Harvard Law Review* 92:549-609.

Davis, K. C. 1972. *Administrative law text*, pp. 157-93. St. Paul, MN: West.

_____. 1977. *Administrative law of the seventies*. St. Paul, MN: West, and Note 8, *infra*.

Downs, A. 1972. Up and down with ecology—the 'issue-attention cycle.' *The Public Interest* 28:41-50.

Dunne, F. P. 1901. *Mr. Dooley's opinions*, p. 26. New York: R. H. Russell.

Edelman, M. 1964. *The symbolic uses of politics*, p. 25. Urbana: University of Illinois Press.

Enthoven, A. C. 1978*a*. Consumer choice health plan, Part I. *New England Journal of Medicine* 298:650-58.

_____. 1978*b*. Consumer choice health plan, Part II. *New England Journal of Medicine* 298:709-20.

Forgotson, E. L., and Cook, J. L. 1967. Innovations and experiments in uses of health manpower—the effect of licensure laws. *Law and Contemporary Problems* 32:731-36.

Herring, E. P. 1936. *Public administration and the public interest*, pp. 213, 397. New York: McGraw-Hill.

Iglehart, J. K. 1978. Carving out a role for states in controlling hospital costs. *National Journal* 10:1045-49.

Knowles, J. H. 1977. The responsibility of the individual. *Daedalus* 106:59-63.

Leiserson, A. 1942. *Administrative regulation: A study in interest representation*, pp. 100-115, 270-71. Chicago: University of Chicago Press.

Locke, J. 1960. *Two treatises of government*, ed. P. Laslett, pp. 348-49. Cambridge: Cambridge University Press.

Lowi, T. J. 1969. *The end of liberalism—ideology, policy and the crisis of public authority*, pp. 55-97, 525-27. New York: W. W. Norton and Co.

Mills, C. W. 1956. *The power elite*, pp. 272-92. New York: Oxford University Press.

Rosenblatt, R. E. 1978. Health care reform and administrative law: A structural approach. *Yale Law Journal* 88:243-53.

Sabatier, P. 1975. Social movements and regulatory agencies: Toward a more adequate—and less pessimistic—theory of 'clientele capture.' *Policy Sciences* 6:302-3.

Schramm, C. J. 1976. The health policy process: The case of OSHA and its administration. Paper delivered at the 104th meeting of the American Public Health Association, October 22, Miami Florida.

Stewart, R. B. 1975. The reformation of American administrative law. *Harvard Law Review* 88:1669, 1684-87, 1711-15.

Thompson, J. D. 1967. *Organizations in action: Social science bases of administrative theory*, pp. 25-38. New York: McGraw-Hill.

Truman, D. B. 1971. *The governmental process*, 2nd ed., pp. 417-21. New York: Alfred A. Knopf.

Five

An Epidemiologic Perspective in Health Services Research

MICHEL A. IBRAHIM

INTRODUCTION

Epidemiology is a scientific discipline concerned with the study of the distribution and determinants of disease, disability, death or health in population groups. It is used as an investigative science to search for causes of disease in populations, and as an applied science in the planning and evaluation of health services. Most epidemiologic inquiry depends on observational, rather than experimental, research methods.

Epidemiologic experiments refer to studies in which subjects are randomly allocated to at least two groups: treatment vs. placebo or stepped-up care vs. regular care. The procedure results in two or more groups which would be comparable on many factors besides the factor under investigation. In contrast, observational methods are based on data gathered on individuals without intervention by the investigator. Observational methods are susceptible to several forms of biases such as selection, information and confounding. The epidemiologist pays considerable attention to the sources and impact of these biases and attempts to avoid them in the design stage or deal with many of them in the analysis phase of the investigation. The quality of an epidemiologic study is judged largely by the kind and degree of bias that might be present.

The objectives, principles and methods of epidemiology are often confused with other disciplines such as clinical research, social research, demography and biostatistics. The confusion arises in part from objectives or methods shared by these disciplines. A comparison of these disciplines and the unique role of each is illustrated in figure 5.1. Drawing upon biologic theories, clinical research is concerned primarily with the diagnosis and treatment of individuals. In contrast, social research is based on social theories and models and is aimed at the understanding of social behavior. While clinic and laboratory records provide primary sources of information in clinical research, population surveys are the primary sources in social research. Furthermore, randomized controlled trials are often employed in clinical research, but observation is the predominant mode of inquiry in social research. The underpinnings of demography and biostatistics are mathematical, probabilistic and biologic theories and models. Population composition, change and dynamics are the main concerns of demography, while the science of biostatistics offers the techniques and tools of health-related investigation. In its pursuit to identify risk factors and to plan and evaluate community intervention programs, epidemiology draws from both the biologic and social theories, and employs more observational than experimental methods. The most distinctive feature of the discipline lies in its ultimate concern with the health status of population groups.

The contribution of epidemiology to the understanding and ultimate prevention or control of major epidemics such as cholera, plague, smallpox and measles is well known. The emphasis was on the germ theory of disease; the microorganisms were identified, vaccines and antibiotics were discovered, and prevention or control of most conditions followed. As these advances reduced the burden of infectious diseases in Western societies and extended life expectancy considerably, modern plagues of heart disease, hypertension, cancer, stroke, obesity, and mental illness have prevailed. Inasmuch as the germ theory is becoming insufficient to explain the widespread occurrence of such conditions, considerable attention has been focused on the important role of environmental, social, behavioral and psychological factors in the genesis and progression of modern ailments.

The study of infectious and chronic diseases, as referred to above, represents a traditional area of application of epidemiology. What, then, is the role of epidemiology in health services research? Many disciplines—medicine, sociology, administration, political science, economics and demography—are involved to a greater or lesser degree in health services research. The distinctive contribution of epidemiology to this area is in the question it attempts to answer. Other disciplines will be concerned, for example, with the organizational structure, financing, personnel, utilization behavior and the like. On the other hand, epidemiology would pose the question: "Does it make a difference in the health status of the population?" In this sense, a health service (or a medical care) program is viewed as one of the independent variables, as one of the determinants, or as a means to an end—the end being the health state of populations. The application of epidemiologic information in the planning and evaluation of health services has received increasing attention in the United States recently. Epidemiologic investigations often require a long period of observation and entail considerable cost. These features limit the usefulness of the field of epidemiology in instances when urgent policy decisions must be made.

The several uses of epidemiology in health services will be illustrated throughout this chapter and will be highlighted by an example of health manpower. The important contribution of epidemiology to health services will be seen from a perspective that is quite different from other disciplines.

FIGURE 5.1: Comparison of Several Disciplines on Their Objectives, Methods and Theories

	Objectives	Methods	Theories & Models
1. Clinical Research	To discover better ways to diagnose and treat individuals	Analysis of clinic and laboratory records, clinical observations and experiences. Randomized clinical trials	Biologic
2. Social Research	To understand social behavior	Surveys of population groups. Collection, analysis and interpretation of social data obtained by observational methods	Social
3. Demography	To understand phenomena of population dynamics—growth, birth, deaths, marriage, divorce, etc.	Collection and tabulation of data from civil registration, census and surveys of population groups	Mathematical Probabilistic, Biologic
4. Biostatistics	To reduce, describe and interpret biologic-related data	Descriptive, inferential and experimental methods	Mathematical, Probabilistic, Biologic
5. Epidemiology	To identify risk factors and to plan and evaluate community intervention trials	Observational and experimental (randomized community trials)	Biologic Social

Reference will further be made to some current and future issues of health services that would rely on or make use of epidemiologic research.

The major principles of epidemiologic research design and analysis from a health service perspective are briefly reviewed below.

RESEARCH DESIGN AND ANALYSIS

The cornerstone of epidemiologic research design employed in the search for causes of disease is exemplified by the prospective cohort study (figure 5.2). The population at risk (e.g., a random sample of the residents in a given town) is examined to identify those with and those without the disease under study. Individuals free of disease may be classified as exposed or not exposed. The term exposure implies exposure to an environmental factor, such as air pollution, or possession of a particular characteristic, such as high blood pressure. The two groups are followed for a period of several years to find out who developed the disease. The risk of developing the disease given the exposure variable, i.e., the relative risk, is calculated as the ratio of two rates: the rate of the disease among the exposed, and the rate of the disease among the not exposed.

The Framingham study of cardiovascular diseases is a good example of this research design. A random sample of the adult residents of the town of Framingham was examined in 1950 to identify the subset of the population which was free of coronary heart disease (Dawber et al. 1951). This cohort of individuals has been followed and monitored since 1950 to document the mortality and morbidity of cardiovascular and related conditions. The mortality and morbidity outcomes within several strata of the cohort, such as levels of blood pressure, serum cholesterol or body weight, were analyzed to estimate the relative risk of what has become widely known as coronary heart disease risk factors. These factors included among others: high blood pressure, elevated levels of cholesterol, obesity, cigarette smoking and physical inactivity.

Occasionally, it is possible to reconstruct exposure data from records and carry out the analysis as in a cohort study. In this case, the population need not be followed over time, resulting in considerable savings in time and money. This approach, the historical cohort, is often used in determining the risk of cancer as a result of exposure to certain elements in occupational settings. Much of our knowledge of industrial hazards has been derived by this method of investigation. The exposure experience of rubber industry workers, for example, was based upon work histories that were subsequently developed into job classifications (McMichael et al. 1976). The frequency and duration of employment within the various classes indicated the type and intensity of exposure in which incidences of cancers of many sites were analyzed.

FIGURE 5.2: The Cohort and Historical Cohort Research Design

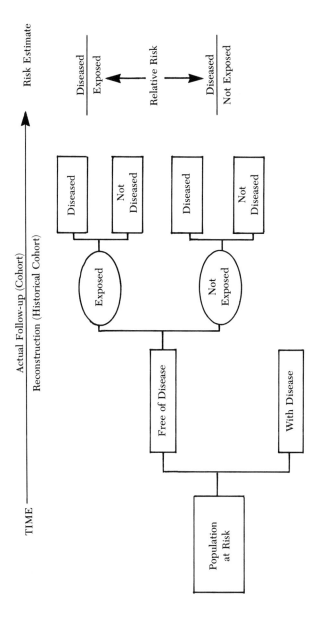

Another important research design in epidemiologic investigations is the case-control study (figure 5.3), which must be distinguished from the study of a case-series in which the investigator estimates the exposure status of the cases with no reference to a control group (Ibrahim and Spitzer 1979). In this study design, the epidemiologist begins with the effect (or disease) and then looks backward in time for the cause (or exposure). The group of individuals with the disease (cases) and a comparable group without this disease or with a different disease (controls) are questioned for the presence or absence of exposure during a defined length of time in the past. Depending on the hypothesis to be tested, medical or occupational records may also be used. The risk of occurrence of the disease in the presence of the exposure factor is estimated by the calculation of what is called an odds ratio, which is based on the frequency of exposure in the cases and controls. The risk of uterine cancer in women taking estrogen during the menopausal period was estimated initially by the case-control method of study.

The case-control study is especially susceptible to selection bias, which could result when subjects are systematically included in or excluded from the case or control groups. Differential recall of past experiences or differential mode of questioning by interviewers of cases and controls could lead to what

FIGURE 5.3: The Case-Control Research Design

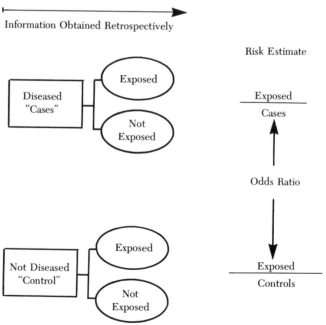

is called information bias. These biases may produce spurious risk estimates and should be avoided or minimized as much as possible. The use of recorded data, objective questions and multiple control groups is highly recommended to lessen the effects of these biases (Ibrahim and Spitzer 1979).

The use of the case-control study in health services research has been limited. A recent study (Clark and Anderson 1979) addressed the question of the potential benefit of the "Pap" smear in preventing cervical cancer. The history of Pap smears over the past five years was obtained from a group of patients with invasive cervical cancer (case group) and from an age-matched neighborhood control (control group). It was found that 32 percent of the cases in contrast to 56 percent of the controls had been screened by Pap smear. The difference between cases and controls persisted after the data were analyzed by age, socioeconomic status, smoking habits and access to medical care.

Although the experimental design in the form of randomized controlled trials (RCT) is used in etiologic research, its main application is in the evaluation of the effectiveness of a vaccine, drug or medical program. The basic elements in a scientific experiment are: (1) the random allocation of subjects into an exposed and an unexposed group; (2) the control of all factors except the one under investigation; (3) changing the intensity of the experimental factor by the investigator; and (4) the double-blind recording of data.

The Hypertension Detection and Follow-up Program (HDFP 1979) consisted of 14 sets of community-based randomized controlled trials throughout the United States. Hypertensive patients were randomly allocated to either a stepped-up hypertension care program or referred to usual sources of medical care. A substantial portion of patients enrolled in the stepped-up care program continued to receive medication and achieve desirable levels of diastolic blood pressure. The five-year mortality from all causes was 17 percent lower in the stepped-up care group than in the referred group. The documentation of the beneficial effects of the stepped-up care led to a nationwide implementation program to control high blood pressure.

The before–after research design is a variant of the cohort design that is commonly employed in health services research. In this design, health indices of a population served by a medical care program are measured before and after the implementation of such a program. Occasionally, the information is reconstructed after the program has been in effect for some time, thereby avoiding the need for a follow-up period. The impact of the program on the health of a population may be estimated only after several of the following measures have been taken: (1) including a comparable control group of a population not receiving the program; (2) taking several measurements while the program is in effect to document a trend, if present; (3) controlling for confounding factors by stratification or multivariate analysis; and (4) monitoring environmental and social factors which could have contributed to the outcome under study.

EPIDEMIOLOGIC PERSPECTIVES IN HEALTH MANPOWER

The epidemiologic contribution to health services research will be illustrated by an example from an important aspect of health care—health manpower. In the late 1960s, several problems in the health manpower needs of the nation were widely recognized, and action was subsequently taken in an effort to resolve them. To alleviate the shortage of physicians, for example, new medical schools were built and the number of medical students increased. Special programs were instituted in the underserved areas (inner city and rural) in order to tackle the maldistribution problem. Increased financial support and number of family medicine programs responded to the proliferation of highly specialized areas of medical practice. Efforts to contain the rising costs of medical care have been vague or nonexistent and have yet to show any results.

Against this background, nurses in expanded roles—nurse-practitioners—emerged as a viable option to remedy the many facets of the health manpower problem. As training programs for nurse-practitioners multiplied throughout the United States, so did political, economic and legislative issues. Some of the questions that were raised include: (1) Would physicians and/or nurses accept the nurse-practitioners? (2) Would the public, and patients in particular, be satisfied with the care received from such a person? (3) Would the nurse-practitioner movement survive economically? and (4) How about licensure—would nurse-practitioners work alone or under the supervision of physicians? The answers to these very important questions require the skills of the political scientist, sociologist, economist and others.

The health services research epidemiologist would want to pose two other questions: Are the clinical skills of nurse-practitioners comparable to those of physicians when employed for conditions cared for by both? And, most importantly, but much more difficult, would it make a difference in terms of favorable outcomes in the health status of the population? Research in this area ranged from simple analysis of tasks and processes of care based on data already available from records to the randomized controlled trial.

ANALYSIS OF DATA ON CLINICAL PERFORMANCE

The performance of a pediatric nurse-practitioner was compared to that of a pediatrician by analyzing data from 182 unselected consecutive charts (Duncan et al. 1971). The 182 children, each having one or more treated physical conditions, were seen first by the nurse and then by the physician. A total of 278 conditions were noted and recorded on the charts by either or both the nurse and the physician. As seen in figure 5.4, the physician and nurse were in total agreement for 86 percent of the conditions. Of the conditions on which they disagreed, only two cases were considered significant: the nurse-practitioner assessed these two cases as questionable red throat infection, while the pediatrician diagnosed one case as pneumonia and the other as meningitis. The authors concluded that the results are indicative of the nurse-practitioners' high competency in assessing medical conditions in children.

The conclusion reached above cannot be made with confidence because of several inadequacies in the research design. Perhaps children could have been randomly allocated initially to the nurse or to the physician and then seen by the other provider. The random allocation would have given each child an equal probability to be seen initially by either provider, and would have resulted in two comparable groups of children. In addition, a more appropriate method of judging concordance between the nurse and the physician would have been to compare their diagnoses against those of a panel of experts. The latter would have offered the external validation source against which sensitivity and specificity of the diagnoses made by the nurse and the physician would have been estimated. The fact that two serious illnesses (pneumonia and meningitis) were misdiagnosed by the nurse as questionable red throat infection may not be dismissed lightly. However, the study was apparently planned *post hoc* and available data had to be used to answer the research question. The findings, though inconclusive, should be suggestive and helpful in generating hypotheses that may be tested by more rigorous methods.

THE DEVELOPMENT AND TESTING OF STANDARD CRITERIA

More elaborate methods have been devised recently to evaluate the quality of medical care (Wagner et al. 1976; 1978). The opinions of a national sample of physicians were sought in regard to the clinical management of an indicator condition: respiratory infections in children. Symptoms, signs, diagnostic tests, and therapeutic action that could be associated with the condition were translated into several "test situations." For each test situation, physicians' opinions were summarized.

An example is given in figure 5.5 in which the percentage of physicians favoring a particular action was analyzed according to two levels of temperature. Depending on the level of temperature, the percentage of physicians who favored a particular action varied from about ten percent to 95 percent. For example, 40 percent of the physicians advised that chest X-rays be taken

FIGURE: 5.4: Comparison of the Assessment of 278 Conditions by a Pediatric Nurse-Practitioner and a Physician

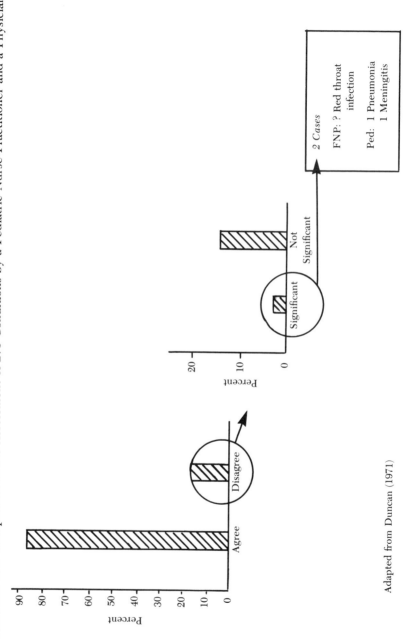

Adapted from Duncan (1971)

FIGURE 5.5: The Percentage of Respondents Favoring Various Actions at Different Levels of Temperature in a Child with Rhinorrhea

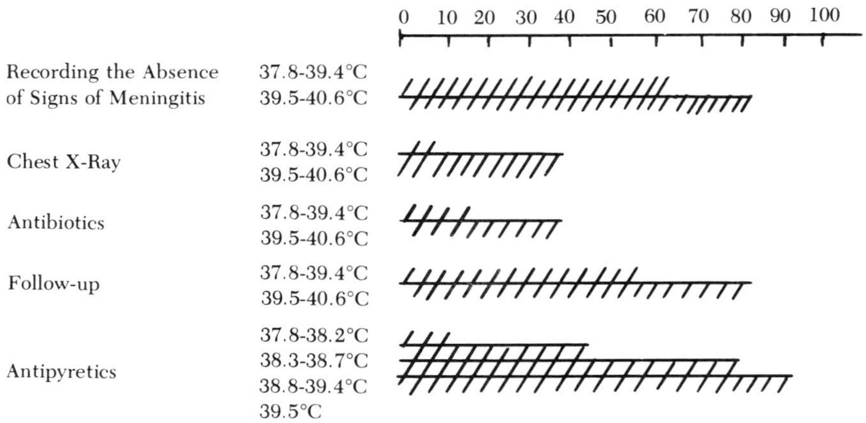

From: Wagner et al. (1978)

TABLE 5.1: Recording of Clinical Tasks Against "Standards" of Practice

"Standard"	Number of Applicable Cases	% Recorded on Chart
History of:		
Exposure History	112	0.9
Prior Treatment	235	17.8
Findings on Physical Examination of:		
Absence of Respiratory Distress	11	18.2
Absence of Signs of Meningitis	123	53.7
Red Pharynx	134	85.8
Diagnostic Tests Needed:		
X-Ray	4	25.0
Throat Culture	127	26.8
Treatment Indicated:		
Oral Decongestants	90	67.8
Antibiotics	278	98.9
Total	1,114	54.4

Adapted from Wagner et al. (1978)

at temperatures above 39.5°C compared to only ten percent at temperatures below 39.5°C. It may be further noted that a larger proportion of physicians favored actions that were relatively innocuous—such as follow-up or giving antipyretics—in contrast to a smaller proportion of physicians whose actions were more substantial, such as prescribing antibiotics or requesting X-rays.

The next step in the research was to develop consensus criteria for the management of respiratory infection in children. This was done on the basis of majority opinion and other rules that are outlined in detail elsewhere (Wagner et al. 1976; 1978).

The actual clinical management of children with this indicator condition may now be evaluated against the standard criteria. Data in table 5.1 show that when, for example, the standard called for obtaining historical information on prior treatment, only 17.8 percent of the applicable cases actually had this information recorded. In contrast, the charts of 99 percent of cases where antibiotic treatment was indicated showed that the treatment was recorded. The above indicates that when the task is important, that is, as perceived by the physician, a larger percentage of cases will have this task recorded in the chart. Another observation is the considerable range in the percentage of tasks recorded in the chart—from 0.9 percent to 98.9 percent.

The strength of the method lies in the way the standard criteria were developed and their potential application to evaluate clinical practice by various providers, including the nurse-practitioners.

A BEFORE–AFTER STUDY

In response to critical health manpower shortages, a nurse-midwife program was established on a demonstration basis in California (Levy et al. 1971). Nurse-midwives are registered nurses, with additional training in obstetrics and gynecology, who are able to manage normal pregnancies. Unfortunately, the California program was terminated after three years of operation. In an attempt to measure the impact of the program on the health status of the population, data were secured on prematurity, infant mortality and other concerns *before* the initiation of the program and *during* its operation. Similar data were collected *after* the termination of the program. Data on the trimester during which prenatal care was received was also documented.

Data on live births and fetal and infant death were obtained from the vital records of the county under study for the three time periods (before, during and after). Infants' birth weights were abstracted from the mothers' obstetric records. Births in the county hospital where the program was administered were compared to other births in the county.

Table 5.2 shows that both prematurity and infant mortality declined during the program, but rose after the program was discontinued. No comparable trend was discerned from the "control" births. Prenatal care received in the first or second trimester also showed the favorable effects of the program.

This example illustrates the exploitation of a "natural" experiment using epidemiologic methods. The research design of a before–after study and a comparison group is a useful and commonly used strategy in the evaluation of health services. Vital records offer a readily available source for outcomes that reflect health status. Note also that having three values (before, during

TABLE 5.2: Prematurity, Infant Mortality and Prenatal Care Before,
            During and After a Midwifery Program

	Community Hospital Births (Program)			Other Births in County	
	Before	*During*	*After*	*During*	*After*
Prematurity Percent	11.0	6.6	9.8	6.0	7.4
Infant Mortality	29.9	26.8	40.2	23.0	25.6
Total Births	345	991	768	1370	1233
	Prenatal Care Received (% of Mothers)				
1st or 2nd Trimester	—	53.7	38.7	77.7	75.4
3rd Trimester	—	34.6	37.2	14.5	13.1
No Known Care	—	11.7	24.1	7.8	11.5

Adapted from Levy (1971)

and after) strengthens the inference more than having only two (before and after). Three points offer the opportunity to look for trends while two points do not.

A RANDOMIZED CONTROLLED TRIAL

The following study represents the most sophisticated attempt to date for the evaluation of medical care rendered by nurse-practitioners (Spitzer et al. 1974; Sackett et al. 1974). Not only was the vigorous strategy of the randomized trial employed, but emphasis was also placed on health outcomes. The latter included social, emotional and physical functions, as well as mortality.

Eligible families in a primary care practice were chosen as the unit of randomization. Families were randomly allocated to a conventional group (physician/conventional nurse) and a nurse-practitioner group. The quality of clinical judgment was assessed for ten indicator conditions and 13 commonly prescribed drugs. Management and prescription criteria were established by a panel of family physicians.

Deaths were identified by a surveillance system during the one year of the trial period. The index of physical function measured the patient's mobility, vision, hearing, and activities of daily living. The emotional function index, ranging from zero (poor) to one (good), considered the patient's feelings of self-esteem, feelings toward others, and thoughts about the future. The social function index assessed the patient's interactions with other people and agencies.

The results in table 5.3 indicate that 65 percent of the care was rated adequate for the conventional group, compared to 70 percent for the nurse-practitioner group. Emotional and social functions were identical in the two groups. Death rate was lower in the nurse-practitioner than in the conventional group, but the difference could be attributed to chance. The two groups

TABLE 5.3: Comparison of Performance and Outcome in the
Conventional and Nurse-Practitioner Patient Groups
at the End of Experiment

	Conventional	*Nurse-Practitioner*
Percent of Care Rated Adequate	65	70
Emotional Function (S.D.)	.58 (.19)	.58 (.19)
Social Function (S.D.)	.83 (.25)	.84 (.27)
Death Rate per Thousand	6.0	2.7

Adapted from Sackett et al. (1974)

also compared well on the use of the 13 prescription drugs (data not shown). By and large, the clinical judgment and the outcome of practice of nurse-practitioners compared favorably with those of the physicians, which led the investigators to conclude that ". . . the nurse-practitioners were effective and safe," and to propose that the delivery of primary care by nurse-practitioners should be further explored.

SOME CURRENT AND FUTURE ISSUES

Aging is perhaps the most important condition with which our society must contend. The population of individuals aged 65 years and older comprises 11 percent of the total population of the Unites States in the 1980s and is expected to reach 17 percent by 2030. This is an increase from 23 million to over 50 million elderly individuals. Women comprise 60 percent of the elderly population, primarily because of differences in life expectancy.

In addition to the increase in absolute numbers and the differences in sex composition, the elderly population presents a special mortality and morbidity profile. Diseases of the heart, malignant neoplasms, and strokes account for three-quarters of all causes of death in this age group. Chronic degenerative diseases and the consequences of their resulting physical disabilities are prevalent in the elderly. However, social isolation, anxiety, loneliness and depression are perhaps the most widespread problems that face the elderly today. The role of epidemiology in the development of data and research strategy for the planning and evaluation of health services for the elderly will certainly expand in the years to come.

Traditionally, women's health has been viewed largely from the maternal perspective. Care during pregnancy has been provided regularly and has been under considerable study in this country and throughout the world. The health of women must now be considered from at least two additional angles. First, the elderly segment, as mentioned above, presents a challenge to those responsible for providing health care and to those responsible for planning and administering our social institutions. In addition to the usual chronic and degenerative diseases, older women also suffer from the loneliness and depression experienced from outliving their spouses. Coupled with the increased crime against the aged, the elderly American woman is perhaps the most vulnerable of all segments of society.

Women employed outside the home comprise another important group that requires attention. Women are now joining the labor force with increasing numbers to satisfy intellectual, social, emotional or financial needs. The nature of the family is rapidly changing as a result. The impact of these changes on the health of women (and of course, men and children) should be of concern to those who conduct research and those who deliver health services.

Another area of contemporary interest is that of health promotion and disease prevention. Changes in the patterns of personal lifestyles (such as engagement in regular physical exercise, consumption of healthful diet, cessation of smoking, and reduction of psychological stress and strain) are being recommended by governmental and voluntary agencies. Such forces are countered by those who are skeptical about the actual value of these lifestyles and are demanding more convincing scientific evidence before advocating any lifestyle changes. The resolution of these differences must await new evidence as well as critical appraisal of existing evidence. Both types of evidence require epidemiologic expertise. As "health promotion and disease prevention" programs are introduced throughout the country, it will be the epidemiologist's responsibility to gather data, establish monitoring and surveillance systems, and design studies that will evaluate the impact of these interventions on the health status of the population.

The workplace will witness continued and expanded attention. As a result of linking cancer to exposure to various toxic substances in industry, epidemiological surveillance and monitoring systems have been put in place to signal hazardous exposure early. These systems require a dynamic data base that includes information on potentially hazardous materials and a complete reporting of mortality and morbidity. More epidemiologic studies are needed to document hypothesized relationships between certain elements in the occupational environment and various diseases. In addition to their use for uncovering causes of diseases occurring in the workplace, epidemiologic approaches are useful for the planning and evaluation of health services that could be provided in the workplace. Health care providers, unions and management are showing increasing interest in arranging for such services. The discipline of epidemiology will be fundamental in answering such questions as what kinds of services should be provided, to whom should they be provided, and how effective will they be?

CONCLUSION

Epidemiology is one of many disciplines that could usefully be applied to address problems in health services. Specifically, epidemiology contributes a set of techniques and methods which are established to answer questions other disciplines cannot answer. Epidemiology defines the types of variables chosen and the way those variables are analyzed. Administration, organization, finance and politics of health care are of utmost importance but they fall short without epidemiologic perspectives. An efficient, cost-effective, well-organized and politically popular health services program should also be well-founded on epidemiologic principles and be shown to have a favorable impact on the health status of the population. The latter is as important a facet of health care as are other concerns. The articulation as well as the resolution of future issues of health services will witness greater reliance on epidemiologic approaches.

REFERENCES

Clarke, E. A., and Anderson, T. W. 1979. Does screening by "Pap" smears help prevent cervical cancer? A case-control study. *The Lancet* 2(July 7):1-4.

Dawber, T. R., Meadors, G. F., and Moore, F. E. 1951. Epidemiological approaches to heart disease: The Framingham study. *American Journal of Public Health* 41:279-86.

Duncan, B., Smith, A. N., and Silver, H. K. 1971. Comparison of the physical assessment of children by pediatric nurse practitioners and pediatricians. *American Journal of Public Health* 61:1170-76.

Hypertension Detection and Follow-up Program Cooperative Group. 1979. Five-year findings of the hypertension detection and follow-up program. *Journal of the American Medical Association* 242:2562-77.

Ibrahim, M. A., and Spitzer, W. O. 1979. The case control study: The problem and the prospect. *Journal of Chronic Diseases* 32:139-44.

Levy, B. S. et al. 1971. Reducing neonatal mortality rates with nurse-midwives. *American Journal of Obstetrics & Gynecology* 109:50-58.

McMichael, A. J., Spirtas, R., Gamble, J. F., and Tousey, D. M. 1976. Mortality among rubber workers: Relationship to specific jobs. *Journal of Occupational Medicine* 18:178-85.

Sackett, D. L., and Spitzer, W. O. et al. 1974. The Burlington randomized trial of the nurse practitioner: Health outcomes of patients. *Annals of Internal Medicine* 80:137-42.

Spitzer, W. O. et al. 1974. The Burlington randomized trial of the nurse practitioner. *New England Journal of Medicine* 290(January):251-56.

Wagner, E. H. et al. 1976. Influence of training and experience on selecting criteria to evaluate medical care. *New England Journal of Medicine* 294:871-76.

Wagner, E. H. et al. 1978. A method for selecting criteria to evaluate medical care. *American Journal of Public Health* 68(May):464-70.

Six

Demography and Health Services Research

LOIS M. VERBRUGGE

INTRODUCTION

Health researchers and planners ask such questions as: "How large will this county's population be ten years from now?" "What percentage of the city's population is Hispanic?" "How do we measure dropout rates for people who joined our clinic's hypertension control program?" "Why do middle-aged women use more health services than younger and older women?" "Do teen-agers have a high risk of low-birth-weight babies, and what are the social and health consequences of early childbearing for mother, father and child?" Good answers to these questions rely on demographic data, techniques and perspectives.

The purpose of this chapter is to identify links between demography and health services research. The term "health services research" shall be used in a general way to include research on health status as well as health behavior. Health services researchers include health professionals, scientists and government agency staff, and the links identified in this chapter pertain to all these groups. Although most of the specific examples refer to the United States, the importance of demography to health services research has no geographical boundaries.

This chapter begins with a definition of demography followed by a discussion on five major areas in which demography makes contributions to health services research: (1) demography's special perspective on human behavior; (2) formulas, techniques, and mathematical models to measure population size, distribution, composition and change; (3) techniques for data collection and analysis; (4) standard terms and definitions for demographic events and population characteristics; and (5) research results and hypotheses about fertility, mortality and migration. This is followed by a section on how health services research is also beginning to influence demographers' work. Finally demography's limitations and future are examined. A list of demography books and journals ends the chapter.

DEFINITION OF DEMOGRAPHY

Demography is the study of the structure and dynamics of human populations. The traditional topics of demography are population size, population change and its components (fertility, mortality, migration), population distribution and population composition. Demographers concerned with fertility study the number and spacing of births, marriage and divorce, contraception and other fertility control practices, and the structure of families and households. Mortality demographers study the timing of death (i.e., the decedent's age) and causes of death. For migration, interest lies in residence changes by individuals and families—where they go, where they come from, and why they move. Figure 6.1 outlines the topics of demography, indicating their respective references to population structure or population dynamics.

There are three main types of demographers: mathematical, technical and social. Mathematical demographers develop and test very general models of population structure and dynamics. Technical demographers measure size and change of particular populations, and they devise methods for collecting and analyzing human population data. Social demographers study relationships between demographic events and other aspects of social life such as attitudes, economic development and socioeconomic status. Social demographers often study individuals, relating personal characteristics to childbearing, age of death, residence changes, and other topics. They sometimes study areas (e.g., nations, counties), relating areal characteristics to rates of fertility, mortality and migration.

FIGURE 6.1: The Topics of Demography

POPULATION STRUCTURE *One Time Point (t_0)*	POPULATION DYNAMICS *Over Time ($t_0 \rightarrow t_1$)*
Population Size	Population Change ("Growth") Fertility Mortality Immigration and Emigration
Population Distribution	Population Movement Internal Migration
Population Composition Sex and Age Marital Status Family and Household Socioeconomic Characteristics (Education, Occupation, Labor Force Participation, etc.)	Changes in Population Composition Population Aging

THE DEMOGRAPHIC PERSPECTIVE

Every scientific discipline has its own special perspective—its preferred units of analysis, assumptions about how they are organized, ways of asking questions, and techniques for analyzing data.

Demography studies the entry and exit of individuals to populations. It aims to measure and understand demographic behavior of individuals and whole collectivities (populations). These two focuses are often distinguished as microstudies vs. macrostudies. For the first focus, demographers generally assume that people make rational decisions about their fertility, marriage and migration behavior. No such assumption is made for mortality since most people would like to defer death as long as possible. For the second focus, demographers assume that population structure and dynamics are part of a large social fabric and that population phenomena are strongly related to social organization, technological development and the natural environment. For both micro- and macrostudies, demographers are interested in the determinants and consequences of demographic events.

The demographic perspective is strongly influenced by the social and behavioral sciences. The principal and most enduring link is with sociology, and demography training programs are usually found within university sociology departments. Demographic theories about individual and population behavior often originate in sociology. (Other common sources of demographic theories are psychology, economics and the biological sciences.)

Although allied with the social sciences, demography has some distinctive features. First, age, sex, marital status and household composition are viewed not merely as "control variables," but as important theoretical factors worthy of close scrutiny. For example, demographers might begin a study by displaying and discussing mortality differentials by sex, but they then go on to ask why those differentials occur. Demography encourages health services research (and other disciplines) to be curious about demographic differentials and to explore reasons for them.

Second, every individual and every population can be located in time and space. Demographers are careful to identify people by both the date and place where events (births, deaths, moves) occurred. This awareness of the specificity of population events naturally leads to an interest in changes over time and comparisons across space. For example, consider the fact that U.S. women who were aged 25–34 in the Depression years had very low fertility rates. Demographers ask: "Do these now-elderly women lack social supports because they have few adult children? How did their fertility in the Depression years compare with that of women in Western Europe?" Demographers' fastidious attention to time and space has helped us to understand (1) the experiences of particular cohorts over their life cycles and (2) differences among populations at a single point in time. Demography encourages other disciplines to be similarly attentive to time and space in their study units and to do comparative analyses when possible.

DEMOGRAPHIC FORMULAS, TECHNIQUES AND MODELS FOR POPULATION MEASUREMENT

Many demographers are engaged in measuring population size, distribution and composition for the present; computing rates of changes over the past; and making projections for the future. For example, the 1980 Census of Population is the basis for population size data for the United States and its subareas. The census also provides information about the age and sex composition of the population, its clustering into households and families, its distribution by state and county, and its social and economic characteristics. When census and vital registration data are joined, rates of fertility and mortality can be computed for the census year. (In noncensus years, population estimates are used instead of census counts.) When two or more censuses are compared, growth rates for particular areas or groups are computed. With census information about age–sex composition and recent growth rates, demographers prepare population projections.

When data are of good quality, demographers can rely on a single data source for accurate population figures. But when data are known or suspected to have large errors, they use multiple sources to estimate population structure and rates. For example, the 1970 Census count of centenarians (people 100+ years old) was thought to be excessive, and a variety of other sources were used to arrive at a good estimate of this age group (Siegel and Passel 1976).

Numerous formulas, techniques, and models have been developed to help demographers describe population structure and dynamics:

Among the many *formulas* for computing rates of fertility, mortality, marriage and migration (see Shryock et al. 1975) are the crude birth rate, age-specific death rate, divorce rate, and net migration rate. Most of these assume that high-quality, detailed data are available, but because this is often not the case for small areas and less-developed countries, demographers have also devised special formulas to use with incomplete data (Brass 1975; Madigan and Herrin 1977).

Techniques for making population estimates and projections have been developed and are well-documented in estimate and projection publications. For example, for many decades demographers have been concerned about how well the U.S. decennial census enumerates the total population. They have devised special techniques to measure coverage error (Siegel 1974; 1975) so we know how many people are missed in each census. (It is encouraging to note that the fraction of people missed has decreased over the past few decades.)

Population *models* state assumptions about fertility, mortality and migration rates and then extrapolate the long-term results. The rates used can be actual or hypothetical ones. The models are general statements of relationships among fertility, mortality, age–sex composition, and growth. Model populations are often compared with real-world population structures to elucidate the intrinsic demographic forces in current populations.

Some well-known demographic models are named logistic growth, stationary populations, stable populations, and reproduction rates. What are the key assumptions for these models?

Logistic growth assumes that a population now growing at rate "r" will eventually reach an upper limit and then cease to grow. A formula allows a researcher to compute that upper limit. The logistic growth model was derived from biology and was formerly applied to human populations as a crude guess of ultimate population size. Because its assumptions are too simple for modern population dynamics, it has been replaced by more complex models.

A stationary population assumes that a population has constant birth rates and death rates year after year, and that these rates equal each other. Population size is constant and age structure is fixed. The stationary population model is also called a "life table population"—it can be viewed as the life cycle of a single birth cohort (e.g., of 100,000 people) and how their deaths stretch across a 100-year period (to equal 100,000 deaths). The stationary model is now widely used to give views of "zero population growth" societies.

The more general stable population model assumes that a population has constant birth and death rates year after year, but the rates do not necessarily equal each other. The population can therefore be growing, decreasing or stationary. (Thus, stationary populations are one type of stable population.) A stable population has a constant growth rate and its age structure is fixed, but the number of people in each age group can change from year to year. Stable population models assume that no immigration or emigration occurs. The models are used now to project the long-term consequences given the persistence of a population's current fertility and mortality rates.

The most popular reproduction rates are the total fertility rate (TFR), gross reproduction rate (GRR), and net reproduction rate (NRR), all of which use fertility rates from a given year and assume that a cohort of young women experience the rates over their lifetime. The TFR states how many children (boys plus girls) 1,000 women will bear if they have these rates. The GRR indicates how many female babies 1,000 women will have if they experience current fertility rates throughout their reproductive ages. For both the TFR and GRR, the women are assumed to survive from the beginning of child-bearing (age 15) to the end (age 49). The NRR indicates the number of female babies for the women, assuming they experience current fertility *and* mortality rates throughout reproductive ages. The GRR and NRR give an idea of a population's ability to replace itself. For example, an NRR of 1,000 means exact replacement (one daughter per mother); 2,000 means each woman replaces herself with two daughters. The TFR, GRR, NRR and other reproduction rates are commonly used to summarize a population's current fertility and its future implications.

Explanations of these models and others are found in standard demography texts (e.g., Shryock et al. 1975).

Health services researchers and planners benefit from demographic formulas, techniques and models in two ways. First, the facts about population size, composition, rates, etc. that demographers produce are needed for good health planning. Planners need data about current and projected population to estimate needs for health services and potential use of those services. National health legislation has had a direct impact on demographers' work. Because of increasing emphasis on local and regional health planning, demographers are producing more data with local-level detail and are developing estimation techniques for small populations. Second, health researchers and planners with some demography training can use the formulas and techniques on their own data to compute rates, to map population distribution, etc. For example, with data on hospital patients and estimates of population size, local health professionals can compute hospital discharge rates for their areas. Health researchers and planners do not make routine use of population models because most models are highly analytical in scope. In summary, demographers provide important descriptive information for health services researchers and planners, and they have developed methods that health workers can use to describe their populations.

TECHNIQUES FOR DATA COLLECTION AND ANALYSIS

Demographers have helped develop techniques which are widely used in health services research and other fields. These include (1) survey research methods, (2) causal models, and (3) demographic techniques suitable for non-demographic data.

Population censuses, population surveys, and vital registration systems are among a nation's first data collection activities. As a result, demographers are often involved early in decisions about census and survey design, field and coding procedures, data storage procedures, and statistical techniques for data analysis. In the United States, the Bureau of the Census has been a major site for development of *survey research methods*, including question wording, interviewing techniques, machine-readable questionnaires, procedures for inputting missing data, and measurement of sampling error. Census Bureau demographers work closely with statisticians to improve the efficiency of data collection and to improve the accuracy and reliability of results. Health researchers adapt procedures from the census and national surveys to their own surveys about health status, health behavior, health professionals and health organizations.

Social demographers study relationships among variables (e.g., between fertility and socioeconomic status). They are interested in finding causal ties among variables, and they tend to be unsatisfied with correlations that have no clear time-ordering or causal rationale. It is not surprising that demographers have helped greatly in the development of *causal models and techniques* for the social sciences (Duncan 1975; Land 1969).

Health researchers can use this causal perspective and its methodology to find sound scientific explanations of health status and health behavior. Knowing that "X causes Y" is far more useful than knowing the "X and Y are related to each other." Causal knowledge is essential for creating viable health programs—programs capable of effecting desired changes in attitudes and behavior.

Some *demographic techniques* are not restricted to population data, but can be used just as easily with data from health surveys and medical records. Examples are standardization of rates, numerator analysis, decomposition of rates, life tables, cohort analysis, and measures of population distribution. A brief description of these techniques and their use in health services research follows.

It is difficult to compare mortality rates from several populations which differ greatly in their age composition because mortality risks vary so much by age. Standardization controls for differences in age composition (or other confounding variables) and enables us to see the true force of mortality in the populations. Similarly, the technique helps in comparing fertility, marriage and migration rates across populations. Of the variety of standardization procedures, the one most appropriate for a given project depends on the population information and rates at hand (Fleiss 1973; Shryock et al. 1975). Health planners can use standardization procedures to compare health status and health behavior of populations which differ greatly in age, sex or social composition. (For more exposition of standardization procedures and some research examples, see Anderson et al. 1980; Hickey et al. 1980; Kleinman 1977; Mantel and Stark 1968; and Stark and Mantel 1966.)

Numerator analysis is used when data are incomplete and rates cannot be computed. For example, we may know the number of deaths for occupation groups in a large company but have inadequate information on the number of people "at risk" in each occupation; thus, we cannot compute rates for each one. With numerator analysis, we can compute an expected number of deaths and compare this with the observed number for each occupation group to see if the group has "excess" mortality. This technique can be very useful to health researchers, who often have health data for specific groups from clinic records but inadequate data on the size of those groups in the general population. To date, there are few research examples even in demography, but the potential value of numerator analysis is great. (See Kupper et al. 1978, for a technical discussion; and Milham 1976, for a research application.)

When demographers observe a change in crude birth rates over time, they question whether it is due to real drops in age-specific fertility rates or to changes in age and marital composition which depress the rate. Decomposition techniques allow them to see exactly how much each factor (age, marriage, fertility rates) contributes to the total change. The technique is appropriate for other demographic phenomena besides fertility. Decomposition is a valuable tool for health planners who want to understand large-scale changes in their communities, e.g., increases in physician visit rates or declines in hospitalization rates. (See Kitagawa 1955, for the technique; and Anderson et al. 1977, for a research example.)

Life tables show how rapidly people exit from a "closed" population (which has no immigration or emigration). Life tables were originally developed for mortality analysis, but they are perfectly appropriate for other types of exit from populations, such as quitting the labor force or leaving the single population to be married. Examples in health services research include discharges from hospitals, dropouts from clinical trials, fecundability (probability of conception), and cessation of contraception. An intriguing health example is the notion of disability-free life—that people exit from the disability-free population when they become chronically ill or die (Sullivan 1971).

The life table is called single-decrement if just one mode of exit is possible. If two are possible (e.g., hospital discharges occur by death or by return to the community), the life table is multiple-decrement. A more complex type is the associated single-decrement table (ASDT) used for mortality analysis; it shows changes in life expectancy if a cause of death, such as cancer, is eliminated or reduced. (See Preston et al. 1972, and Shryock et al. 1975, for life table techniques. See Chiang 1968 and Jordan 1975 for statistical theory behind life tables. Tsai et al. 1978 present an interesting discussion of ASDTs for cardiovascular diseases, cancer and motor vehicle accidents in the United States.) Examples of how life tables can be used in health services research can be found in Elandt-Johnson (1973), Greville (1974), and Sullivan (1971). Their value in analysis of contraceptive use and effectiveness is discussed in Potter (1966) and Tietze and Lewit (1973).

Cohort analysis is a strategy for looking at cross-sectional data from several points in time. The interest is to trace how specific cohorts (usually birth cohorts) change as they grow older, how age groups differ in behavior, and how the population as a whole differs from one historical time period to another. Thus, one hopes to distinguish three effects in the time-series data: cohort, age and period. Cohort analysis offers a clear perspective on the data and also some specific statistical techniques for analyzing them. (There are currently a variety of recommended procedures, and refinements in them are being made frequently. For state-of-the-art discussions, see Fienberg and Mason 1978; Glenn 1977; and Mason et al. 1973.) Cohort analysis has obvious applications to longitudinal health surveys which study panels over a long time or which do cross-sectional surveys every few years. For an early example of cohort analysis in health research, see Greenberg et al. (1950).

Population distribution measures summarize how people are concentrated or dispersed geographically. Two popular measures are population potential and the Gini index. Population potential indicates the concentration of people around a given spot. By computing population potential for numerous small areas (such as census tracts in a city), one can determine which areas are most accessible to the total population. The Gini index measures how unequally people are distributed in a large area, e.g., if a country's population is highly concentrated in big cities. One number is computed and used to show the degree of concentration for the entire area. Measures of population distribution can help health planners choose specific locations for clinics and hospitals, understand access problems to current services, and plan overall distribution of services in a large area. (For a review of distribution measures, see Chapters 5 and 6 of Shryock et al. 1975.)

The National Center for Health Statistics has issued a publication of special pertinence to health students and researchers. The *Statistical Notes for Health Planners* is a series of occasional papers that gives explicit directions about analysis techniques (many of them demographic) for local health planners. To date, the series has covered measures of infant mortality, mortality, migration, cause of death, need for and supply of mental health services, and use of cause-specific death rates for health service areas.

STANDARD TERMS AND DEFINITIONS

Demography's terminology is an important contribution to health services research. Years of experience with population censuses, national population surveys and vital registration have resulted in a set of categories and definitions for population characteristics and places, such as age, marital status, family, metropolitan area, and occupation. The U.S. Bureau of the Census and the United Nations have worked extensively on demographic terminology, and they present clear definitions in their respective publications. Demographic terminology is now conventional throughout population research. It is eminently clear and seldom altered.[1] A few examples of Census terms follow.

1. "Age" is an individual's age at his or her last birthday.
2. "Single" means never-married. (Unfortunately, in popular usage the term means not-married. This has caused confusion, and it is recommended that health researchers use the standard demographic definitions of marital statuses.)
3. A "family" is two or more persons in a household who are related by blood, marriage or adoption. "Household" is a more encompassing term, referring to all persons in a given housing unit. In turn, a "housing unit" is a place currently occupied or intended for occupancy as separate living quarters. In "separate living quarters," occupants have exclusive use of a kitchen or cooking area and/or direct access to their living area from the outside or through a common hall. (This example shows how terms are embedded in others. Little is taken for granted in demographic terminology; virtually everything is defined.)
4. An "alien" is a U.S. resident who is not a U.S. citizen.

Demographic terms and definitions are appropriate for use by researchers in many fields, including health services research, and they should be adopted whenever possible. The U.S. Bureau of the Census and United Nations definitions sometimes differ, and researchers should use the ones that match their scope (domestic vs. international).[2] Standardized terminology ultimately helps make scientific products comparable and cumulative. It is especially important for linking results from two different disciplines, such as demographic research on fertility and health services research on prenatal and postnatal care.

UNDERSTANDING DEMOGRAPHIC BEHAVIOR: SOCIAL DEMOGRAPHY

Social demography is concerned with the determinants and consequences of fertility, mortality and migration for individuals and for societies. Social demographers often start with descriptive analysis, looking at trends over time or differentials among population groups. For example, they may discuss birth rates over a decade or differences in birth rates among income groups. To get ideas about why changes or differences occur, they scrutinize rates for specific population groups (e.g., age-, sex- and race-specific rates). Explanatory analysis tests hypotheses developed during the descriptive phase. Demographers usually take theories about individual and social behavior from the social sciences, and then modify them to fit a particular topic. They then state hypotheses and test them statistically.

Social demography's concerns are very close to those of health services research. There are certainly numerous links between fertility, mortality, migration and population composition on the one hand, and health status, health services use and health expenditures on the other. For example, pregnancy is accompanied by prenatal and postnatal medical care. Illness or injury precedes death, and death often occurs in a hospital or nursing home. Poor health causes some people to move to more comfortable climates or to places with special medical services; for others, poor health prevents residence moves. Age and sex groups differ greatly in their illness and injury rates, and in their needs for and use of health services. Changes in birth, death and migration rates in a city alter the population's needs for health services.

Let us look at these links in a more theoretical way and then consider some key research issues that incorporate demographic variables into health services research and also health planning.

THE LINK BETWEEN DEMOGRAPHY AND HEALTH

Most questions linking demographic and health variables take this form:

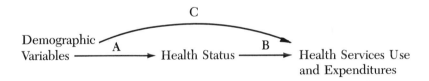

A asks how age, sex, fertility history, marital status, etc. affect health. For example, we know that health status varies sharply by age. *B* considers how health status prompts health services use and health expenses. For example, research shows that poor health is the strongest predictor of health services use; all social and demographic variables are secondary to it. *C* shows how the number of people, their geographic mobility, their age and sex, and other demographic characteristics directly influence health services and expenses. For example, men and women differ in their attitudes about the worth of medical care; apart from their actual health status, women are more likely to visit physicians than are men.

A great deal of health research has focused on these linkages.[3] In that research, demographic variables are determinants and health variables are consequences. Analysis of any link (A,B,C) can be descriptive or explanatory. We can also ask questions of this form:

$$\text{Health Services Use and Expenditures} \xrightarrow{\quad D \quad} \text{Health Status} \xrightarrow{\quad E \quad} \text{Demographic Variables}$$

D and E ask how health services and expenses influence people's health status and how that, in turn, influences their fertility, age at death, cause of death, probability of marriage, and decisions to move. Here, health variables are determinants and demographic variables are consequences. Questions like D and E are often very difficult to answer, and there has been relatively little research on them.

Most of the research issues discussed below are of the form A, B or C. This reflects the weight of research work to date; it does not mean these types of issues are more important than D or E issues.

RESEARCH ISSUES

Fertility

Some important questions about fecundity, childbearing decisions, fertility control, the timing of births, and infant health clearly link demography with health services research.

Fecundity (the ability to reproduce) is affected by a woman's health. Venereal disease, poor nutrition, and very low or very high body weight delay menarche, suppress ovulation, and hamper implantation of fertilized ova. (See Frisch 1978, and McFalls 1979; for a contrasting view, see Bongaarts 1980.) Together, health researchers and demographers are working to identify causes of subfecundity which can be alleviated by personal and public health actions.

Increasingly, childbearing is a conscious choice made by a couple. Genetic characteristics and health problems of both partners are taken into account in *decisions to have children*. Some of the important factors are blood-type compatibility of parents, diabetes, female alcoholism, and genetic disease. As knowledge about high-risk factors grows, health staff must develop better counseling skills to help couples make satisfying choices about childbearing and adoption.

Social demographers survey the frequency and types of *fertility control* used by the population, a factor which can change rapidly in response to shifts in laws and preferences. In the past decade, there has been a notable shift in the United States from the pill and IUD to sterilization and abortion (Ford 1978; Forrest et al. 1978; Westoff and Jones 1977). Survey data give valuable information to health professionals who plan fertility control services and who must respond quickly to changes in public desires and requests.

Demographers are also involved in research on the success and safety of contraceptives and abortion. Together with epidemiologists and statisticians, they conduct longitudinal studies of users to assess the effectiveness, side effects, acceptability, and long-term health effects of various methods. Even if a method passes these tests, it may not be used widely because of political constraints or limited access. For example, the safety of first-trimester abortions has been amply demonstrated, but access is restricted because of public laws, physician attitudes, and hospital policies (Lindheim, 1979). Health services researchers can examine access problems and devise remedies for them.

Adolescent pregnancy and childbearing are currently troublesome issues in the United States. Adolescents are responsible for a sizable fraction of all U.S. births (in 1978, 11 percent of all babies were born to girls under age 19). Social demographers are trying to determine the causes of high teenage fertility, especially the personal and peer group factors that prompt girls to become sexually active and pregnant. Research shows that teenage sexual activity has been rising rapidly and, although more teens use contraception, they use less effective methods than a decade ago (Zelnik and Kantner 1980). There is active research on how early childbearing affects the mother's physical health, emotional health, and socioeconomic status, and how the child's health and education are affected. We now know that early childbearing often truncates a young woman's education, hampers her chances of marriage or remarriage, and jeopardizes her economic welfare (Card and Wise 1978; Furstenberg 1976; Trussell 1976; Weeks 1976). Teenage mothers tend to have more children and have them closer together than women who start childbearing later (Trussell and Menken 1978). The social and intellectual development of children born to teenagers is inhibited (Baldwin and Cain 1980). To meet the special prenatal and postnatal needs of teens and their children, health planners are adapting local health services to assure privacy and sensitive, continuous care. They are also developing health programs to influence teens' attitudes and contraceptive behavior, in the hope of averting adolescent pregnancies and births.

Increasingly, American women are delaying the timing of their first birth and are spacing their total births more closely (Ryder 1973). Little is known about how *delayed childbearing and close spacing* affect the health of women and their children.

There is also a macroperspective on childbearing: during reproductive ages, women actively use health services for *obstetrical care* and for gynecological services. By examining birth, marriage and divorce rates for a given area, projections of future reproductive-age women and births can be made. Health planners use these projections to estimate needs for OB/GYN and pediatrics services and to plan for appropriate service sites and staff.

Some questions about fertility and health are especially important for developing countries. How short spacing, high parity, and large family size impair women's and children's health has been studied in several countries (McCook 1976; Taylor et al. 1976). Also, whether family planning services should be integrated with regular health and maternal and child health services is a subject of debate among population planning experts.

Demographers are also studying *infant health* to further decrease infant mortality rates and improve survivors' long-term health. What characteristics of the mother and father lead to low birth weight, delivery complications, neonatal death, and problems in physical and mental development? Research shows that important factors are mother's age (under 20 or over 35), low socioeconomic status, mother's smoking, little or no prenatal care, and poor nutrition during pregnancy (see Bouvier and van der Tak 1976; MacMahon et al. 1972; Menken 1972; Shapiro et al. 1968; Slesinger 1973; and Surgeon General 1979).

Marriage and Family Composition

How do marital status and domestic situations influence a person's health status and access to care during illness?

Demographic data show that *married people* enjoy better health status than nonmarried people, and that divorced and separated people have the worst health status (Verbrugge 1979). Social demographers are intrigued by these differences and are trying to determine how marriage enhances physical and mental well-being. It is also possible that health influences marital status, i.e., poor health could reduce a single person's marriage prospects and increase a married person's chances of becoming divorced. Health professionals should be aware of the difficulties that nonmarried people face and offer comprehensive services to boost their physical and emotional health.

Another intriguing issue is how *family characteristics and living arrangements* affect the health of household members. Are large families or those with young children especially likely to spread infectious diseases among members? (See Dingle et al. 1964; and Monto and Ross 1977, for some evidence.) Do family members tend to acquire similar chronic conditions during their lifetimes, and do they tend to die from similar causes? If so, how much is this due to shared lifestyles, similar environmental exposures, and similar genetic background? Do adults living alone have higher morbidity than those who have adult companions at home? Kobrin and Hendershot (1977) have shown that people living alone have higher mortality rates than others, but there are no studies of the relationship between living arrangements and health. When an individual has serious and long-term health problems, difficult decisions must be made about home care, intermediate care, and institutionalization. How important are family factors, such as the availability of a spouse or nearby kin? For example, women over age 65 are much more likely to be in nursing homes than men those ages. This is partly because older women tend to be widows and have few opportunities for home care, whereas older men are more likely to be married and can rely on their spouse for home care when ill. Demographers' knowledge of family and household composition is an asset in designing research and interpreting results on all of these topics.

Mortality

Exactly how are illnesses and injuries related to death? What accounts for large differences in death rates among some population groups? Where do older people prefer to die, and what impact does this have on health services?

For many decades, health workers have used mortality rates as indicators of health status. But concern about functional limitations during life has increased, and more-direct data from health surveys are now preferred. The theoretical separation of *morbidity and mortality* now gives us the chance to study carefully the causal ties between health and death.

Illness and death are strongly linked in real life; people are ill or injured (even if briefly) before they die. Both macro- and microresearch are needed on the links. First, researchers should compare morbidity and mortality rates for a given disease, such as hypertension, and observe if population differentials are similar.[4] Descriptive studies like this promise fascinating insights into how illnesses and causes of death are reported and how a population's overall morbidity experience compares with its ultimate causes of death.

Second, surprisingly little is known about how a person's illness and injury experiences actually influence death. For example: (1) When people have multiple health problems, which one is most likely to cause death? (2) How do particular diseases, such as diabetes, cause cardiovascular degeneration and boost overall risks of death (see Manton and Stallard 1980)? (3) How does medical care intervene between morbidity and death? Does it mainly relieve symptoms, or does it actually increase longevity? This question has generated a great deal of debate (Carlson 1975; Illich 1976; Powles 1973), but conclusions are yet unclear. The effectiveness of medical care is a difficult issue, and much research will be required before answers become available.

Population groups vary in their mortality rates. Sex *mortality differentials* are especially large—the average life expectancy at birth of U.S. males is eight years less than for females. Race and socioeconomic differentials are also notable. What are the health risks and health profiles of these groups? How much are the mortality differentials due to different lifestyles, occupational hazards, exposure to pollutants, and stress?

Sex differentials are especially interesting. They may be partly due to genetic differences as well as to the different risks associated with lifestyle. "Early" death in men also has a powerful impact on the physical, mental and social well-being of women. Widows suffer grief, stress, loneliness, and often a decline in economic status (especially if a husband dies before retirement age). These problems can adversely affect a woman's physical health. We need to know more about the health consequences of widowhood (for both sexes), and health professionals must be ready to assist the widowed as they cope with loss and attempt to develop new lifestyles.

Increasingly, the aged are asking to *remain at home* or have hospice care just before death. This trend necessitates changes in medical care services for elderly patients, and it encourages innovation and flexibility on the part of physicians and other health professionals.

Migration and Population Distribution

How do migration patterns and residential density influence needs for health services in local areas?

Migrant laborers and illegal immigrants pose special problems for health research and planning. These groups tend to have very poor health. Because of their transience or illegal status, it is difficult to obtain good data on their health status and to provide good-quality, continuous health care to them. Concern about illegal immigrants is especially great now because of heavy inflows from Mexico into the southwestern states. Demographers are engaged in estimating the numbers and locations of these people (Heer 1979), so that health and social welfare agencies can design appropriate services.

The past decade has witnessed other migration flows, notably the shift of *elderly people* to southern climates (Barsby and Cox 1975) and that of all age groups from urban to nonurban areas (Morrison and Wheeler 1976). The concentration of retirees in the Sunbelt imposes new demands for medical and health services there, and the dispersion of people into nonmetropolitan areas increases the need for good rural services. Demographic estimates and projections allow health planners to anticipate these flows, so they can ultimately provide adequate services.

How important is poor health as a *reason for moving*? What benefits do the ill hope to derive from a move? By contrast, poor health can inhibit mobility if people fear that a shift will increase stress or cause discontinuous medical care. A great deal of research has been done on decisions to move (Lansing and Mueller 1967; Ritchey 1976; Rossi 1955; Shaw 1975), but there has been little specific attention to health as a factor in residence changes.

It is widely believed that high *population density* in households and neighborhoods is detrimental to health, but research evidence shows that negative effects are not large or pervasive (Choldin 1978; Freedman 1975; Severy 1978; Verbrugge and Taylor 1980). The negative effects of high population density may be related to specific conditions, e.g., the inability to cope with noise coupled with inadequate soundproofing in housing structures. Demographers are actively investigating relationships between population density and health effects.

Population distribution in a metropolitan area has important implications for the placement and utilization of health services. Most urban residents can choose among several alternatives from which to obtain health care. What are the selection criteria for regular care and emergency care? We know a great deal about levels of health services utilization, but not much about how people evaluate the resources available to them. Microdata on utilization can be combined with macrodata on population distribution to assist health planners in decisions about new facilities and augmenting services in existing ones.

Population Composition

How does age–sex composition affect a population's health status and needs for health care?

A society which has low fertility and low mortality rates over many years becomes "old," having a large percentage of elderly people. *Population aging* has important implications for health and health care needs because the elderly often have chronic conditions and functional limitations and some require extended hospital and nursing home care.

Demographers are making local and national projections of the elderly population (U.S. Bureau of the Census 1977). In addition, social demographers are trying to understand how population aging influences economic productivity, consumer behavior, voting behavior, community participation, and social ties (Siegel 1976). To make sound decisions about health facilities and equipment, health planners must have substantial information about recent and projected changes in age composition for their locales and also about overall social characteristics of "old" populations.

Sex ratios also have a strong impact on a population's medical needs. Up to age 65, the number of males and females in each age group is quite equal (106 males per 100 females at birth, 88 per 100 at ages 60–64). But women predominate in the over-65 age group—there are 68 men per 100 women. The gap widens for the very elderly (85+), where there are only 45 men per 100 women. Older women tend to have more chronic ailments but less severe ones than older men (Verbrugge 1982). They need more ambulatory care and monitoring but less hospitalization. Further, many common gerontological health problems are more likely to affect older women than older men (e.g., arthritis, osteoporosis, vision dysfunction, hypertension, senile dementia). Thus, health issues for the aged population are sometimes virtually "women's issues." Gerontological health research and planning must keep women's needs and desires clearly in mind (without forgetting the presence and needs of elderly men).

HEALTH DEMOGRAPHY

The influence of demography's contributions to health services research and planning is not unilateral. Demographers are becoming more interested in health as an important factor in their research. For example, some demographers are exploring how maternal nutrition affects fertility; how increased child survival in developing countries encourages families to bear fewer children; how morbidity influences the timing and cause of death; and how changes in health affect family stability. For these issues, again, health variables are determinants and demographic variables are consequences. (See links *D* and *E* on page 138.) Other demographers, who take health itself as the dependent variable, ask how demographic factors affect health status and health behavior. (See links *A*, *B*, and *C* on page 137 and the examples cited in the previous section.)

This new branch of demography is called health demography,[5] and the scientists involved therein rely greatly on information and perspectives from health services research.

THE LIMITATIONS AND FUTURE OF DEMOGRAPHY

Demography is a conservative science characterized by fastidious collection of data and clear reporting of results. Its approach is highly quantitative, and it strongly favors statistical testing of hypotheses. Demographers shun idiographic, anecdotal and "case" evidence, although these sources can provide important clues about real-world relationships. Demography is not a particularly imaginative or daring discipline. Few demographic theories are truly proprietary—most originate in other social sciences and are then modified, often greatly. To date, microtheories about individual behavior are among the best elaborated, while macrotheories about relationships among a society's population, economy, technology, and environment are less well developed. There are few bridges between micro- and macrolevels, i.e., theories that show how individuals respond to and ultimately influence large social processes and organization.

Demography is a "small" science with a well-defined array of study variables. This feature offers some benefits since demographers can focus closely on their specific tasks and topics, but a disadvantage is that demographers often need skills in other disciplines such as sociology, statistics or economics in order to make notable scientific contributions. Demography is properly an adjunct to the social and behavioral sciences rather than a full-fledged science in itself. For a thoughtful discussion of demography's scientific status and achievements, see Nam (1979).

The next few decades will see important contributions in technical and social demography. Technical demographers will develop procedures for making sound population estimates and projections for local areas. They will improve techniques for studying mortality, especially for analyzing multiple causes of death (Manton and Poss 1979; Manton et al. 1980) and increased life expectancy associated with the eradication of certain diseases (Keyfitz 1977; Tsai et al. 1978). With statisticians, they will develop efficient sampling schemes to gather large and complex samples of the U.S. population that might, ultimately, replace the full-enumeration census. Strategies for cohort analysis will be refined. Social demographers will accumulate more information about factors that affect fertility, mortality and migration. Their threories will become more generalizable, i.e., less focused on specific periods or places. Contributions will continue to center on micro- rather than macrotheories. Social demographers will undoubtedly be more cognizant of health in their research. For another viewpoint on the coming decade's demographic contributions, see Preston (1978).

As a scientific discipline and as a profession, demography's future is secure. Its importance in academic research and social planning will increase. Demography will remain integrated with the social sciences, but it will be used more and more by allied disciplines such as health services research, community medicine, education, urban planning, and social work.

CONCLUSION

The major contributions of demography to health services research and planning are:

1. Demography encourages health researchers to view demographic variables as theoretically interesting, i.e., to explain differences among population groups rather than simply report them. Demography also encourages careful studies of a single cohort's lifetime experiences and comparisons across cohorts and populations.

2. Demographers produce information about population structure and dynamics that is useful to health services researchers and planners in understanding and improving health.

3. Health researchers use demographic formulas and techniques to analyze population data they themselves collect.

4. Demographers have helped to develop survey research methods and causal analysis techniques that are widely used in the health sciences.

5. Some techniques, originally created for demographic data, have broad utility and can be readily applied to health data. Examples are standardization of rates, numerator analysis, decomposition of rates, life tables, cohort analysis, and population distribution measures.

6. Demography offers standard terms and definitions for population characteristics which should be adopted by health services researchers.

7. Social demography offers research information about how demographic phenomena (fertility, mortality, migration) affect health status and health services use. Demographers can help in designing research methods to test hypotheses about health status and health behavior, and to interpret the results.

8. Some demographers are now studying health variables intensively in their own research. Work in health demography will strengthen ties between demography and health services research.

The links between demography and health services research are not merely potential—they are active in both teaching and research sites. Students of health planning, health administration, and health education often receive demographic training that increases their ability to interpret demographic information for the populations they serve and also to analyze population data themselves. The most exciting links, however, come from the scientific questions and research projects that join demographers and health services researchers. Marvelous and enduring scientific information emerges from such collaboration.

NOTES

1. A few contemporary changes in the United States merit comment. Concepts of race, ethnicity, and household head status have changed dramatically in the 1970s and 1980s. Census definitions are being modified accordingly. The changes will enhance the relevance of current data, but they will hamper comparisons with previous census data.

2. In addition, agencies of the U.S. government often differ in their "standard" definitions. From time to time, agencies confer to create more consistent terminology for particular projects, but there is no overall government effort to do so. The Office of Federal Statistical Policy and Standards (OFSPS) (1978) has promulgated a few standard terms for use by all agencies. Although several terms

need updating, the OFSPS handbook is very useful. (Note: Effective 1981, OFSPS is renamed the Office of Information and Regulatory Affairs and is within the Office of Management and Budget.)

3. Note that these questions focus on populations as potential *users* of health services. Populations also provide the *providers* of those services. Demography can aid studies of health manpower, but its contribution to studies of health status and health behavior is much larger. I have therefore chosen not to consider the link between demography and health manpower.

4. We expect parallel results, e.g., age groups with high morbidity will usually have high mortality, but occasionally there may be striking differences. For example, women have higher rates of self-injury, but men have higher rates of suicide (Jarvis et al. 1976). Do women "try less hard" to kill themselves?

5. Some readers will notice the similarity between health demography and social epidemiology. Many research questions are the same in the two fields, but the perspectives, techniques of data collection and analysis, and key variables differ somewhat. There are superb opportunities for collaboration between health demographers and social epidemiologists.

REFERENCES

Anderson, J. E., Chang, M.C. E., and Fook-Kee, W. 1977. A component analysis of recent fertility decline in Singapore. *Studies in Family Planning* 8(November):282-87.

Anderson, S., Auquier, A., Hauch, W. W., Oakes, D., Van Daele, W., and Weisberg, H. I. 1980. *Statistical methods for comparative studies.* New York: John Wiley & Sons.

Baldwin, W., and Cain, V. S. 1980. The children of teenage parents. *Family Planning Perspectives* 12(January–February):34-43.

Barsby, S. L., and Cox, D. R. 1975. *Interstate migration of the elderly.* Lexington, MA: Lexington Books.

Bongaarts, J. 1980. Does malnutrition affect fertility? A summary of evidence. *Science* 208(May):564-69.

Bouvier, L. F., and van der Tak, J. 1976. Infant mortality—progress and problems. *Population Bulletin* 31(April). Washington, D.C.: Population Reference Bureau Inc.

Brass, W. 1975. *Methods for estimating fertility and mortality from limited and defective data.* Chapel Hill, NC: International Program of Laboratories for Population Statistics, University of North Carolina.

Card, J. F., and Wise, L. L. 1978. Teenage mothers and teenage fathers: The impact of early childbearing on the parents' personal and professional lives. *Family Planning Perspectives* 10(July–August):199-205.

Carlson, R. J. 1975. *The end of medicine.* New York: John Wiley & Sons.

Chiang, C. L. 1968. *Introduction to stochastic processes in biostatistics.* New York: John Wiley & Sons.

Choldin, H. M. 1978. Urban density and pathology. In *Annual Review of Sociology*, ed. R. H. Turner, vol. 4, pp. 91-113. Palo Alto, CA: Annual Reviews, Inc.

Dingle, J. H., Badger, G. F., and Jordan, W. S. 1964. *Illness in the home.* Cleveland: The Press of Case Western Reserve University.

Duncan, O. D. 1975. *Introduction to miltiequation models.* New York: Academic Press.

Elandt-Johnson, R. C. 1973. Age-at-onset distribution in chronic diseases: A life table approach to the analysis of family data. *Journal of Chronic Diseases* 26:529-45.

Fienberg, S., and Mason, W. 1978. Identification and estimation of age-period-cohort models in the analysis of discrete archival data. In *Sociological methodology 1979*, ed. K. F. Schuessler, pp. 1-67. San Francisco: Jossey-Bass Inc.

Fleiss, J. L. 1973. *Statistical methods for rates and proportions.* New York: John Wiley & Sons.

Ford, K. 1978. Contraceptive use in the United States, 1973-1976. *Family Planning Perspectives* 10(September–October):264-69.

Forrest, J. D., Tietze, C., and Sullivan, E. 1978. Abortion in the United States, 1976-1977. *Family Planning Perspectives* 10(September–October):271-79.

Freedman, J. L. 1975. *Crowding and behavior.* San Francisco: W. H. Freeman.

Frisch, R. E. 1978. Menarche and fatness: Reexamination of the critical body composition hypothesis. *Science* 200(June 30):1506-13.

Furstenberg, F. F., Jr. 1976. *Unplanned parenthood: The social consequences of teenage childbearing.* New York: Free Press.

Glenn, N. D. 1977. *Cohort analysis.* Beverly Hills, CA: Sage Publications.

Greenberg, B. G., Wright, J. J., and Sheps, C. G. 1950. A technique for analyzing some factors affecting the incidence of syphilis. *Journal of the American Statistical Association* 45:373-99.

Greville, T. N. E. 1974. United States life tables by dentulous or edentulous condition, 1971 and 1957-58. *Vital and Health Statistics*, series 2, no. 64, DHEW/HRA 75-1338. Rockville, MD: National Center for Health Statistics.

Heer, D. M. 1979. What is the annual net flow of undocumented Mexican immigrants to the United States? *Demography* 16(August):417-23.

Hickey, R. J., Clelland, R. C., and Clelland, A. B. 1980. Epidemiological studies of chronic disease: Maladjustment of observed mortality rates. *American Journal of Public Health* 70(February):142-49.

Illich, I. 1976. *Medical nemesis.* New York: Random House.

Jarvis, G. K., Ferrence, R. G., Johnson, F. G., and Whitehead, P. C. 1976. Sex and age patterns in self-injury. *Journal of Health and Social Behavior* 17:146-55.

Jordan, C. W., Jr. 1975. *Life contingencies*, 2nd ed. Chicago: Society of Actuaries.

Keyfitz, N. 1977. What difference would it make if cancer were eradicated? An examination of the Taeuber paradox. *Demography* 14(November):411-18.

Kitagawa, E. M. 1955. Components of a difference between two rates. *Journal of the American Statistical Association* 50:1168-94.

Kleinman, J. C. 1977. Age-adjusted mortality indexes for small areas: Applications to health planning. *American Journal of Public Health* 67(September):834-40.

Kobrin, F. E., and Hendershot, G. E. 1977. Do family ties reduce mortality? Evidence from the United States 1966–1968. *Journal of Marriage and the Family* 39:737-45.

Kupper, L. L., McMichael, A. J., Symons, M. J., and Most, B. M. 1978. On the utility of proportional mortality analysis. *Journal of Chronic Diseases* 31:15-22.

Land, K. C. 1969. Principles of path analysis. In *Sociological methodology 1969*, ed. E. F. Borgatta, pp. 3-37. San Francisco: Jossey-Bass Inc.

Lansing, J. B., and Mueller, E. 1967. *The geographic mobility of labor.* Ann Arbor, MI: Survey Research Center, Institute for Social Research.

Lindheim, B. L. 1979. Services, policies and costs in U.S. abortion facilities. *Family Planning Perspectives* 11(September–October):283-89.

MacMahon, B., Kovar, M. G., and Feldman, J. J. 1972. Infant mortality rates: Socioeconomic factors. *Vital and Health Statistics*, series 22, no. 14. Rockville, MD: National Center for Health Statistics.

Madigan, F. C., and Herrin, A. N. 1977. New approaches to the measurement of vital rates in developing countries. Reprint Series, no. 18. Chapel Hill, NC: International Program of Laboratories for Population Statistics, University of North Carolina.

Mantel, N., and Stark, C. R. 1968. Computation of indirect-adjusted rates in the presence of confounding. *Biometrics* 24:997-1005.

Manton, K. G., and Poss, S. S. 1970. Effects of dependency among causes of death for cause elimination life table strategies. *Demography* 16(May):313-27.

Manton, K. G., and Stallard, E. 1980. Mortality of the chronically impaired. *Demography* 17(May):189-206.

Manton, K. G., Stallard, E., and Poss, S. S. 1980. Estimates of U.S. multiple cause life tables. *Demography* 17(February):85-102.

Mason, K. O., Mason, W. M., Winsborough, H. H., and Poole, W. K. 1973. Some methodological issues in analysis of archival data. *American Sociological Review* 38:242-57. (See also comments in *American Sociological Review*, 1976, 41.)

McCook, A. S. 1976. *Health and population: Research and policy issues, annotated bibliography*, vol. 3, no. 2. Washington, D.C.: Interdisciplinary Communications Program, Smithsonian Institution.

McFalls, J. A., Jr. 1979. Frustrated fertility: A population paradox. *Population Bulletin* 34(May). Population Reference Bureau Inc., Washington, D.C.

Menken, J. 1972. The health and social consequences of teenage childbearing. *Family Planning Perspectives* 4(3):45-53.

Milham, S. 1976. Occupational mortality in Washington State 1950–1971. Vol. 1, NIOSH Research Report, HEW/NIOSH 76-175-A.

Monto, A. S., and Ross, H. 1977. Acute respiratory illness in the community: Effect of family composition, smoking, and chronic symptoms. *British Journal of Preventive and Social Medicine* 31(June):101-8.

Morrison, P. A., and Wheeler, J. P. 1976. Rural renaissance in America? *Population Bulletin* 31(October). Population Reference Bureau Inc., Washington, D.C.

Nam, C. B. 1979. The progress of demography as a scientific discipline. *Demography* 16(November):485-92.

Office of Federal Statistical Policy and Standards. 1978. *Statistical policy handbook.* Washington, D.C.: U.S. Department of Commerce.

Potter, R. G. 1966. Application of life table techniques to measurement of contraceptive effectiveness. *Demography* 3:297-304.

Powles, J. 1973. On the limitations of modern medicine. *Science, Medicine, and Man* 1:1-30.

Preston, S. H. 1978. The next fifteen years in demographic analysis. In *Social demography*, eds. K. E. Taeuber, L. L. Bumpass, and J. A. Sweet, pp. 299-313. New York: Academic Press.

Preston, S. H., Keyfitz, N., and Schoen, R. 1972. *Causes of death: Life tables for national population.* New York: Academic Press.

Ritchey, P. N. 1976. Explanations of migration. In *Annual review of sociology*, ed. A. Inkeles, vol. 2, pp. 363-404. Palo Alto, CA: Annual Reviews, Inc.

Rossi, P. H. 1955. *Why families move: A study in the social psychology of urban residential mobility.* Glencoe, IL: The Free Press.

Ryder, N. B. 1973. Recent trends and group differences in fertility, and The future growth of the American population. In *Toward the end of growth*, ed. C. F. Westoff, pp. 57-68 and 85-95. Englewood Cliffs, NJ: Prentice-Hall, Inc.

Severy, L., ed. 1978. Crowding: Theoretical and research implications for population-environment psychology. *Journal of Population* 1(Fall).

Shapiro, S., Schlesinger, E. R., and Nesbitt, R. E. L., Jr. 1968. *Infant, perinatal, maternal, and childhood mortality in the United States.* Cambridge, MA: Harvard University Press.

Shaw, R. P. 1975. *Migration theory and fact: A review and bibliography of current literature.* Philadelphia: Regional Science Research Institute.

Shryock, H.S., Siegel, J. S., and associates. 1975. *The methods and materials of demography*, rev. ed., U.S. Department of Commerce, Bureau of the Census. Washington, D.C.: Government Printing Office.

Siegel, J. S. 1974. Estimates of coverage of the population by sex, race, and age in the 1970 census. *Demography* 11(February):1-23.

———. 1975. Coverage of population in the 1970 census and some implications for public programs. *Current Population Reports*, series P-23, no. 56. Bureau of the Census, U.S. Department of Commerce. Washington, D.C.: Government Printing Office.

———. 1976. Demographic aspects of aging and the older population in the United States. *Current Population Reports*, series P-23, no. 59. Bureau of the Census, U.S. Department of Commerce. Washington, D.C.: Government Printing Office.

Siegel, J. S., and Passel, J. S. 1976. New estimates of the number of centenarians in the United States. *Journal of the American Statistical Association* 71(September):559-66.

Slesinger, D. P. 1973. A study of infant mortality in Wisconsin, 1969. Working Paper 73-12. Center for Demography and Ecology, The University of Wisconsin–Madison.

Stark, C.R., and Mantel, N. 1966. Effects of maternal age and birth order on the risk of mongolism and leukemia. *Journal of the National Cancer Institute* 37:687-98.

Sullivan, D. F. 1971. A single index of mortality and morbidity. *Health Services Reports (HSMHA Health Reports)* 86(April):347-54.

Surgeon General, Office of the Assistant Secretary for Health and. 1979. *Healthy people*, DHEW/PHS 79-55071. Washington, D.C.: Government Printing Office.

Taylor, C. E., Newman, J. S., and Kelly, N. U. 1976. Interactions between health and population. *Studies in Family Planning* 7(4):94-100.

Tietze, C., and Lewit, S. 1973. Recommended procedures for the statistical evaluation of intrauterine contraception. *Studies in Family Planning* 4(February):35-42.

Trussel, T. J. 1976. Economic consequences of teenage childbearing. *Family Planning Perspectives* 8:184-91.

Trussel, T. J., and Menken, J. 1978. Early childbearing and subsequent fertility. *Family Planning Perspectives* 10(4):209-18.

Tsai, S. P., Lee, E. S., and Hardy, R. J. 1978. The effect of a reduction in leading causes of death: Potential gains in life expectancy. *American Journal of Public Health* 68(October):966-71.

U.S. Bureau of the Census. 1977. Projections of the population of the United States: 1977 to 2050. *Current Population Reports*, series P-25, no. 704. Washington, D.C.

Verbrugge, L. M. 1979. Marital status and health. *Journal of Marriage and the Family* 41:267-85.

————. 1982. Women and men: Mortality and health of older people. In *Aging in society: Selected reviews of recent research*, ed. M. W. Riley, B. B. Hess, and K. Bond. Hillsdale, NJ: Lawrence Erlbaum.

Verbrugge, L. M., and Taylor, R. B. 1980. Consequences of population density and size. *Urban Affairs Quarterly* 16(December):135-60.

Weeks, J. 1976. *Teenage marriages: A demographic analysis*. Westport, CT: Greenwood Press.

Westoff, C. F., and Jones, E. F. 1977. Contraception and sterilization in the United States, 1965-1975. *Family Planning Perspectives* 9(July–August):153-57.

Zelnik, M., and Kantner, J. F. 1980. Sexual activity, contraceptive use and pregnancy among metropolitan-area teenagers: 1971–1979. *Family Planning Perspectives* 12(September–October):230-37.

REFERENCES FOR FURTHER READING

Some major references on the demographic perspective, demographic techniques and models, and social demography are listed below. A fine bibliography and key demography journals are also cited. For details about demographic terminology and for data on population size, distribution, composition and change, readers should consult reports published by the U.S. Bureau of the Census and the United Nations.

THE DEMOGRAPHIC PERSPECTIVE

Hauser, P. M., and Duncan, O. D., eds. 1959. *The study of population*. Chicago: University of Chicago Press.

DEMOGRAPHIC FORMULAS, TECHNIQUES AND MODELS

Barclay, G. W. 1958. *Techniques of population analysis*. New York: John Wiley & Sons.

Coale, A. 1972. *The growth and structure of human populations: A mathematical investigation*. Princeton, NJ: Princeton University Press.

Keyfitz, N., and Flieger, W. 1971. *Population: Facts and methods of demography*. San Francisco: W. H. Freeman & Co.

Pollard, A. H., Yusuf, F., and Pollard, G. N. 1974. *Demographic techniques*. Australia: Pergamon Press.

Shryock, H. S., Siegel, J. S., and associates. 1975. *The methods and materials of demography*, rev. ed. U.S. Department of Commerce, Bureau of the Census. Washington, D.C.: Government Printing Office.

Spiegelman, M. 1968. *Introduction to demography*, rev. ed. Cambridge: Harvard University Press.

Stockwell, E. G. 1976. *The methods and materials of demography*. (Condensed version of Shryock and Siegel). New York: Academic Press.

United Nations. Manuals of methods of estimating population. *Population studies* (Series A), Nos. 10, 23, 25, 42, 46, 47, 54, 55. New York: Department of Economic and Social Affairs, 1952–1974. See also issues of *Studies in methods* (Series F) and *Statistical papers* (Series M).

SOCIAL DEMOGRAPHY

Bogue, D. 1969. *Principles of demography*. New York: John Wiley & Sons.

Ford, T. R., and DeJong, G. F., eds. 1970. *Social demography*. Englewood Cliffs, NJ: Prentice-Hall, Inc.

Matras, J. 1970 *Populations and societies*. Englewood Cliffs, NJ: Prentice-Hall Inc.

The human population. *Scientific American* (reprint of articles in September 1974 issue). San Francisco: W. H. Freeman & Co.

Thomlinson, R. 1975. *Population dynamics: Causes and consequences of world demographic change*, 2nd ed. New York: Random House.

United Nations. 1973. The determinants and consequences of population trends. *Population studies* vol. 1, (Series A), No. 50. New York: Department of Economic and Social Affairs.

BIBLIOGRAPHY

Population Reference Bureau. 1976. *Sourcebook on Population 1970–1976*. Washington, D.C.: Population Reference Bureau Inc. Lists and describes demography books, periodicals, data sources, and training programs.

JOURNALS

Demography. Social, technical and mathematical demography.
Family Planning Perspectives. Fertility and family planning in the U.S.

International Migration Review. Interdisciplinary journal of migration research.
Journal of Population. Psychological aspects of demographic behavior.
Population and Development Review. An international focus.
Population Index. A quarterly publication which abstracts demographic articles in
    other journals.
Studies in Family Planning. An international focus on family planning.

Seven

Economics and Health Services Research

PART ONE:

An Introduction to Health Economics

RALPH E. BERRY, JR.

PART TWO:

Health Economics and Collaborative Research Opportunities

ROGER D. FELDMAN

PART ONE

This chapter addresses from the economic perspective the substance of economics, applications to health services research, the findings generated by such applications, the particular policy relevance of the specific efforts and opportunities for interdisciplinary collaboration.

WHAT IS ECONOMICS?

Economics is the science of scarcity. In its most fundamental form, economics is concerned with the allocation of scarce resources. If resources were not scarce there would be no economic problem, there would be no economic issues, and there would be nothing for economists to be concerned about (at least not qua economists). But resources are scarce—they are exceedingly scarce relative to the uses to which they might be put to satisfy our individual and collective wants. And it is this relative scarcity that makes important the fundamental questions that are the concern of economics: How is society to allocate its scarce resources? What goods and services are to be produced? Since we can't have all that we might want, certain choices must be made. By what process are these choices to be made, and what specifically will be the eventual choices? Moreover, different goods and services can be produced and provided in different ways. Given that a particular output is to be forthcoming, how might it be produced? Choices need to be made in the use of scarce resources in production—the familiar question of whether to use technology which relies more heavily on capital or labor, for example. In different contexts with different relative scarcities of resources, the appropriate mix of capital and labor can be expected to vary.

Finally, quite apart from what is produced and how it is accomplished there is the question critical to all individual members of a society or economic system: Who gets what? How is the output of a society to be distributed among its members? This, then, is the concern of economics and economists in general. The concern is with scarcity and with the allocation of scarce resources. Economists get involved with a variety of issues, but basically they are concerned with the way society answers such fundamental questions as what to produce, how to produce, and to whom to distribute the fruits of its productive capacity.

The first two questions relate to the relative efficiency of the allocation of resources—that is, how well a society is doing, how much it is getting for the resources it is using. The last question relates to the equity of the income distribution that evolves.

What do economists concern themselves with when they reflect on the health services sector? That's right, the same issues and the same set of concerns! Indeed, the health sector of most economies exhausts a significant part of societies' scarce resources. In the United States at the present time, our health sector represents something in the order of ten percent of our aggregate capacity to produce goods and services. The general concern of economics would seem most appropriate in the context of health services. Are we producing the right aggregate amount of health services? Is ten percent of our GNP the appropriate response to what we ought to produce relative to alternatives? Or how about within the health sector? Given the aggregate expenditure on health care and medical services, should we be producing the mix of services that currently prevails? Would a different mix be more appropriate? Would our society be better off in some sense if we had more of certain medical care services and less of others, for example? Or how about the way that medical care is distributed among our population?

If one reflects on the health and medical care sector, its record in recent times, and certainly upon the criticism leveled from both without and within the sector, one can gain an appreciation of the relevance of addressing the fundamental economic questions to this large and growing sector of our economy. Some 20 years or so ago, physicians regularly pointed out that the United States was not doing particularly well on a comparative basis with other industrial societies in terms of life expectancy, infant mortality, age-specific mortality, and so forth. For emphasis, they would add that this was in spite of the fact that we spent more in both absolute and relative amounts on medical care. Of course, they were asking questions of the first kind: "What are we producing? What are we getting for the significant proportion of our scarce resources that are allocated to the medical care sector?" More, they were obviously suggesting—at least by implication—that we would (could) be better off in some sense if we altered our allocation either to the sector or within the sector, or both.

Or consider the performance of the health sector in recent years in terms of the rate of inflation of health care costs. Now of course this inflation is not a problem of recent vintage, but represents a phenomenon with a long history that has actually intensified in recent years. But is this inflation not symptomatic of some phenomena that might be uncovered by asking questions of the second kind? How are we allocating resources within the health care sector? After all, the inflation is indicative of an increase in the resource cost or opportunity cost of health care. Would not a better understanding of just how health care is produced and how choices are made within this sector provide the basis, perhaps, of improving the allocation of resources?

Finally, the issues of access to care, maldistribution of manpower, and the relationship between poverty and health have long been of some policy concern. Are those concerns not related to questions of the third kind? There are equity considerations along geographic, income and other dimensions that could be addressed to some advantage in general social welfare terms.

WHAT IS THE THEORETICAL FRAMEWORK OF ECONOMICS?

Economics is the science of scarcity and it is, in the last analysis, a behavioral science. The behavior of concern is that related to economic activities and choices when choices need to be made. The theoretical framework that underlies virtually all economics is essentially derived from the principles of maximization subject to constraint. Given that resources are scarce and hence that choices must be made, the question is how well can any choice serve to satisfy the chooser. Whether our concern is with consumers faced with a set of choices and the constraint of their income, or a producer faced with a set of choices and the constraint of technology available, or whatever, the basic nature of the problem is the same. Do consumers go on random walks in selecting goods and services? What motivates firms in deciding how much to produce, to sell or to charge? The economists' answers to these questions are that economic actors will seek to maximize something and that their behavior can be understood and predicted in such terms. This is perhaps a bit oversimplified, but it serves to emphasize the common theoretical framework upon which most economic theory is based and hence most economic research rests.

The basic tool kit of economists is composed of the scissors of supply and demand, and in each instance the traditional and most common version of the tool is derived essentially from the principle of maximization subject to constraint. Thus, the demand comes from individual consumers or household units that are assumed to be maximizing their utility or satisfaction subject to an income constraint and the prices given in the several markets for the various goods and services among which they may choose. On the supply side, in the simplest case, producers are assumed to be maximizing their profit subject to the constraints imposed by the technology available, market demand, and the prices they face in hiring or purchasing inputs or resources. Taken together, of course, the demand for and supply of any good or service make up the market.

And, of course, the market is the basic mechanism for allocating scarce resources—and a significant amount of economic research goes into studying markets. The principal grist for the mill of economics research is going behind the demand curve, going behind the supply curve, and looking at the structure, conduct and relative performance of specific markets.

WHY HEALTH CARE MARKETS?

It would undoubtedly be the case that economists would study health care markets as a natural course of events. There are several reasons why this is so. First, there is the sheer size, scope, and magnitude of the health sector. This is a large and growing sector of the economy and as such it is bound to draw some attention from those whose livelihood involves studying that economy. Then there is the derivative potential policy relevance of health services research. The sector is probably of even more relative significance in the context of public policy than it is in the context of the overall economy.

Still, for quite some time, there has been enough interest on the part of certain economists in the health care sector that it would be appropriate to refer to a subdiscipline of health economics. The integrity of health economics as a subdiscipline of economics probably derives from the complexity of issues surrounding the question "Are health care markets different?" Economists have been drawn to this field in some part by the challenge of resolving this question.

Very few markets can be characterized as perfectly competitive, and a variety of market imperfections obtains in virtually all markets. Indeed, a principal purpose of economists analyzing the structure, conduct, and relative performance of specific markets is to assess the extent to which market imperfections result in particularly nondesirable outcomes. If health care markets are different, it is not because there are market imperfections per se, but because there are so many, simultaneously.

Health care markets may be imperfectly competitive because of the scarcity of sellers, which could be due to limited entry, collusion among sellers, or inability of the market to support more than one seller. Scarcity of sellers gives each some control over prices or quantities of goods sold (one good may be quality); therefore, to pursue socially undesirable goals such as restricting output and accumulating monopoly profits. This problem is compounded by the high costs of information in health care markets. It is important to realize that the cost of acquiring information is not a waste of resources and that information is not free in other industries. What is special about health is that sellers can often make it difficult for consumers to obtain good information (Feldman and Begun 1978).

Medical expenses are often large relative to consumers' incomes and they are risky. People normally buy insurance against large, risky losses. In this respect, health insurance is not different from fire or auto insurance. However, because of the difficulty of assigning dollar values to adverse health outcomes, health insurance policies typically reimburse consumers for medical expenses. Consumers thus lose the incentive to shop for reasonably priced medical care, which makes maintaining competition more difficult.

Health care is also marked by externalities (situations where individuals do not consider all the costs or benefits of their actions). The unassisted competitive economic system will not devote enough resources to goods that involve positive externalities and will result in too much of those goods that involve negative externalities. Clearly, health care markets are characterized by externalities. Again, externalities are not unique to health care markets, but they represent an additional consideration.

Finally, medical care markets may have trouble reaching equilibrium. Normally, sellers cut prices when they can't sell as many goods as they had planned. But some observers (Fuchs 1972) claim to find persistent excess supply for surgery, as evidenced by high prices and low workloads per surgeon. There may be excess demand for other goods such as physicians' house calls.

Still another appeal of the health sector is the extent of what Feldstein (1974) has referred to as nonstandard behavior in its several markets. Economists have been intrigued by the intellectual challenge of contributing to the theory of nonprofit enterprises, for example. What motivates enterprises that are formed and operated on a nonprofit basis? Some progress has been made in solving this puzzle—and it has evolved essentially from the principles of maximization subject to constraint—but definitive models or explanations of the behavior of nonprofit enterprises probably remain to be specified and certainly remain to be demonstrated. Then there is the special nature of the relationship between patient and physician that at times puts supply side actors on the demand side of the market. When the consumer-patient enters the market for health services, does he encounter a physician entrepreneur or an agent? It makes a difference to the patient, of course, but it also makes a difference analytically. Indeed, such nonstandard behavior can be viewed as market imperfections in a strict sense, and the analysis of health care markets is both more difficult and more interesting as a consequence. Dr. Feldman discusses several cases of nonstandard behavior in Part Two.

While economists are probably attracted to health economics by the intellectual challenges, e.g., the theory of nonprofit enterprises, their contributions derive in large part from the ability to analyze markets and assess market imperfections. Generally, these contributions take the form of going beyond the demand and supply curves and looking at the structure, conduct and relative performance of specific health care markets. Thus, the principal grist for the mill of health economics research is essentially the same as that for economics research in general.

Together, the problems of market imperfection and the motivation of sellers constitute "nonstandard economic behavior." The opportunity to develop models of nonstandard behavior constitutes perhaps the major intellectual challenge of the study of health care to economists. These opportunities are elaborated upon by Dr. Feldman in Part Two.

WHAT HAVE ECONOMISTS LOOKED AT AND WHAT HAVE THEY FOUND?

It is not our present purpose to provide more than a general overview of the relevant literature. (Several good summaries of recent work in health economics are Feldstein (1974), Grossman (1977), and Newhouse (1978a).) But it is appropriate to summarize briefly the principal factors that economists have investigated and comment briefly on what they have found.

Some attention has been paid to the relationship between medical care and health in the production function sense. For example, Auster, Leveson and Sarachek (1969) have estimated a production function for health. There have been other attempts, but theirs is representative and perhaps the most widely cited.

Economists use production functions to assess the technical relationship between inputs (the scarce resources) and outputs (the goods and services that are desired). Indeed, the production function is central to the analysis of the supply side of the problem. (Theoretically, the cost function is derived from the production function; empirically, analysis of cost functions has dominated research on the supply side—especially hospital cost research.)

Among the health production function studies, the major "discovery," if you will, is probably a demonstration of the obvious—that medical care has not been particularly unique in producing good health; that other factors are not only important to health status, but are more important.

The major problem with these production function studies of the relationship between medical care and health has been the general inability to measure the output. What is health, good health or health status? Indeed, most such studies have actually relied on measures of the absence of health as surrogates. Thus, most researchers have selected dependent variables such as mortality, morbidity or work loss days for their studies.

In general, the demand side of health and medical care has been well researched. Moreover, in relative terms demand analysis has progressed somewhat further than supply analysis. Demand studies have usually employed econometric techniques to estimate a traditional demand equation with the quantity of services dependent on the service's own price, the prices of substitutes and complements, income, insurance, and such surrogates for consumer taste parameters as race, sex, age and education. Albeit most researchers have specified rather complete demand equations, the state of knowledge has been advanced by varying the emphasis on the several factors likely to influence demand as well as the preciseness with which the several independent variables are approximated.

Thus, for example, earlier demand studies such as that by Rosenthal (1970) tended to concentrate on the effect of price on the quantity demanded. Given the widespread contention that medical care consumption was not responsive to price but was determined exclusively by technical medical considerations, the early demand studies that demonstrated some price elasticity, i.e., responsiveness of quantity demanded to the price charged, were of significance.

Of course, considerable care must be taken in interpreting price elasticity results because of the importance of insurance in the medical care sector—especially in the case of hospital services which have been the subject of much demand analysis. Later demand studies that specifically accounted for the fact that the net price paid by the patient depends on both the gross price charged and the extent of insurance coverage, such as that by M. Feldstein (1971), facilitated the interpretation of price elasticity estimates. Additional demand studies that have concentrated on the role of insurance in demand, such as those by Phelps and Newhouse (1972) and Rosett and Huang (1973), have served to clarify still further the interrelated influences of price and insurance. Finally, several recent studies, including those by Acton (1972) and Grossman (1972), have introduced the patient's time as an integral part of the total price.

In general, the demand for medical care is price-inelastic—the degree of responsiveness is less than proportional—but there is a significant relationship between price and the quantity demanded. In the case of physicians' services, for example, a ten percent price increase might be expected to lead to a one or two percent decline in the quantity demanded. The quantity of hospital services demanded appears to be somewhat more responsive, but still inelastic—perhaps a three to five percent quantity response for a ten percent price change. Other medical care goods and services are even somewhat more responsive to price changes. And the quantity demanded is also responsive to patient time.

Of course, insurance coverage is a critical characteristic of the market for medical care. It is of paramount significance in the case of hospital services. On the one hand, insurance or other third-party coverage serves to lower the net price of the good or service in question to the consumer. At a lower price the good or service in question is more desirable, other factors being the same. On the other hand, third-party payers are likely to reflect more reliable sources of revenues to suppliers. On balance, insurance can be expected to stimulate demand and result in a larger proportion of the scarce resources of concern flowing into the medical care sector. Moreover, within the sector, because insurance coverage is not proportional across types of services, one might expect the allocation of resources to be distorted relative to what would be obtained if there were no third-party coverage.

Although most demand studies in the health sector have tended to emphasize own-price elasticity, some research has begun to analyze the influence of substitutes and complements. (Economists refer to the responsiveness of the quantity demanded of one good to the price of another as the cross-elasticity of demand.) Davis and Russell (1972), for example, estimated the cross-elasticity of inpatient hospital care with respect to the price of outpatient services and found the expected direct relationship. M. Feldstein (1971) included the numbers of general practitioners and medical and surgical specialists per capita in his demand equation for hospital care. His findings suggest that general practitioners represent substitutes for hospital care and specialists represent complements.

Most demand studies have found the income elasticity—degree of responsiveness of quantity demanded to income—for medical care expenditures in general to be in the order of 1.0. Essentially this means that a given percentage increase in income can be expected to lead to a proportional increase in the amount expended on medical care. In the case of hospital services, income elasticities have generally been found to be rather low. The studies of Anderson and Benham (1970) and P. Feldstein and Carr (1964) are representative. Moreover, the effect of income on medical care expenditures appears to have declined over time. This is undoubtedly related to the fact that over time insurance coverage has increased significantly.

Even this somewhat brief and incomplete review of demand studies indicates the volume of research that has been completed. As noted above, the demand side has been well researched, and the results are essentially indicative of the effort. One problem of some note, however, has been the inability to date to capture product heterogeneity adequately in the dependent variable. Very little has been done to account for product differences in the demand function. This is, of course, of particular significance, in the case of medical care, where quality differences in general or differences in the complexity of the scope of services, in the case of hospital care, are ubiquitous.

Finally, there is a significant gap in the state of knowledge on the demand side that should be mentioned. Not enough is known about the role of the physician in determining the demand for other medical care goods and services. This is of particular concern in the case of hospital services. Are hospital services final goods, or intermediate goods, for example? Estimating a demand equation in which the quantity of hospital services is dependent on their respective prices, other prices, and such consumer characteristics as income, insurance coverage, race, age, sex and education is equivalent to assuming that hospital services are a final good. Virtually all empirical demand studies have followed this route. An alternative perspective would view the consumer's demand to be for medical care. Physicians would be viewed as entrepreneurs who combine several inputs, including their own time and hospital services, to produce medical care. The demand for hospital services, in effect, would be a derived demand. P. Feldstein (1966) outlined such a perspective in some detail and others have alluded to it often, but little if any empirical demand research has been based on this conceptual model.

Is the demand for hospital services to be considered in the context of consumers maximizing their satisfaction as would be the case if they are treated as a pure final good? Or is it to be considered in the context of physician entrepreneurs maximizing their utility as would be the case if they are treated as a pure intermediate good? It seems likely that neither extreme represents the state of the real world. An alternative that is intermediate and has considerable intuitive appeal would treat the physician as an agent for the patient in the market for hospital services. This is a relatively new idea and holds much promise for learning more about the role of the physician in determining the demand for hospital services.

The supply side of health and medical care has received considerable attention as well. Reinhardt (1972), for example, estimated a production function of physicians' services. Perhaps the most significant of Reinhardt's findings was that physicians tend to employ only half as many aides as would be maximally profitable. One implication, of course, is that physicians do not particularly like to manage. There is some psychic cost to the burden of administration.

Much of the research on the supply side of the market for physicians' services has looked at the supply of physicians in terms of their numbers, and especially the geographic and specialty choices of physicians. The relative emphasis of the research has undoubtedly been affected over time by the concern over a potential physician shortage. This concern seems to have passed—the apparent geographic maldistribution of physicians in particular and of health manpower and health services in general, and the issues of specialty choices that did not always appear to match the kinds of physician services that the population might need or want.

In general, economic research has tended to demonstrate that certain economic factors do have some influence—income, for example, is of some concern to young physicians choosing specialties and, to some extent, geographic location. But as one might expect, institutional characteristics such as available residencies are of some importance in specialty choice. A variety of factors related to the desirability of a location, prior exposure to it, and the availability of complementary medical facilities are of significant importance in the geographic location decisions of physicians.

On the supply side of the market for hospital services, considerable research effort has been devoted to hospital cost analysis. Most of the earlier cost studies concentrated on the question of whether or not hospital services were produced subject to economies-of-scale. On balance, the weight of evidence is that economies-of-scale, however significant statistically, are not particularly significant in absolute terms. Lipscomb, Raskin and Eichenholz (1978) have analyzed the data from most cost studies and approximately constant returns to scale can be inferred from the long-run data. This is consistent with the findings of M. Feldstein (1968) for British hospitals and Evans (1971) for Canadian hospitals. The latter two studies are significant in this regard because the availability of case-mix data in England and Canada allows case-mix differences to be taken into account and hence avoids a source of bias that prevails in most cost studies of U.S. hospitals.

In the short run, marginal costs tend to be significantly below average costs—that is, it is considerably less expensive to treat an additional case at the margin than it costs on average overall. This result is rather consistent among all cost studies and has some relevance for public policy in the context of cost containment.

WHY ARE THINGS THE WAY THEY ARE?

There are probably three things that contribute to an explanation of why things are the way they are in the health sector. First, markets work to allocate scarce resources primarily by the process of prices that signal scarcity values—scarcity values of the resources used to produce goods and services and scarcity values of the goods and services themselves. In the health sector, these scarcity values are scrambled so that it is difficult to ascertain the real scarcity value as perceived by consumers because they often do not face the real price or cost due to insurance. Moreover, because providers are usually reimbursed at cost by third parties, they have little incentive to assess the comparative cost and scarcity value of goods or resources.

Second is the phenomenon discussed in the previous section, namely, that the market for certain health services, most particularly that for physicians' services, has the peculiar characteristic of supply-side actors on the demand side of the market.

Finally, there is the special nature of certain markets such as that for hospital services which are characterized by the dominance of nonprofit enterprises. As discussed above, not enough is known about the behavior of nonprofit enterprises to allow confident predictions of their behavior in every context.

WHAT IS THE POLICY RELEVANCE OF HEALTH ECONOMICS?

On balance, we can express some cautious positive comments regarding the policy relevance of health economics. The positiveness would obviously refer more to the relevance for policy than to examples of past policy successes.

In essence, economic research in the health services context has come a considerable way in the past couple of decades. Much is known about the several markets that make up the health sector. Certainly, for example, we have a sufficient knowledge of the range of price elasticity estimates to be able to assess the potential for the impact of certain policy interventions on the demand side. Thus, quite apart from its political acceptance, previous economic research would be sufficient to predict the general impact of restricting health insurance to catastrophic insurance. The same research allows some reasonable predictions to be made about the potential impact of various national health insurance proposals.

Somewhat less is known about the supply response to changes in the market environment. Indeed, if research gaps are to be closed to some advantage, they will undoubtedly be those that concern the supply-side phenomena. Both the physician-agent—the supply-side actor who is often on the demand side—and the nonprofit enterprise represent issues of some concern for future research.

Indeed, it seems reasonable to note that the failure to date of public policy efforts to contain medical care cost inflation can be understood best in terms of the failure to understand or account for reactions of suppliers when faced with new constraints. Thus, we come full circle in a sense. We need to understand the objectives of economic actors—just what it is that they are trying to maximize—if we are to expect to have success in causing them to modify the behavior by changing one or more of the constraints that they face in their markets.

PART TWO

WHAT IS THE PLACE OF ECONOMICS AMONG THE SOCIAL SCIENCES?

The principle of maximization subject to constraint, which underlies virtually all of economics, lends itself easily to mathematical formulation. Mathematics enables economists to state complex problems in precise terms and manipulate them with an ease that would probably be impossible without the use of mathematics. Other social sciences, notably political science and sociology, have shared the inclination of economics in the use of mathematics.

The concept of equilibrium is especially important to economists. Once individuals have made their best constrained choice, they will tend to maintain that behavior until disturbed by a new set of circumstances. These may arise as the chooser receives new data regarding the scarcity of goods and services, as the chooser's wealth changes, or as his/her preferences regarding alternative choices change. Since economists (as distinct from sociologists) have little to contribute to understanding how preferences are formed, they assume that they are constant during the time period of the problem. The assumption of constant preferences provides a stable foundation for predicting how choosers respond to new situations, and in the hands of a gifted practitioner such as Becker (1976), economic theory can explain phenomena as diverse as marriage, fertility, crime and altruism.

However, there is not unanimous agreement within the profession with regard to some fundamental theoretical assumptions. A trenchant criticism has been raised from within the economics profession by Marxist critics like Bowles and Gintis (1975). Marxists claim that preferences are changed by the very processes that the economic system uses to solve the problem of scarcity. The economic system transforms raw materials into products, and workers with given skills and consciousness into workers with altered skills and consciousness. The imperative governing this transformation is, of course, the imperative of capitalism which requires a skilled but docile workforce to turn out commodities and gullible consumers to keep buying them, lest the market become glutted. While most economists would not accept this entire argument, they are at least bothered by parts of it, as evidenced by the continuing ambiguity within the profession regarding the social value of advertising.

Another characteristic that distinguishes economists from other social scientists is their peculiar relation to data. Most economists depend for their livelihood on analyzing some type of data, whether it be the supply of money or cycles in the hog market. Yet they rarely collect the data themselves. Most economists have never conducted a survey or taken a course in research design, and, as a consequence, their research methods look primitive, especially to psychologists.

Once economists get the data in hand, however, their analytic techniques sharply rival those of other social sciences in sophistication and ingenuity. Economists have made notable contributions to science, especially in the areas of linear programming and estimation of simultaneous equations models.

Why do economists have this schizophrenic relation to data? One reason is that economic data are harder to collect than psychological or sociological data. Captive audiences of freshmen students are not usually a good population for economists to study. In addition, much of the data sought is owned by, or cannot be collected without the cooperation of, organizations which have a proprietary interest in the data. It is often best to let the organizations collect the data and to use it with their permission.

Reliance on data collected by the organizations under study, e.g., the American Medical Association, the American Hospital Association, and Blue Cross health insurance plans, raises the possibility of conflict of interest. Yet economists have been among the most perceptive critics of medicine, hospitals and health insurance. The real danger associated with using secondary data is that it is often poorly suited for testing economic theories. Key variables may have to be constructed or approximated and are sometimes missing altogether. This comment recalls a conversation between an economist and a sociologist: "Economist: 'Is there no concept so vague that sociologists won't theorize about it?' Sociologist: 'Is there no dataset so bad that economists won't analyze it?' "

Economic problems are not well-suited to data collection under laboratory conditions. For example, it is very hard to elicit trustworthy answers to the question "How much would you be willing to pay to reduce the probability of accidental death by one percent?" in the laboratory. Fortunately, the real world contains enough natural variation for economists to study. People take risks every day. By observing wage differentials connected with risky jobs, Thaler and Rosen (1976) were able to impute a willingness to pay for lifesaving!

The fact that economists (American economists, at least) usually turn to the real world for data is a source of both weakness and strength. The cost of collecting data increases when we go to the real world, and this reinforces the tendency among economists to rely on data collected by others. On the other hand, enough natural variation can almost always be found in the United States if economists cast their nets widely enough. For example, local government spending per capita in major U.S. cities shows over a three-fold variation, even after adjusting for cost of living differences. The success of applied economics in the United States, compared to its relative aridity in Europe, may partly be due to greater opportunities in this country for observing natural economic variation.

There may be some economic problems for which natural variation is insufficient or where it is confounded by the tendency of human subjects to self-select into the treatment group. In these cases, economists may conduct social experiments. Two well-known examples are the New Jersey income-maintenance experiment and the RAND health insurance experiment (Pechman and Timpane 1975; Newhouse 1974). However, social experiments have their own problems of execution and inference, notably, the difficulty of distinguishing temporary from permanent behavior changes, and the tendency of human subjects to react abnormally when their behavior is being observed (Rivlin 1974). Some economists have reacted to these problems by devising techniques for purging selectivity bias from natural data (Lee 1977; 1978). But social experiments will remain in the economists' tool kit, and the conduct of experiments offers a chance for economists to cooperate with more experimental social scientists.

How Can Social Scientists Collaborate in Health Services Research?

Nearly all health economists, if asked for a reference on the production of health, the demand for medical care, or the supply of physicians' and hospital services, would cite one of the studies just mentioned. This is evidence for the broad scope of agreement among researchers in this field. But there are other topics of active discussion and occasional disagreement among health economists. Four such topics will be discussed here: the role of physicians as consumers' agents, theories of hospital behavior, the effect of group practice on physicians' incentives, and the market for health insurance.

The topics all represent examples of "nonstandard" economic behavior. As explained earlier, the motives of producers in nonstandard markets may differ from economists' usual assumptions of profit maximization.

Nonstandard cases abound in health economics. The suppliers of health care are generally nonprofit institutions or professionals. Consumers have virtually unlimited purchasing power (due to insurance) but severely limited information and, therefore, must rely heavily on the advice of providers. And markets may clear only with a significant amount of nonprice rationing.

These problems all require modifications or extensions of the economist's basic paradigm. However, at the same time, they may offer the greatest opportunities for health economists to collaborate with other social scientists, because nonstandard economics may be the standard bread-and-butter research of other social sciences. To give but one example, sociologists have often studied the evolution and conduct of professional associations (Begun 1977). Since most personal health services are produced by professionals, and since professionals are influenced by economic as well as social forces, this area offers a good opportunity for economists to join forces with sociologists.

Reference to the role of physicians as consumers' agents will illustrate this point in greater detail. A relatively ignorant patient may delegate authority to a physician, as M. Feldstein (1974) says, "with the hope that the physician will act for him as he would for himself if he had the appropriate expertise." The physician thus becomes the consumer's agent. However, the agency relation may not be perfect because the physician, as provider of services, stands to make money or save time according to the advice given to the patient. In areas with "too many" physicians, the physician may advise the patient to use more services. This not only benefits the patient (assuming that more services are at least slightly helpful), but it also maintains the physician's income. In other areas with "too few" physicians, a physician may not fully exploit his/her power to raise prices, but decide instead to ration scarce services to the most-deserving (in some sense) patients.

Economists have tested the agency hypothesis indirectly by deducing and searching for certain consequences associated with a scarcity or surplus of providers. Rafferty (1971), for example, showed that less-serious hospital treatments are postponed when there is substantial pressure on capacity. But Newhouse and Marquis (1978b) found conflicting evidence in the following ingenious test: if physicians make the decisions, then patients' demands should not be sensitive to variables that are imperfectly perceived by the physician, e.g., the appropriate insurance variable in an individual demand equation is the area's insurance coverage, and the individual's insurance policy is irrelevant.[1] Yet, consumers in the RAND health insurance experiment had significantly different expenses for ambulatory physicians' services depending on the plan in which they were enrolled.

The most recent direct test of the agency hypothesis was done by Fuchs (1978). He obtained a linear prediction of the number of surgical operations per capita as a function of price and surgeons per capita and exogenous variables related to the demand for surgery. The positive estimated coefficient of the surgeons per capita variable was interpreted to indicate that physicians can shift the demand for surgery.

In the absence of a theory of the agency relation, one should be cautious about interpreting the results of existing empirical studies. An adequate theory must explain how physicians' target income is set or, to put the issue differently, when does an area have "too few" physicians and when does it have "too many"? Physicians per capita has been used as an empirical proxy for the theoretical variable. However, Sloan and Feldman (1978) recently showed that, if demand is pushed outward when there are more physicians per capita, then high per capita income and insurance coverage should, inter alia, cause the opposite effect. This is clearly unacceptable.

If the notion of target income is to have value, it must be related to factors in the physician's background and environment, and the relation should extend beyond simplistic, ad hoc stories about "keeping up with the Joneses." Surely, some of the factors related to target income must be of interest to medical educators and sociologists.

The fully elaborated agency theory must also account for forces that limit the physician's ability to reach the target income. Sloan and Feldman (1978) relied on a general aversion to demand curve-shifting. Medical ethics might be more to the point. Can someone tell us, precisely, what are the costs of being a bad agent?

The second opportunity for the social sciences to collaborate in health services research is the economic behavior of hospitals. Most nongovernment U.S. hospitals, and a disproportionate share of hospital beds, are not-for-profit. What are the implications of not-for-profit organizations for hospital behavior?

The economic approach to this question, following our usual paradigm, is to postulate an objective function which is maximized subject to constraints. An example of the objective function, popularized by M. Feldstein in his seminal study of hospital cost inflation (1971), is $U = U(Q,q)$, where the arguments of the function are quantity (Q) and quality (q) of service ("service intensity" can be used interchangeably with quality). The hospital maximizes this function subject to a cost function for quantity and quality, $C = C(Q,q)$; patient care demand, $D = D(Q,q,P,I)$, where P and I are price and insurance variables; and the nonprofit budget constraint that total revenue equals total cost, or $PQ = C$.

Formal maximization of the objective function subject to constraints yields a set of equations that can be solved for optimal levels of the hospital's choice variables, Q and q. The change in choice variables with respect to exogenous factors can also be examined via "comparative statics" analysis.

This analysis provides a very useful framework for organizing casual observations about hospital behavior, especially the observation that hospital prices have increased faster than the general price level for about 30 years. According to M. Feldstein (1971), the process starts when consumer demand increases due, say, to better insurance coverage. Hospitals can respond to demand pressure by increasing the number of bed-days, but they can also switch to higher-priced methods of providing care without reducing the occupancy rate of beds. If the latter course is preferred, price and service intensity will rise simultaneously to restore market equilibrium—a result which, in fact, dominates post-World War II experience.

Although this theory has helped economists to organize their observations, it is very difficult to devise a direct test of the theory itself. This is because the analytic predictions of the theory differ quantitatively but not qualitatively from standard profit-maximization. The "first-order" conditions for constrained maximization usually indicate that a nonprofit utility-maximizing hospital will purchase inputs beyond the profit-maximizing level. This occurs for two reasons: inputs may directly yield utility, i.e., status or prestige, to the hospital; and the nonprofit budget constraint requires that all potential profits get spent on inputs. But it is extremely difficult to estimate differential input demand functions for nonprofit and proprietary hospitals, especially because the for-profits differ so much that they do not provide a valid control group.

The problem would be solved if it could be shown that nonprofit hospitals respond "perversely" when exogenous market variables change, e.g., not cutting back the size of residency programs when residents' wages rise. Unfortunately, this is not the case—both nonprofit and proprietary hospitals tend to conserve inputs that are relatively expensive (Feldman and Yoder 1980).

A more promising opportunity might be to identify the goals of relevant groups in the hospital—physicians, trustees and administrators—and the situations in which each group is likely to have the upper hand. This approach would use the structure-conduct-performance paradigm shared by industrial organization in economics and organization theory in sociology (Scherer 1971; Blau 1970; Thompson 1967).

Pauly has already done some work along these lines (1973; 1978). His organization theory is rather simple: physicians run the hospital as a cooperative partnership that seeks to maximize their net incomes. But the simplicity of the theory is matched by the neatness of his test of it. Broadly speaking, his hypothesis is that, if identifiable characteristics influence physicians' decision making, these characteristics will also affect hospital costs. The most important medical staff characteristic, according to Pauly, is the concentration of output among attending physicians. When output is concentrated among a few physicians and they share some input costs, each one will bear a larger share of the common costs. Thus, in ordering services for their own patients, each physician will be more cost-conscious. In addition, it may be easier to detect and discipline noncooperative partners when output is concentrated among few physicians.

Pauly embeds his theory of collective action in a standard hospital cost function. He finds that total hospital cost is lower, controlling for admissions and case mix, when output is concentrated.

The interesting theoretical question to consider is, "Why don't less-concentrated hospitals adopt policies to discourage resource overutilization?" Clearly, such policies are available. Evidence indicates that some hospitals directly control staff members' privileges (Clarkson 1972). Maybe others do not because the costs of control are prohibitive. We will assume that there is a fixed cost per physician of control, shown by height OF in figure 7.1; marginal cost is assumed to be a nondecreasing function of staff size and to decline if output is concentrated among few physicians. The losses from cheating (which equal the benefits of control) are shown in figure 7.2. Each physician's incentive is to use OA of a common input, where the marginal revenue product (MRP) of the input equals his/her share of the input price. If all physicians have equal output shares, and they all cheat, the loss to each from cheating is area BCD.[2] The size of this area is approximately equal to

$$\frac{W^2 (1 - 1/M)^2}{2\beta}$$

where β is the absolute value of the slope of the MRP curve.

It can be seen that the loss rises if the MRP curve is more elastic (β is smaller) or the input is more expensive. Differentiating the loss with respect to staff size shows that $d \ loss/dM > 0$ and $d^2 \ loss/dM^2 < 0$. The loss (benefit) function is also plotted in figure 7.1.[3]

It will be in each physician's self-interest to vote for resource-saving polices if the private benefits exceed his/her costs. This point occurs at staff size M_1 in a concentrated-output hospital and a larger staff size, M_2, in an unconcentrated hospital.[4] This proposition could be tested by examining hospitals' resource allocation rules in relation to staff size, concentration and input markets.

This is just one example of the industrial organization/organization theory research that can be done on hospitals. In general it will be advantageous to identify hospital decision makers and their incentives. The technique of constrained maximization can be used to derive testable propositions about the relation between hospital structure on one hand and hospital conduct and performance on the other.

Hospitals are not the only places where physicians practice together. Increasingly, ambulatory medical care is delivered by physicians in group practices. One should not be surprised if some of the same problems of collective decision making that arise in hospitals also carry over to group practices. This idea has been pursued formally by Sloan (1974) who showed that:

> Total scale-adjusted, nonphysician costs rise as the group size increases because the individual physician member bears an increasingly smaller proportion of the financial consequences of the failure to control costs. Where both revenues and costs are shared, the financial return to individual effort falls as group size rises. A negative relationship between effort and group size is predicted when both revenues and costs are shared. (pp. 53-54)

Casual observations tend to support Sloan's predictions. Physicians in multispecialty groups, for example, are more likely to have a formal managerial structure than those in general practice or single specialty groups. Managerial structure may represent an effort to control or, at least, to atten-

FIGURE 7.1: Costs and Gains per Physician of Resource-Saving Policies

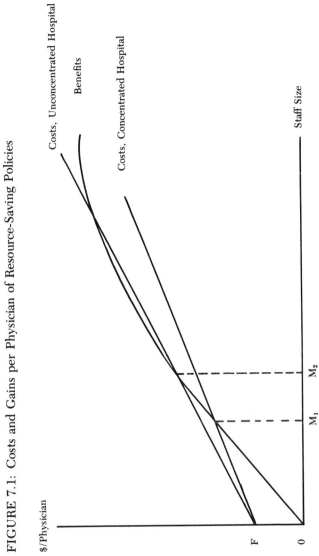

$/Physician

Costs, Unconcentrated Hospital

Benefits

Costs, Concentrated Hospital

F

0

M₁ M₂

Staff Size

FIGURE 7.2: Losses per Physician from Cheating

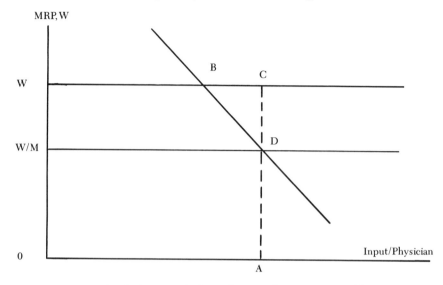

uate noncooperative behavior. And, multispecialty groups are likely to need this formal control mechanism because physicians in one specialty "may be rather poor judges of whether expenditures related to another field will increase group profits" (Sloan 1974).

Formal testing of Sloan's propositions has been delayed by lack of acceptable data. Newhouse (1973) had previously shown that overhead costs per physician visit (all nonphysician costs except costs of ancillary services and space) were higher in practices that shared costs than in those that did not. His sample was limited to the private practices of 20 single specialty groups or solo practitioners in Los Angeles. In addition to the small sample size, the group practices represented 11 different specialties; therefore, Newhouse's single output variable, office visits, may not accurately measure product differences between groups.

Recently, however, data have been collected by Mathematica Policy Research, Inc. specifically to examine the effect of cost- and revenue-sharing arrangements on physicians' incentives (Held and Reinhardt 1979). The Mathematica survey, sponsored by the National Center for Health Services Research, covers 6,400 physicians in almost 1,000 group practices.

The tightness of the link between an individual physician's effort and income was measured on a scale from one to ten. Gross billings per physician, adjusted for other variables, were found to be sensitive to the incentive variable. According to Mathematica's estimate, a change along the scale from one to ten—from very loose to very tight—increased total annual billings per full-time physician by about 12 percent.

Groups also appeared to be "intuitively aware" that the economic incentives to be productive diminish as group size increases. Larger groups were more likely than small groups to base compensation on productivity. And even prepaid groups, which typically use salary or capitation-based compensation, were cognizant of productivity: they were more likely than fee-for-service groups to use explicit productivity guidelines.

The incentive structure of prepaid group practices will most likely be an active research topic for the next several years because, among other reasons, (1) prepaid groups now serve seven million Americans, and (2) hospitalization rates for prepaid group members are about 30 percent below those of comparable populations with conventional health insurance (Veit 1978; Luft 1978). This is surprising, because one expects sicker people and people with greater perceived medical care needs to join prepaid groups selectively. Clearly, either physicians or consumers in prepaid groups must have an incentive to hold down hospitalization rates.

Feldman explored this puzzle in a recent working paper (1979). He hypothesized an objective function for physicians with leisure goods and services per patient as arguments (the latter argument may be interpreted as "quality of care"). If a group uses capitation-based compensation, then adding patients to a physician's list increases his/her income but makes it more difficult to maintain the accepted level of services per patient. As a result, physicians may supply fewer services per patient than are demanded at the money price of zero dollars. Further, this apparent "underservice" may be in the patients' best interest, because otherwise they would use too much care, in the sense that the marginal value of care at zero dollars must certainly be less than the marginal cost of producing care.

This research (which is now purely speculative) links physicians' incentives to a final topic—the market for health insurance. At the present time, 92 percent of hospital expenditures are insured (Newhouse 1978c). Yet, we know almost nothing about the market for insurance, not even whether a rise in the relative price of medical care increases the demand for insurance. To quote Newhouse (1976): "I believe that the effect of such inflation on demand for insurance is highly uncertain at the present time. . . ."

Ignorance may be highly costly in this area, especially if there is a substantial "feedback" effect from medical care prices to health insurance. Then, as M. Feldstein (1973a) has suggested, more complete insurance coverage will lead to higher medical care prices, higher prices to more insurance, and so on in what may be a vicious circle. Although Feldstein does not believe that this is the case, we are amazed that even the plausible existence of instability has not led to much greater interest (or concern) in the market for insurance.

Most private insurance policies are purchased by employers for their employees; the details of the policies often are determined by collective bargaining agreements. Therefore, to understand the market for insurance, three groups require examination: employees, management and labor.

Most economists would agree that the health insurance system created by the interaction of these groups is far from ideal. Insurance "scrambles" the scarcity value of medical care resources as perceived by consumers because they do not face the real price or cost of using resources. The typical health insurance policy pays a high fraction of small and moderate bills but imposes a variety of limits on use and an overall ceiling on benefits (M. Feldstein 1973*b*). Thus, prices are especially scrambled for less-serious health problems which might otherwise be financed on a pay-as-you-go basis. In addition, insurance distorts the choice of location where these problems are treated, because insurance coverage of a given treatment is usually more complete if the patient is hospitalized.

Why have the three involved groups—employees, employers and labor unions—allowed the system to evolve in this way? Employees, clearly, have an incentive to receive compensation in the form of insurance rather than wages because employer payments for insurance are excluded from their taxable income. Likewise, employers have an incentive to give insurance fringe benefits because they are exempt from the employer's share of the social security payroll tax. Yet, neither of these facts explains why the type of insurance purchased should be of such an inferior variety.

An equally puzzling question is why management and labor have so calmly accepted the escalating cost of health insurance benefits. Management, which prides itself on cost-control and employs efficiency experts in its factories, has been remarkably unwilling to do anything about the inefficient structure of health insurance benefits. Labor has refused to budge from its "first-dollar, full-cost" bargaining position even though the high costs of health insurance benefits must surely reduce the wage and benefit gains available elsewhere.

Enthoven (1979) has offered the following explanation of the current impasse:

> Employers have seen health benefits as a way of attracting qualified employees to their company, or as a way of discouraging unionization. Union leaders have seen health benefits as a prize to be won at the bargaining table, and as a way of making the union the worker's benefactor. Both emphasize benefits to the employer or union, and not the use of this medical purchasing power to create a market of competing provider groups in the community. (p.149)

However, as health insurance costs become an albatross around the necks of both employers and unions, the situation may change. Some companies, such as R.J. Reynolds Industries, may go into the health care business on their own, offering company-sponsored prepaid group practices. In other cases management and unions may fight it out, as happened in 1978 when coal mine owners attempted to bargain for reduced health benefits.

These situations offer ideal opportunities for collaborative social science research. What are the factors, for example, which predispose management and labor to accept new approaches to health insurance benefits? What are the social costs and benefits involved? How can innovative insurance policies be marketed successfully? Answers to these questions will require the skills of experts in industrial relations, economics and marketing, to name but three disciplines. The market for health insurance deserves to be and will be an active research field for some time to come.

NOTES

1. Survey data, e.g., the Physician's Practice Cost Surveys conducted by the National Opinion Research Center, indicate that physicians can estimate the percentages of their patients with Medicaid, Medicare, Blue Shield and other health insurance plans. There is no evidence, however, that they perceive the details of an individual patient's private insurance policy, such as deductibles and copayment (and whether or not these provisions have been met at a particular time).
2. If the price of a common input is W dollars per unit and there are M staff physicians, then each physician's share of the input price is W/M. Each physician orders OA units of the input and ultimately pays the full cost of $OWCA$ dollars. The cost of the marginal BC units of the input exceeds its value by BCD dollars.
3. In hospitals with unequal output shares, the position of the benefits function depends on the distribution of power among staff physicians. Physicians with small output shares have the most to gain from resource-saving policies, since they pay the bills for heavy resource-users. The number of potential gainers per loser is greater in concentrated hospitals. If all physicians share in the right to make decisions, then the benefits function shifts upwards in concentrated hospitals.
4. The maximum feasible staff size for resource-saving policies is also larger in concentrated-output hospitals.

REFERENCES

Acton, J. P. 1972. Demand for health care among the urban poor, with special emphasis on the role of time. R-1151-OEO/NYC, October. Santa Monica, CA: The RAND Corporation.

Anderson, R., and Benham, L. 1970. Factors affecting the relationship between family income and medical care consumption. In *Empirical studies in health economics*, ed. H. Klarman, pp. 73-95. Baltimore: The Johns Hopkins University Press.

Auster, R. D., Leveson, I., and Sarachek, D. 1969. The production of health: An exploratory study. *Journal of Human Resources* 4(Fall):411-36.

Becker, G. S. 1976. *The economic approach to human behavior*. Chicago: University of Chicago Press.

Begun, J. W. 1977. *Professionalism and the public interest: Price and quality in optometry*. Unpublished Ph.D. dissertation, University of North Carolina at Chapel Hill.

Blau, P. 1970. A formal theory of differentiation in organizations. *American Sociological Review* 35(April):201-18.

Bowles, S., and Gintis, H. 1975. The problem with human capital theory—A Marxian critique. *American Economic Review* 65(May):74-82.

Clarkson, K. W. 1972. Some implications of property rights in hospital management. *The Journal of Law and Economics* 15(October):363-84.

Davis, K., and Russell, L. The substitution of hospital outpatient care for inpatient care. *Review of Economics and Statistics* 54(May): 109-20.

Enthoven, A. C. 1979. Consumer-centered vs. job-centered health insurance. *Harvard Business Review* (January–February):141-52.

Evans, R. G. 1971. 'Behavioral' cost functions for hospitals. *Canadian Journal of Economics* 4(May):198-215.

Feldman, R., and Begun, J. W. 1978. The effects of advertising: Lessons from optometry. *Journal of Human Resources*, Supplement. 13:247-62.

Feldman, R. 1979. The economic theory of health maintenance organizations. Mimeo, Center for Health Services Research, University of Minnesota.

―――――, and Yoder, S. 1980. A theoretical analysis of GME financing. In *Medical education financing*, ed. J. Hadley. New York: Prodist.

Feldstein, M. S. 1968. *Economic analysis for health service efficiency*. Amsterdam: North-Holland Publishing Co.

―――――. 1971. Hospital cost inflation: A study of nonprofit price dynamics. *American Economic Review* 61(December):853-72.

―――――. 1973a. The welfare loss from excess health insurance. *Journal of Political Economy* 81(March–April):251-80.

―――――. 1973b. The medical economy. *Scientific American* 229(3):151-59.

―――――. 1974. Econometric studies of health economics. In *Frontiers of quantitative economics II*, eds. M. Intriligator and D. Kendrick. Amsterdam: North-Holland Publishing Co.

Feldstein, P. J. 1966. Research on the demand for health services. *Milbank Memorial Fund Quarterly* 44(July):128-65.

―――――, and Carr, W. J. 1964. The effect of income on medical care spending. *Proceedings of social statistics section*. American Statistical Association, pp. 93-105.

Fuchs, V. R. 1972. Health care and the United States economic system: An essay in abnormal physiology. *Milbank Memorial Fund Quarterly* 50(April):211-37.

―――――. 1978. The supply of surgeons and the demand for operations. *The Journal of Human Resources*, Supplement. 13:35-56.

Grossman, M. 1972. On the concept of health capital and the demand for health. *Journal of Political Economy* 80(March–April):223-56.

―――――. 1977. A survey of recent research in health economics. *The American Economist* 21(Spring):14-20.

Held, P. J., and Reinhardt, U., eds. 1979. *Analysis of economic performance in medical group practices*. Princeton, NJ: Mathematica Policy Research.

Lee, L. F. 1977. *Estimation of limited dependent variables models by two stage methods*. Unpublished Ph.D. dissertation, University of Rochester.

_____. 1978. Unionism and wage rates: A simultaneous equations model with qualitative and limited dependent variables. *International Economic Review* 19(June):415-33.

Lipscomb, J., Raskin, I. E., and Eichenholz, J. 1978. The use of marginal cost estimates in hospital cost-containment policy. In *Hospital cost containment: selected notes for future policy*, eds. M. Zubkoff, I. E. Raskin, and R. S. Hanft, pp. 514-37. New York: Prodist.

Luft, H. S. 1978. How do health-maintenance organizations achieve their savings? *The New England Journal of Medicine* 299(June 15):1336-43.

Newhouse, J. P. 1973. Economics of group practice. *The Journal of Human Resources* 8(Winter):37-56.

_____. 1974. A design for a health insurance experiment. *Inquiry* 11(March):5-27.

_____. 1976. Inflation and health insurance. In *Health: A victim or cause of inflation?*, ed. M. Zubkoff. New York: Prodist.

_____. 1978a. Insurance benefits, out-of-pocket payments, and the demand for medical care: A review of the recent literature. *Health and Medical Care Services Review* 1(July–August):2-15.

_____, and Marquis, M. S. 1978b. The norms hypothesis and the demand for medical care. *The Journal of Human Resources*, Supplement. 13:159-82.

_____. 1978c. The erosion of the medical marketplace. R-2141-1-HEW, December. Santa Monica, CA: The RAND Corporation.

Pauly, M. V., and Redisch, M. 1973. The not-for-profit hospital as a physicians' cooperative. *American Economic Review* 63(March):87-100.

Pauly, M. V. 1978. Medical staff characteristics and hospital costs. *The Journal of Human Resources*, Supplement. 13:77-111.

Pechman, J. A., and Timpane, P. M., eds. 1975. *Work incentives and income guarantees*. Washington, D.C.: The Brookings Institution.

Phelps, C., Newhouse, J. 1972. Coinsurance and the demand for medical services. R-964-OEO, May. Santa Monica, CA: The RAND Corporation.

Rafferty, J. A. 1971. Patterns of hospital use: An analysis of short-run variations. *Journal of Political Economy* 79(January–February):154-65.

Reinhardt, U. 1972. A production function for physician services. *Review of Economics and Statistics* 54(February):55-66.

Rivlin, A. M. 1974. How can experiments be more useful. *American Economic Review* 64(May):346-54.

Rosenthal, G. 1970. Price elasticity of demand for short-term general hospital services. In *Empirical studies in health economics*, ed. H. Klarman, pp. 101-17. Baltimore, MD: The Johns Hopkins University Press.

Rosett, R., and Huang, L. 1973. The effect of health insurance on the demand for medical care. *Journal of Political Economy* 81(March–April):281-305.

Scherer, F. M. 1971. *Industrial market structure and economic performance*. Chicago: Rand McNally & Company.

Sloan, F. A. 1974. Effects of incentives on physician performance. In *Health manpower and productivity*, ed. J. Rafferty. Lexington, MA: Lexington Books.

————, and Feldman, R. 1978. Competition among physicians. In *Competition in the health care sector: Past, present, and future*, ed. W. Greenberg. Germantown, MD: Aspen Systems Corporation.

Thaler, R., and Rosen, S. 1976. The value of saving a life: Evidence from the labor market. In *Household production and consumption*, ed. N. E. Terleckyj. New York: Columbia University Press.

Thompson, J. D. 1967. *Organizations in action*. New York: McGraw-Hill Book Company.

Veit, H. R. 1978. The HMO alternative. Office of Health Maintenance Organizations, DHEW. *Focus* 1(December):2.

Eight

Health Services Research: A Cross-Disciplinary Retrospective

THOMAS CHOI and JAY N. GREENBERG

This chapter is divided into three major segments: (1) a summary and comparison of the previous chapters in terms of their theoretical frameworks, assumptions and contributions to health services research; (2) a discussion of areas of potential interlinkages among the several perspectives in health services research with a particular emphasis on research methodology; and (3) some perceptions on the setting of health services research and the potential for cross-disciplinary cooperation.

It should be said as a caveat that this chapter is not, and cannot be, the final arbiter of interdisciplinary research in health. However, this chapter will, in part, highlight opportunities, the need for and barriers of interdisciplinary cooperation as an extension of what has been alluded to in various ways by the chapter authors.

SUMMARY

In this section we will organize thoughts abstracted from each chapter for comparative analysis.

THEORETICAL FRAMEWORKS

Table 8.1 summarizes selected information provided by the authors regarding each perspective to provide a clear view of the different perspectives. However, two problems appear common to summaries of this type: (1) summaries are grossly simplified versions and therefore do not do justice to the complete text; and (2) because subject matter and writing styles differ, the summaries of each perspective are not always directly comparable. The goal is to highlight what the authors have to say (and how they say it) rather than to homogenize style and content into a procrustean mold for the expediency of greater uniformity in reporting.

As table 8.1 shows, under the theoretical framework column, the theoretical thrust of sociology is its emphasis on constraints imposed by elements external to the individual. This implies that individual attitude and behavior

TABLE 8.1: Health Services Research by Selected Perspectives

	Theoretical Framework	Assumptions	Contributions to Health Services Research
Sociology	1. Structural-functional: social facts paradigm 2. Conflict: social definition paradigm 3. Symbolic interaction: social behavior paradigm	1. Presence of social structure, patterned behavior 2. Study of collectivities preferred 3. Structural constraints on behavior	1. Knowledge about implementation of policies 2. Interorganizational relationships used to illuminate organizational transactions 3. Development of independent variables to explain health-related attitudes and behavior
Political Science	1. Competing and varied 2. No political science theory of health	1. Inequality exists 2. Nature of politics governed by redistributive, regulatory, distributive system	1. How diverse elements affect policy and change
Jurisprudence	1. No clear theory 2. Group interests	1. Precedents are important. 2. Medical transactions are like contracts.	1. Knowledge about rule making and policy making 2. Knowledge about social change
Epidemiology	1. Biological 2. Social	1. Health status is measurable. 2. Causes of health status change are measurable.	1. Knowledge about health status of population groups 2. Knowledge about detecting disease in populations
Demography	1. Social demography 2. Population dynamics 3. Technological demography	1. Age, sex, marital status, and household composition have consequences. 2. Individual and population may be located through time and space.	1. Improve knowledge regarding survey research methods. 2. Improve health planning. 3. Explain population differentials.
Economics	1. Behavioral science of scarcity	1. Maximize gains subject to constraint.	1. Estimation of production functions 2. Econometric techniques 3. Estimation of demand curves 4. Description of market conditions

are consequences of the environment. Given this framework, studies such as those related to physician behavior or patient behavior are usually conducted along the theme of how the environment constrains action. The environment for the individual may include, but is not limited to, the hospital, home or general social context. The sociological framework, therefore, may be applicable to a variety of settings, health services being only one such area. This perspective emphasizes the sociology *in* health services vis-à-vis the sociology *of* health services.[1]

Similarly, political scientists argue from the perspective that there are many paradigms which can explain health issues, and these paradigms are competing and varied in substance. Therefore, no overarching political science theory exists, much less a single theory of health.

In contrast, economics operates from a more central underlying theme— that scarce resources affect a variety of societal actions. On the other hand, epidemiologists and demographers borrow from other disciplines, but the nature of their inquiry and their products bears the unique characteristics of their own perspectives. Finally, jurisprudence claims no clear theory of its own, but rather is preoccupied with the unraveling of the process of rule making and policy making, which either leads to or formalizes social change.

ASSUMPTIONS OF THE PERSPECTIVES

Shortell accurately describes those assumptions of sociology which have particular relevance to health services research. In essence, these assumptions underscore the importance of social and organizational structure (as a form of behavioral constraint) over individual will and motivation. Indeed, if health services research may be described in an overly simplified fashion as research which examines the organization of health services and the activities related to the organization of such services, then sociology emphasizes the first part of the research domain. Sociology emphasizes the structure and organization of health services delivery and the inherent constraints which influence all transactions in the health arena.

Political science operates from the assumption that inequality exists within society. Who gets health care differs quantitatively and qualitatively across population groups. The reasons for these differences are bases of political science inquiry. It is the nature of the political system which impacts on who gets care, what type of care, and why. And the nature of politics is governed by whether policies are redistributive, regulatory or distributive.

Jurisprudence takes the view that the content of the issue, be it health or otherwise, is often subjugated in importance to the nature and content of legal precedents—that courts are precedent-oriented rather than just issue-oriented. In other ways, jurisprudence resembles other perspectives in that there is no particular arena called the jurisprudence of health. All medical transactions are treated like other contractual transactions, i.e., the rules and regulations which govern the formalization and execution of contracts apply to health just as they do to other arenas. In sum, the contractual approach attempts to be content-free. Thus, jurists examine health transactions through the contracts model.

Despite the fact that epidemiology and demography borrow heavily from other sciences, theoretical assumptions of epidemiologic and demographic perspectives are strictly their own. Epidemiologists assume that health status is an identifiable and measurable outcome and that the causes of changes in health status are similarly measurable using epidemiologic techniques.

Demography, as stated by Verbrugge, borrows heavily from sociology, psychology, economics and the biological sciences. Like epidemiologists, demographers have established their own focuses, ways of asking pertinent questions, and ways of analyzing data. Demographers assume the importance of characteristics such as age, sex, marital status and household composition in affecting a number of variables related to health. Furthermore, demographers work from the assumption that time and place in regard to persons or populations have systematic consequences on health demands and planning.

Aside from crediting the social and biological sciences for their theoretical contributions, epidemiologists and demographers ask investigative questions unique to their perspectives but couched in the framework of other sciences. Epidemiology and demography are further intertwined by common concerns: epidemiologists are concerned with the health status of population groups, and population groups, of course, are the primary concern of demographers.

The underlying assumption of economics is, namely, that the maximization of gains, subject to constraints, is applicable to health as to other areas. For consumers, what is being maximized is assumed to be utility or personal preferences; for profit-oriented organizations, what is being maximized is assumed to be income; and for nonprofit organizations, what is being maximized is still debated among economists. As Feldman points out, collaborative research on nonprofit organizations may be particularly fruitful in light of this uncertainty.

RELEVANCE OF THE PERSPECTIVES (CONTRIBUTIONS)

The relevance of the various perspectives may be described in three areas: (1) impact on policy, (2) impact on methodology and (3) impact on theory particular to one's perspective.

Impact on Policy

All six approaches in this book implicitly or explicitly state the relevance of their perspectives in terms of contributions to policy formulation, implementation or analysis. While the chapters on epidemiology and demography do not specifically mention contributions to policy matters, the influence of the two fields on policy is undeniable. Verbrugge notes, for example, that demographers' contributions have helped planners directly to improve health care. Moreover, at a minimum, demography may be seen to have an indirect impact on health policy formulation. Epidemiologists claim that "an efficient, cost-effective, well-organized and politically popular health service program should also be well-founded on epidemiologic principles and be shown to have a favorable impact on the health status of the population" (Ibrahim, Chapter Five). Thus, epidemiology cannot be divorced from health policy.

Impact on Methodology

While policy concern is clearly germane to all six perspectives and therefore a means of common dialogue, one area that is consistently emphasized and updated in health services research is methodology. Recent achievement in research methods in health services research cannot be attributed to any single one of the six perspectives since health issues are sufficiently complex that no perspective can justifiably claim credit as the sole contributor to methodological breakthroughs. Instead, what accomplishments there have been (and what gaps there still exist in methods) are consequences of interdisciplinary health services researchers.

A common need of all six perspectives is the development of a clear measure or of a set of clear measures of health status. Such a measure or set of measures will provide a gauge on health status and/or health outcome of specific interventions. From a research point of view, health status is useful as both an independent as well as a dependent variable. While measurement skills exist in various ways and levels across disciplines, such skills have the greatest impact if used in a cross-disciplinary fashion so as to ensure the feasibility of the measure(s) for use in the broadest sense.

Some of the best health status measures of recent vintage bear this type of interdisciplinary approach (Ware et al. 1980). These measures are disease-specific and tested for reliability and validity. The contribution to methods of such work is in empirically operationalizing a subject's level of illness severity. The potential application of these methods assists in identifying not only individual illness severity but also aggregates illness severity and the levels of severity treated by a particular health care facility. Health status measures, once quantified, are potentially useful in helping to establish treatment standards, i.e., to assure quality of care, and cost standards for a similar level of illness severity. This is not unlike recent developments in classifying case mix of patients for assessing length-of-stay and hospital cost (Fetter et al. 1980).

Another recent contribution to methods is in computer modeling of physicians decision-making processes. Gustafson et al. (1976; 1978) have done a variety of work in this area in modeling the process of how physicians judge patient illness severity. His work is further replicated and extended elsewhere (Choi et al. 1981).

Simulation of physician decision-making processes is particularly important in circumstances where physician judgment is called for but where physician presence is not always feasible. Take for example an emergency situation where paramedics and an advanced life support unit are summoned. In the best of all circumstances, a physician would be present to diagnose the level of patient severity and administer corresponding treatment. Since a physician's presence is not likely under these circumstances, the ability to simulate physician judgment in order to assess accurately the patient's condition becomes critically important. Research in this area of simulation by means of severity scales has made important strides and a definite contribution to methodology (Champion and Sacco 1976; Brekke et al. 1981).

Another important contribution of health services research to methods is in the realm of clinical decision analysis.[2] This is an area which has only recently attained its proper recognition and no doubt is an area that will receive far greater attention.

Clinical decision analysis systematically brings a variety of information to bear on whether treatment should be administered to a particular patient or set of patients, given a particular set of health problems.

Modeling physician decision-making processes takes into account physician intuition, physician experience, patient characteristics, financial cost information, and probability of favorable health outcome. Such models serve as an important aid in decision making. Many applications, from cost-effectiveness assessments to educating physicians in formalized thinking, are yet to be fully realized.

Clinical decision analysis provides a method critical to projecting the optimal odds on the side of proper diagnoses, treatment and recovery. Recent publications on the subject amplify the usefulness of clinical decision analysis and show promise of wider acceptance in time. Again, clinical decision analysis is an area in which various disciplines and perspectives converge, e.g., statistics, theory, health services administration, medicine, epidemiology, economics, political science, psychology and sociology. (For further reading, consult Weinstein and Fineberg 1980; McNeil et al. 1978; Bunker et al. 1977; and Elstein et al. 1978.)

Impact on Theory

In the arena of health services research, research activities designed to resolve problems have spawned some important by-products—namely contributions to disciplinary and theoretical concerns—which in turn show promise in assisting future problem solving.

In health economics,[3] for example, significant contributions have been made toward the estimation and interpretation of consumer demand curves. Acton (1972; 1975) showed that nonprice variables, such as waiting time in a physician's office, may be important determinants of demand. Arrow (1963) earlier emphasized the importance of the physician, in his role as patients' agent, in determining the position of the demand curve. In subsequent studies researchers have attempted to quantify the physician's influence, but Sloan and Feldman (1978) have emphasized the difficulty of separating the demand-generating power of physicians from indirect effects, e.g., shorter waiting times in areas with high physician density. This difficulty should be recognized in all professional services over which providers have better information than consumers.

Other economists have made significant contributions to the problem of measuring quality differences in demand studies. Although the relevant theory was developed elsewhere (Becker and Lewis 1973; Rosen 1974), the problem of quality variation is especially pronounced in health care. Health care services, unlike electric power and corn (two subjects of classic demand analyses), are inherently heterogeneous. Goldman and Grossman (1978), Feldman (1979), and Begun and Feldman (1981) have proposed essentially similar techniques to control for product heterogeneity by the relation between price and product characteristics. An interesting offshoot of the same theory was the Thaler and Rosen (1976) paper cited in Chapter Seven that measured wage differentials on risky jobs to estimate the willingness to pay for lifesaving.

A final contribution of health economics to demand studies has been in the measurement of price and insurance variables. Newhouse and Phelps (1974) and Newhouse, Phelps and Marquis (1979) have pointed out the pitfalls of using incorrect or improperly measured variables. Keeler, Newhouse and Phelps (1977) investigated the implications of deductibles in insurance policies and showed that there is an upper range for optimal deductibles.

There is a close link between these studies and the second major area to which health economics has contributed: the analysis of insurance markets. Arrow (1963; 1965), who explored the theory of riskbearing, showed how it is optimal for a risk-averse consumer to have complete indemnity insurance against all risks, provided that policies can be purchased at fair advantage and with no administrative charges. However, Pauly (1968) produced a counter-example: complete insurance may not be desirable when the presence of insurance affects consumers' behavior (this phenomenon is called "moral hazard" in the insurance literature). Pauly's challenge defined a research agenda that was soon fulfilled in two major papers by M. Feldstein (1971; 1973). In the first, Feldstein showed that insurance is a significant contributor to hospital inflation; in the second, he measured the welfare cost of excess health insurance to the American economy. Feldstein's admonition can be applied to other insurance markets where moral hazard is present (federal flood insurance, for example).

A third major contribution of health economics has been to the theory of nonprofit organizations. This area has already been discussed in some detail in Chapter Seven, but major papers by Newhouse (1970), M. Feldstein (1979), and Pauly and Redisch (1973) on the objectives of nonprofit hospitals immediately come to mind.

A fourth and final contribution of health economics has been to advance knowledge of the behavior of regulated industries. The health care industry is heavily regulated by providers of services and the government. Economists have examined the consequences of both types of regulation. The study of provider regulation owes much to a classic paper by Kessel (1970), which claimed that the American Medical Association is an entry-limiting cartel. In the same vein, Benham (1972) and Feldman and Begun (1978; 1980) showed that consumers pay higher prices as a consequence of professional control.

Among the numerous studies of government regulation, Sloan and Steinwald (1980*a*; 1980*b*) have recently examined the effects of regulations on hospital costs and input use. Among other findings they conclude that prospective reimbursement of hospitals has had, at best, a small negative effect on costs and resource use. Of general interest to economists, they find that regulated enterprises anticipate the threat of regulation and thereby are able to escape their effects.

Taking the sociology of health as another example, information regarding determinants of physician performance provided important clues to the power of the organization in shaping physician behavior (Rhee 1976; Scott et al. 1976, 1979; Palmer and Reilly 1979). Beliefs and attitudes impact upon another form of behavior—namely, patient compliance (Hershey et al. 1980). Such research, however, provides strong bases to discourage any cavalier assumptions about direct and logical association between attitudes and behavior. Human behavior also is strongly shaped by external forces, beyond personal beliefs. The sociology of health literature provides evidence that forces such as environment and norms are far more persuasive in shaping behavior than are the internal attitudes of individuals.

Similar analogies concerning contributions to theory through applied health services research may be drawn in political science. For example, Banfield (1961) documented how micropolitics can thwart important outcomes, as in the case of circumventing the construction of a clearly needed hospital in Chicago. Because jurisprudence, demography and epidemiology are more "applied-oriented" (see section entitled "Application Bent"), byproducts from work done within these perspectives may not have as strong a theoretical impact. Nonetheless, discoveries within these perspectives have generalizability or transportability to other arenas. In jurisprudence, studies about emergency rooms and Hill-Burton laws have strong effects on regulations in general. Epidemiological methods of isolating problem areas contribute also to crime-solving techniques by increasing the odds of isolating the perpetrator(s) of crime. Demography, which identifies population trends in relation to health care needs (e.g., nursing homes), also contributes information necessary to social security agencies, economic forecasters, and training programs for health care providers.

CROSS-DISCIPLINARY PERSPECTIVE

The six perspectives can be conceptually grouped in several ways, their proximity varies according to different schemes. Three such conceptual schemes are identified: (1) theoretical eclecticism, or the extent to which each of the six perspectives is composed of a mixture of perspectives; (2) application bent, or the extent to which the perspective itself is oriented toward problem solving; and (3) paradigm vs. methods orientation, or the extent to which the thrust of the perspective is paradigm- or research methodology-based.

THEORETICAL ECLECTICISM

Sociology, political science and economics are three traditional branches of social sciences. While there are many subbranches of knowledge within each of the three disciplines, all three originate as self-sufficient domains. While this description is applicable also to jurisprudence, jurisprudence differs in that it is eclectic, encompassing many facets of social life such as economics and politics. Similarly, epidemiologists and demographers openly acknowledge the eclecticism of their respective perspectives.

Many principles of epidemiology and demography are based on substance borrowed from other perspectives, as acknowledged in Chapters Five and Six. Sociology, political science and economics share similar properties as self-encompassing domains, whereas jurisprudence, epidemiology and demography are more openly affected by changes in other disciplines. One implication of the eclectic perspectives, with their tradition of incorporating concepts from other disciplines, is that they perhaps facilitate working across disciplines.

APPLICATION BENT

Some perspectives more than others are geared toward application[4]—the directness with which a particular perspective engages in problem-solving actions. "Directness" refers to the problem-solution orientation of precepts within a given perspective. Some disciplines are action-, decision- or problem-oriented, at least relative to others.

Jurisprudence is the most application-oriented of the six perspectives. Jurisprudence is instrumental in the court actions and rule making which govern the conduct of health-related procedures and implementation. Demography and epidemiology are oriented toward identifying population trends, such as the differentiation of birth rates or risk factors within specific groups, and gravitate toward problem isolation and resolution. Compared to jurisprudence, demography and epidemiology as a group, the disciplines of economics, sociology and political science tend toward the more traditional academic emphasis in conveying concepts, theories and generalizations. The difference between these traditional academic disciplines and the more applied perspectives is relative, not absolute. Economics, sociology and political science are theoretically oriented and, as such, are relatively removed from direct problem solving. Thus, they provide a methodology for framing issues which may bear upon ultimate problem resolution, but their orientation is in the perpetuation and testing of scientific knowledge rather than in problem resolution per se.

PARADIGM AND METHODS CONTINUUM

The six perspectives may also be distinguished by another criterion—namely, the degree to which the perspectives are paradigm- or research method-oriented. Paradigm[5] orientation refers to the amount of attention paid to (1) the traditional theories, concepts and instrumentation of a particular school of thought, and (2) the extent of effort expended to achieve consistency among the abstract or underlying concepts used in a traditional theory and the empirical variables selected to represent them. Sociology and political science tend to be more paradigm-oriented than the other perspectives; i.e., concepts, theories and measurements are used to maintain or bring continuity to a tradition or context. In sociology a great deal of emphasis is placed on (1) how one's research does or does not reflect the tradition of a major theory, and (2) to what extent selected research variables actually achieve construct validity. For example, a significant amount of energy is devoted to validating concepts such as social class, religiosity and self-esteem which are almost never measured apart from a particular theoretical context.

The degree of such emphasis differs in economics, demography and epidemiology. Economics (usage here refers primarily to microeconomics) serves to illustrate the point: although the discipline is well grounded in theory, the actual research conducted does not pay special homage to or seek security in any particular theory or theorist. Moreover, the variables used in research do not generally undergo any extensive validation to ensure congruence between the variables selected to estimate the underlying constructs and the underlying constructs themselves. In fact, there exists a general implicit modus operandi in economics—that face validity of data suffices. Concomitantly, economics gravitates toward the use of variables which are inherently the least cumbersome to quantify, without particular regard to the theoretical context into which these variables may or may not fit.

This is not to imply a lack of concern with measurement errors on the part of the economics discipline; in fact, some of the most important contributions to measurement error estimation may be found in economics literature. However, the types of measurement error to which economists usually address themselves—namely, reliability errors—are very different from errors in validity. The former deals with the consistency of variables used to estimate the underlying construct, and the latter deals with the equivalence of variables used relative to the underlying construct.

As stated previously, economics has a particular affinity toward variables which lend themselves readily to quantification. Economics, demography and epidemiology share a preference for variables which can be straightforwardly operationalized. In demography and epidemiology, the nature of the subject matter coincides well with such a preference because concepts such as birth rates, population shifts and degree of risk are inherently operationalized. Economics is not paradigm-grounded in the sense that variables are not expected to be strictly reflective of tradition or of the professed underlying construct. Thus, being paradigm-free, typical economics variables are inherently quantifiable. Therefore, the distance between theory and data is much shorter than in sociology and political science.

DISTANCE BETWEEN THEORY AND DATA[6]

In health services research, all social sciences employ certain methodological approaches in their investigative processes. However, the distance between theory and data, or operational gaps, is greater or of greater concern in some social sciences than in others. This relative distance between theory and data not only reflects the orientation of the perspectives (e.g., paradigm-dominant vs. paradigm-free), but also impacts upon the development of the various perspectives. In sociology, for example, development tends primarily toward the extension and tests of paradigms, with methods playing a supportive, though systematic and substantial, role. Conversely, economics underscores the importance of analytical methods (such as regression analysis) with less emphasis on the goodness of fit between the empirical model and the theoretical base.

In sociology, as in political science, the preponderance of the discipline is in the generation and extension of paradigms that are generally complex and not easily operationalized. Concepts such as hospital structure, systems, and organizational subculture pose particular difficulties to the researcher in closing the gap between concepts and data. Among sociologists, for example, a great deal of effort goes into measurement reliability and validity to ensure that conceptual models and empirical systems are isomorphic.

In economics, demography and epidemiology, the concepts used (relative to those used in sociology, jurisprudence and political science), are often expressed and expressable in parsimonious mathematical terms. Thus, empirical specification (operationalization) for economists, demographers and epidemiologists is an inherent part of the study of basic concepts, and their theories tend to be much closer to the data by virtue of their preference and the nature of their subject matter. Some overly simplified examples here might illustrate the point: concepts such as sick days, age cohort, staff size, infant mortality and odds ratio imply operations inherent in these variables, and, therefore, language is less likely to be divided into conceptual and empirical components.

It is not by accident that the chapters on economics, demography and epidemiology appear to be relatively more methodological than the others. Even though economists use abstract concepts such as utility to derive certain results, however, they generally do not dwell on these abstract concepts to the point of validating the existence and measurement of such constructs. Abstract concepts are simply assumed to exist, and the validity of the assumptions as a rule is not tested. Variables and data used to reflect these underlying constructs are relegated to certain types of variables which meet the criteria of accessibility and quantifiability.

The perception of methods-orientation is generally reinforced by the choice of emphasis by the practitioners of the respective perspectives. Economists start with certain abstract constructs but quickly move on to dealing with the empirical relationships through the use of clearly quantified variables. To what extent these variables are valid indications of the underlying construct is not the focus of the economist's orientation.

In addition to the selection of clearly quantifiable variables, the use of analytical methods such as multiple regression further underscores the methods-orientation of economics. The analytic relationships between straightforward quantifiable variables become the central concern of economics, and it is partly this emphasis on the part of economists that reinforces the impression of methods-orientation in contrast to paradigm-orientation. Despite a lack of preoccupation with the soundness of the measurement of the variables, economists do not seem overly concerned with this impression. To use a simple analogy, they appear more interested in chemical compounds and in the process of their formation rather than in the proper identification of the elements which form the compound.

In contrast, sociologists and political scientists see methodology as a way of testing the soundness of paradigms (or the proper identification of elements, to extend the analogy). This puts method in a particular perspective, that it is an aid to substantiating ideas. However, method has a more basic impact in sociology and political science—it often constrains and shapes theoretical thinking. Moreover, method (and resulting operation) is neither necessarily nor automatically defined in the paradigms even though it is clearly an inherent part of the sociological and political science disciplines.

While the subject matter of economics, demography and epidemiology is inherently more methodological than that of other fields, this bent appears to constrain the disciplines somewhat from either expanding into theoretical issues that are not straightforwardly measurable or from dealing with problems posed by abstract concepts. Because the traditions of these perspectives seem to argue against expansion into verification of abstract concepts, the contributions of these disciplines are often made in the area of analysis rather than in the creation of theoretical concepts and the measurement of variables.

In paradigm-dominant perspectives, the interest in and emphasis on methodology is by no means slighted, just as the converse is true of method-dominant perspectives. A significant portion of sociological literature concentrates on methodological concerns such as structural equations, path analysis, factor analysis, and smallest-space analysis. However, methodology is only one of several areas of concentration in sociology. Chapter Two reinforces the general impression that sociology is a discipline rich in concepts about activities in society. However, the chapter does not venture to discuss how these concepts are measured and used in analysis because such measurement and analysis are regarded as but several of many topics of concern to sociologists.

In the pursuit of measurement reliability and validity, sociologists have borrowed heavily from psychometricians (e.g., Cronbach 1951; Lord and Novick 1968). Sociologists emphasize techniques of multiple regression as applied to sociological variables just as economists emphasize the use of econometrics. Regressing patient compliance on variables such as patient education level, health beliefs, social class, and locus of control serves as an example. The complexity of the variables requires the amalgamation of psychometric techniques (measuring concepts and assessing the reliability and validity of measurement) with economists' (especially econometricians') multiple linear regression techniques. A number of articles combine these techniques and provide excellent examples of such amalgamation (Jacobson and Lalu 1974; Blalock 1968; Costner 1971). This promotion of interplay between methodological techniques borrowed from psychometrics and econometrics is an important methodological contribution of sociology. More importantly, perhaps, the feasibility of connecting the two sets of techniques opened the door for amalgamation of concepts used in different disciplines.

POTENTIAL COOPERATIVE VENTURES

The assertion that sociology and political science are similar is not likely to be challenged as would be a claim that the boundaries between sociology and economics are indistinct. We have portrayed sociology as paradigm-dominant and economics as paradigm-free. Concomitantly, we have indicated that economics gravitates toward methodology. These differences need not be construed to mean that a methodological or theoretical chasm exists between paradigm-dominant and paradigm-free perspectives. Recent approaches in both sociology and economics, for example, show a blending of disciplinary boundaries. Harrison C. White (see Leinhardt 1981) writes from a sociological perspective on a topic traditionally reserved to economists: markets, real markets dealing with transactions for goods or services. White reviews markets as a sociological phenomenon. Editor Leinhardt commented on White's paper:

> White views markets as a structured system of roles. Differentiated and distinct firms or producers are linked together through communication ties. By virtue of this communication, firms are able to observe each other's production and revenue behavior. Adjustments result from these observations, a market becomes institutionalized as firms search for optimal niches, and the distribution of market shares equilibrates. White argues that neoclassical economic theory has important failures, including the fact that it cannot specify market boundaries or discriminate a producer's market from an entire industrial economy. These failures can be overcome, however, when markets are understood to be demonstrable social structures built by the interlocking joint perceptions and decisions of actors much as the social structure of affect in a group is a consequence of the interlocking affective choices of the members. White's approach is behavioral and concrete; it is based on the observable, tangible tension between buyers and sellers setting the terms of trade. His approach is in direct contrast to the emphasis on intangible cogitation of utility by producers and consumers that has motivated economic theorists. As a consequence of his focus on tangible interactions, White is able to lay out an eminently sociological research program, one extending traditional sociological field research methods to the study of economic markets. (1981, pp.xi-xii)

Manski (1981), an economist, gives a contrasting view of how contemporary economic techniques of modeling, estimation and forecasting can have utility in sociology. Taken together, the works of White and Manski call for new joint undertakings between sociology and economics. White's paper shows how traditional economics could be understood better by the application of sociological principles, and Manski's paper shows the converse. Yet the impact of both articles is not so much a divergence of scholarly opinions as a convergence of conclusions that sociology and economics stand much to gain from one another, both theoretically and methodologically, through cooperative efforts.

Chapter Seven emphasizes several potential areas for collaboration among various social science perspectives. One major area for possible cooperation has not yet been mentioned: social scientists who are adept at data collection could work with economists to obtain reliable and valid data needed by economists. Economists, as Feldman indicated, rarely collect primary data of their own. Unfortunately, some of the reasons given for not doing so are not entirely convincing in light of the equally difficult circumstances faced by other social scientists, primarily sociologists, psychologists and political scientists, in collecting their own data.

The issue of data collection clearly goes beyond the mechanical act of information solicitation. Indeed, it is an integral part of measurement—one which links the conceptual and the empirical levels. Data primarily collected by others (i.e., secondary data) may not be testable by Sloan's theory (see page 174), but the more fundamental problem is the inability to integrate concepts and data systematically.

Collaboration between economists and social scientists adept at data collection could simply facilitate the gathering of data needed by both. No doubt collaboration in data collection has meaning at the theoretical and analytical levels also. Use of secondary data not only compromises comprehensive analysis but severely handicaps any systematic tests of theory. The conclusions reached by a joint research endeavor would therefore not be limited to fragmented information or piecemeal results. Such collaboration will also make possible the execution of projects of the type so clearly suggested by Feldman (see pages 170-79).

HEALTH SERVICES RESEARCH SETTING: POTENTIAL FOR CROSS-DISCIPLINARY COOPERATION

This final section returns to and extends a pivotal point raised in the first chapter. Chapter One suggests that if the primary goal of health services research is the development of instrumental knowledge, then the use of social science methods of inquiry may not be optimal. Methods of social science inquiry are geared to theory development rather than problem solving.

Training health services researchers for applied research and problem solving holds a certain appeal. Health services researchers with such training ideally would allow no other agendas (e.g., generating theory, publishing in a discipline-based journal) to compete with their primary goal—to produce results of direct utility to the client.[7] Training such a group of researchers is an appealing but elusive goal because of the number of technical and social factors that confound a strict problem-solving orientation in health services research.

TECHNICAL FACTORS

First, if health services researchers restrict themselves to resolving problems for specific clients and do not concern themselves with theory generating, then ultimately the problem-solving process will be based on techniques not easily generalized from one situation to another. Techniques are then derived from scratch for each problem to be solved, and each assignment is novel in that the role of research is not to accumulate evidence nor to extract and generate principles and theories. In the long-run, health services research will be inefficient and costly to the client for lack of history and tradition.

Second, it is unlikely that anyone could teach the conduct of health services research in a theoretical vacuum. Just as engineering cannot be taught without a grounding in physics, research problems in health services and other arenas must be framed in some general context. Political scientists, for example, may view the 1965 passage of the Medicare bill as a consequence of compromises among significant political parties. Sociologists may see the same event in terms of the general constraints of the larger social fabric, forging and forcing an inevitable solution. Economists may see the bill as a consequence of economic feasibility. An atheoretical researcher may have no real context within which to explain the phenomenon or to conduct research. It is important to underscore that today's applied research is made possible by the basic, disciplinary research foundations of yesterday, and that curtailing disciplinary research today may be the death knell for health services research of tomorrow.

Finally, the quality of research must be judged against some collective norm or standard that reflects disciplinary emphases of peers. Peer judgment removes from the client some of the burden of judging the soundness of analyses and corresponding recommendations. On the other hand, research efficiency can be adversely affected if research is conducted primarily to satisfy peer judgment criteria rather than to meet clients' needs. It is in relation to this potential problem that our call for atheoretical research makes the most sense to clients. Unfortunately, while peer judgment of research quality has its attendant flaws, there is as yet no better solution.

SOCIAL FACTORS: RELATIONSHIP OF HEALTH
SERVICES RESEARCHERS AND SOCIAL SCIENTISTS

For now and the foreseeable future, health services researchers constitute a subset of the larger domain of social scientists in the sense that all scientists grapple ultimately with theoretical principles. Health services researchers are linked with social scientists by two commonalities: (1) a common reference group of scientists in their individual disciplines, and (2) the professional standards set by these groups. But to the extent that health services researchers are trained under and share the goals of social science disciplines, their professional effectiveness is largely determined by the reference group or standards promulgated therein.

Chapter One describes a major difference between health services research and social science: health services research may be predominantly instrumental in nature whereas academic social science gravitates toward work that may or may not be instrumental. Another important difference, covered earlier in this chapter, involves the desirability of interdisciplinary work among health services researchers vis-à-vis academic social scientists. Health services researchers are accordingly judged by at least two additional sets of performance criteria: (1) the ability to meet the needs of an external set of clients and (2) the ability to work with other health services researchers from different disciplines and backgrounds.

Given the scope of most health issues, the satisfaction of client needs often requires the collective contribution of health services researchers from several disciplines. Client support is important because it is from clients that researchers often obtain funding. Typical clients may be state legislatures; policy makers at different levels and settings; medical personnel, including physicians, nurses, administrators and public officials; funders, both local and national; and major corporations and businesses.

CLIENT IMPACT ON THE HEALTH SERVICES RESEARCH SETTING

The addition of client consideration in health services research and the competing demands (at least in terms of time) between a client's needs and those of the differing reference groups create a work setting that is potentially both counterproductive and challenging to researchers.

The literature is replete with examples of how organizational structure affects performance (Rhee 1976; Scott et al. 1979). The health services researchers' work structure has to be sufficiently fluid to capture new resources at any given moment. The impact of such a structure may preclude systematic and sustained research projects.

In fact, to health services researchers, clients' needs frequently take precedence because of their real-world deadlines and political timing. Indeed, the demands of clients and those of professional reference groups are frequently at odds. Clients want immediate answers to specific problems, while the professional reference groups want methodical analyses that provide long-term, generalizable conclusions. To the extent that the availability of unconditional research funds is decreasing, the competition for research time between clients' needs and disciplinary goals will become increasingly pronounced. Satisfying one group (clients or reference group) may often mean denying (or at least delaying) the satisfaction of the other.

This kind of work environment potentially precludes a proactive approach to research as the call upon health services researchers by clients traditionally has been random, unpredictable and usually in haste as needs arise. The professional response of health services researchers therefore becomes reactive in nature. Such reactivity may hinder, if not actually preclude, the methodical nurturing across disciplines. The likelihood of mutual understanding and symbiotic cooperation is potentially relegated to a less important status.

Because the survival of health services researchers is largely dependent upon client support, the work structure is arranged in such a way as to maximize the likelihood of meeting client needs. This structure primarily involves the formation of organizational coalitions and liaisons between clients and research centers. Activities of health services research are therefore more likely to be dictated by the nature of these coalitions rather than by indigenously prescribed long-term goals.

The structure of the work setting is, therefore, by definition highly interorganizational in nature. In essence, the nature of research activities is tied to the stability of various coalitions, and the slightest fluctuation in a coalition between clients and researchers affects the activities of the research organization. The open-systems nature of the research organization renders health services researchers vulnerable to external changes.

These interorganizational relationships are not formed overnight or by sheer coincidence. Substantial energy is directed toward maintaining rapport with clients, wherein lies an inherent irony: the tension between the desire to satisfy clients on one hand and to meet professional standards on the other. In other words, forming coalitions with clients can easily become an end in itself rather than a means to the end of doing sound research. It is, in part, the open-systems nature of research organizations which convolutes the ends and the means. The activities of research are decidedly not proactive. The goals of health services research are very likely defined by the moment, according to the immediate needs of specific clients, rather than by long-term strategy geared to projected needs in the health services arena.

To the extent that the external support system changes, the internal organization of research changes concomitantly to adapt itself to the support environment. The internal research organization is, therefore, resource-dependent upon the external support system and thus not well insulated from external forces. To survive, i.e., to obtain external resources, health services research organizations must be adaptive. Adaptability generally translates to mean diversification—research is conducted on many fronts and by different groups which must obtain resources from a variety of places to avoid reliance on a single source.

Such diversification places researchers in distinct subspecialties, usually along the lines of special areas within social science disciplines. Thus, economists work in specific economic areas, political scientists in others. Consistent with the open-systems model, each specialist is constrained in a soloist role, apart from others, moving in concert primarily with the ebb and flow of resources.

Through a chain of actions and reactions, then, the external resource-dependent health services research organizations are pressured into a federation of semiautonomous sections, each pursuing resources specific to its own specialty. Such a federation in essence fragments health services research and reinforces its individualistic interests. Depending on one's value system, this fragmentation may be a price worth paying for the survival of the research organization. Any organizational integration of various perspectives may be too cumbersome to react quickly in terms of funding opportunities. The intent of probing the bifurcated world of health services research is to underscore the unlikelihood that researchers in such an open system would have the luxury of planning together as a collective body and interacting proactively in a joint venture.

In summary, the structure of the work setting of health services researchers may be described as one which is arranged to maximize sensitivity to external demands, primarily the needs of clients. This type of structure may have a counterproductive effect on both satisfying professional reference groups and promoting interdisciplinary cooperation.

If the goal is to provide instrumental information to clients, then under current conditions the overall content of health services research will tend to be fragmentary. However, if the content of health services research is designed to enlarge upon disciplinary interests, then its very survival may be at stake. There is no easy solution to the dilemma, but the key lies in changing the nature of disciplinarian expectations. Until very recently, health services researchers played a dual role—in response to their clients and to their respective disciplines. However, as current research support dwindles, the disciplines seem to be shifting toward a more pragmatic emphasis in research. Sociology departments offer an example: formerly maintaining their distance from applied research, they now judiciously offer courses and programs in applied, evaluative and policy research. The common underlying theme for all such research is relevance—relevance to the client, now a disciplinarian emphasis.

The environmental elements of health services research may therefore converge. That is, client and disciplinarian expectations may both increasingly underscore relevance or instrumental knowledge. If history repeats itself and pragmatism again prevails, the environment of health services researchers and the demands made upon them will be far less divided.

NOTES

1. The distinction being made originally by Mechanic (1978) and appropriately repeated by Shortell in Chapter Two.
2. It is not correct to claim this as an indigenous contribution of health services research since decision analysis has been part of the business school graduate curriculum for the last 15 years. The adaption of decision analysis for clinical usage, however, is properly a methodological contribution of health services research.
3. The kind assistance of Roger Feldman in preparing this section is gratefully acknowledged.
4. This judgment is not to be confused with usefulness. For example, a particular perspective may not be directly applicable to specific problem solving, but it may nevertheless provide a framework which is useful in elucidating the issues related to the particular problem at hand.
5. For an extensive discussion of paradigm, refer to Kuhn (1962).
6. For an excellent treatment of the distinction between the conceptual level (theory) and the empirical level (data) and methods designed to reconcile the two levels, see Blalock (1968). It is important to recognize the two levels as being distinct and that bridging the two levels becomes an important methodological interest in sociology.
7. The term clients is used advisedly and refers to those who need immediate solution to problems from health services researchers. Clients are to be distinguished functionally from sponsors. Sponsors are those who support health services research with very broad agendas. This distinction between clients and sponsors parallels the distinction made between short-term goals and long-term goals of health services researchers in Chapter One.

REFERENCES

Acton, J. P. 1972. Demand for health care among the urban poor, with special emphasis on the role of time. R-1151-OEO/NYC, October. Santa Monica, CA: The RAND Corporation.

————. 1975. Nonmonetary factors in the demand for medical services: Some empirical evidence. *Journal of Political Economy* 83(June):595-614.

Althauser, R. P., and Heberlein, T. A. 1970. Validity and multitrate and multimethod matrix. In *Sociological methodology*, eds. E. Borgatta and G. W. Bohrnstedt. San Francisco: Jossey-Bass, Inc.

Arrow, K. J. 1963. Uncertainty and the welfare economics of medical care. *American Economic Review* 53(December):941-73.

————. 1965. *Aspects of the theory of risk-bearing*. Helsinski: Yrjo Jahnssonin Saatio.

Banfield, E. 1961. *Political influence*. New York: Alfred A. Knopf.

Becker, G. S., and Lewis, H. G. 1973. On the interaction between the quantity and quality of children, Part 2. *Journal of Political Economy* 81(March–April):S279-S288.

Begun, J. W., and Feldman, R. D. 1981. *A social and economic analysis of professional regulation in optometry.* DHHS Publication no. (PHS) 81-3295 (April). Washington, D.C.: Government Printing Office.

Benham, L. 1972. The effect of advertising on the price of eyeglasses. *Journal of Law and Economics* 15(October):337-52.

Blalock, H. M., Jr. 1968. The measurement problem: A gap between the languages of theory and research. In *Methodology in social research*, ed. H. M. Blalock, Jr. New York: McGraw-Hill Book Company.

Brekke, M. L., Campion, B. C., Choi, T., and Long, L. A., with Brekke, M. J. 1981. Pre-hospital criticality and prognosis. Paper presented at the Annual Meetings of the University Association for Emergency Medicine, April. San Antonio, TX.

Bunker, J. P., Barnes, B. A., and Mosteller, F. 1977. *Costs, risks, and benefits of surgery.* New York: Oxford University Press.

Champion, H. R. and Sacco, W. 1976. Quantitation of injury. In *Proceedings* of First Conference on Cybernetics and Society.

Choi, T., Brekke, M. L., Campion, B. C., and Long, L. A. 1981. Feasibility of simulating physicians' judgment of patient severity. Paper presented at the Annual Meetings of the American Public Health Association, November. Los Angeles.

Costner, H. L. 1971. Theory, deduction, and rules of correspondence. In *Causal models in the social sciences*, ed. H. M. Blalock. Chicago: Aldine Publishing Company.

————, and Schoenberg, R. 1973. Diagnosing indicator ills in multiple indicator models. In *Structural equation models in the social sciences*, eds. A. S. Goldberg and O. D. Duncan. New York: Seminar Press.

Cronbach, L. J. 1951. Coefficient alpha and the internal structure of tests. *Psychometrika* 16:297-334.

Elstein, A. S., Shulman, L. S., Sprefka, S. A. et al. 1978. *Medicare problem solving: An analysis of clinical reasoning.* Cambridge: Harvard University Press.

Feldman, R. 1979. Price and quality differences in the physicians' services market. *Southern Economic Journal* 45(January):885-91.

————, and Begun, J. W. 1978. The effects of advertising: Lessons from optometry. *Journal of Human Resources*, (Supplement). 13:247-62.

————, and Begun, J. W. 1980. Does advertising of prices reduce the mean and variance of prices. *Economic Inquiry* 18(July):487-92.

Feldstein, M. S. 1971. Hospital cost inflation: A study of nonprofit price dynamics. *American Economic Review* 61(December):853-72.

————. 1973. The welfare loss from excess health insurance. *Journal of Political Economy* 81(March–April):251-80.

Fetter, R. B. et al. 1980. Case mix definition by diagnosis-related groups. *Medical Care.* 18(February):supplement.

Goldman, F., and Grossman, M. 1978. The demand for pedatric care: A hedonic approach, Part 1. *Journal of Political Economy* 86(April):259-80.

Gustafson, D. H., and Halloway, D. C. 1976. A decision theory approach to measuring severity in illness. *Health Sciences Research* 10:97-106.

————, Frylock, D., and Rose, J. 1978. Transportability methodology. Unpublished paper from the Severity Index Project, Center for Health Systems Research and Analysis, University of Wisconsin, Madison.

Heise, D. R., and Bohrnstedt, G. 1970. Validity, invalidity, and reliability. In *Sociological methodology*, eds. E. F. Borgatta and G. W. Bohrnstedt. San Francisco: Jossey-Bass Inc.

Hershey, J. D. et al. 1980. Patient compliance with antihypertension medication. *American Journal of Public Health* 70(October):1081-89.

Jacobson, A. L. and Lalu, N. M. 1974. An empirical and algebraic analysis of alternative techniques for measuring unobserved variables. In *Measurement in the social sciences*, ed. H. M. Blalock, Jr. Chicago: Aldine Publishing Company.

Keeler, E. B., Newhouse, J. P., and Phelps, C .E. 1977. Deductibles and the demand for medical care services: The theory of a consumer facing a variable price schedule under uncertainty. *Econometrica* 45(April):641-55.

Kessel, R. A. 1970. The AMA and the supply of physicians. *Law and Contemporary Problems* 35(Spring):267-82.

Kuhn, T. S. 1962. *The structure of scientific revolutions*. Chicago: University of Chicago Press.

Leinhardt, S., ed. 1981. *Sociological methodology*. San Francisco: Jossey-Bass Inc.

Lord, F. M., and Novick, M. R. 1968. *Statistical theories of mental test scores*. Readings: Addison-Wesley.

Manski, C. F. 1981. Structural models for discrete data: The analysis of discrete choice. In *Sociological methodology*, ed. S. Leinhardt. San Francisco: Jossey-Bass Inc.

McNeil, B. J. et al. 1978. Fallacy of the five-year survival in lung cancer. *The New England Journal of Medicine* 299:1397-1401.

Mechanic, D. 1978. *Medical sociology*, 2nd ed. New York: Free Press.

Newhouse, J. P. 1970. Toward a theory of nonprofit institutions: An economic model of a hospital. *American Economic Review* 60(March):64-74.

————, and Phelps, C. E. 1979. On having your cake and eating it too: Econometric problems in estimating the demand for health services. R-1149-NC, April 1974; revised version with M. S. Marquis, R-1149-1-NC, October 1979. Santa Monica, CA: The RAND Corporation.

Palmer, H. R., and Reilly, M. C. 1979. Individual and institutional variables which may serve as indicators of quality of medical care. *Medical Care* 17(July):693-717.

Pauly, M. V. 1968. The economics of moral hazard. *American Economic Review* 58(June):531-37.

————, and Redisch, M. 1973. The not-for-profit hospital as a physicians' cooperative. *American Economic Review* 63(March):87-100.

Rhee, S. O. 1976. Factors determining the quality of physician performance in patient care. *Medical Care* 14(9):733-50.

Rosen, S. 1974. Hedonic prices and implicit markets: Product differentiation in pure competition. *Journal of Political Economy* 82(January–February):34-55.

Scott, W. R., Forrest, W. H., and Brown, B. W. 1976. Hospital structure and post-operative mortality and morbidity. In *Organizational research in hospitals*, eds. S. Shortell and M. Brown. Chicago: Blue Cross Association.

Scott, W. R., Flood, A. B., and Ewy, W. 1979. Organizational determinants of services, quality, and cost of care in hospitals. *Milbank Memorial Fund Quarterly/ Health and Society* 57:234-64.

Sloan, F. A., and Feldman R. 1978. Competition among physicians. In *Competition in the health care sector: Past, present, and future*, ed. W. Greenberg. Germantown, MD: Aspen Systems Corporation.

Sloan, F. A., and Steinwald, B. 1980*a*. Effects of regulation on hospital costs and input use. *Journal of Law and Economics* 23(April):81-109.

Sloan, F. A., and Steinwald, B. 1980*b*. *Insurance, regulation, and hospital costs*. Lexington, MA: D. C. Heath, Lexington Books.

Thaler, R., and Rosen, S. 1976. The value of saving a life: Evidence from the labor market. In *Household production and consumption*, ed. N. E. Terleckyj. New York: Columbia University Press.

Ware, J. E., Davis-Avery, A., and Brook, R. H. 1980. *Conceptualization and measurement of health for adults in the health insurance study: Vol. VI, analysis of relationships among health status measures*. R-1987/6 HEW, November. Santa Monica, CA: The RAND Corporation.

Weinstein, M. C., and Fineberg, H. V. 1980. *Clinical decision analysis*. Philadelphia: W. B. Saunders Company.

Author Index

Lexicon

About the Editors

THOMAS CHOI is Assistant Professor at the Center for Health Services Research at the University of Minnesota. His research interests center on the governance and management of university hospitals, emergency medical services, and health promotion. He teaches measurement issues and organizational theory. Dr. Choi received his doctorate in sociology from the University of Minnesota and taught at Johns Hopkins University before returning to Minnesota.

JAY N. GREENBERG is an Assistant Professor at the Center for Health Services Research and a faculty member of the Humphrey Institute of Public Affairs at the University of Minnesota. His research interests include long-term care, health planning and policy, and methodological issues in the evaluation of health services. Dr. Greenberg's current research centers on the delivery and financing of long-term care. He received a Sc.D. in Health Services Administration from Harvard. In July 1983 Dr. Greenberg will join the faculty of Brandeis University and will serve as the Associate Director for Research of the University Health Policy Consortium.

Randall Library – UNCW

RA440.85 .S63 1982

Social science approaches to health services resea

NXWW

304900282422–